SOCIOLINGUISTICS

'This text book is enormously enabling. Not only does it comprehensively provide the basic theory and method at the right level, but beginners have the means and the models so that they can "get their hands dirty" with real data and real problems in doing Sociolinguistics.'
William Downes, *University of East Anglia*

'The whole structure and approach is satisfying to read and rewarding to use.'
Clive Grey, *Edge Hill College of Higher Education*

Routledge English Language Introductions cover core areas of language study and are one-stop resources for students.

Assuming no prior knowledge, books in the series offer an accessible overview of the subject, with activities, study questions, sample analyses, commentaries and key readings – all in the same volume. The innovative and flexible 'two-dimensional' structure is built around four sections – introduction, development, exploration and extension – which offer self-contained stages for study. Each topic can also be read across these sections, enabling the reader to build gradually on the knowledge gained.

Sociolinguistics:
❏ provides a comprehensive introduction to Sociolinguistics
❏ draws on a range of real texts, from an interview with Madonna to articles in international newspapers and classroom discourse
❏ uses real studies designed and conducted by students
❏ provides classic readings by the key names in the discipline from Milroy and Holmes to Fairclough and Cameron

The accompanying website providing weblinks and extra resources for lecturers, teachers and students can be found at **http://www.routledge.com/textbooks/sociolinguistics**

Written by an experienced teacher and author, this accessible textbook is an essential resource for all students of English language and linguistics.

Peter Stockwell is Senior Lecturer in the School of English Studies at the University of Nottingham, UK, where his interests include Sociolinguistics, stylists and cognitive poetics. His recent publications include *Cognitive Poetics: An Introduction* (Routledge, 2002), *The Poetics of Science Fiction*, *Investigating English Language* (with Howard Jackson), and *Contextualized Stylistics* (edited with Tony Bex and Michael Burke).

Series Editor: Peter Stockwell
Series Consultant: Ronald Carter

ROUTLEDGE ENGLISH LANGUAGE INTRODUCTIONS

SERIES EDITOR: PETER STOCKWELL

Peter Stockwell is Senior Lecturer in the School of English Studies at the University of Nottingham, UK, where his interests include sociolinguistics, stylistics and cognitive poetics. His recent publications include *Cognitive Poetics: An Introduction* (Routledge, 2002), *The Poetics of Science Fiction, Investigating English Language* (with Howard Jackson), and *Contextualized Stylistics* (edited with Tony Bex and Michael Burke).

SERIES CONSULTANT: RONALD CARTER

Ronald Carter is Professor of Modern English Language in the School of English Studies at the University of Nottingham, UK. He is the co-series editor of the forthcoming *Routledge Applied Linguistics* series, series editor of *Interface*, and was co-founder of the Routledge *Intertext* series.

OTHER TITLES IN THE SERIES:

Sociolinguistics
Peter Stockwell

Pragmatics and Discourse
Joan Cutting

Grammar and Vocabulary
Howard Jackson

FORTHCOMING:

World Englishes
Jennifer Jenkins

Practical Phonetics and Phonology
Beverley Collins & Inger Mees

Child Language
Jean Stilwell Peccei

Stylistics
Paul Simpson

SOCIOLINGUISTICS

A resource book for students

PETER STOCKWELL

Routledge
Taylor & Francis Group

LONDON AND NEW YORK

First published 2002 by Routledge
2 Park Square, Milton Park, Abingdon, Oxon, OX14 4RN

Reprinted 2003, 2005

Routledge is an imprint of the Taylor & Francis Group

© 2002 Peter Stockwell

Typeset in 10/12.5pt Minion by Graphicraft Limited, Hong Kong
Printed and bound in Great Britain by TJ International Ltd, Padstow, Cornwall

British Library Cataloguing in Publication Data
A catalogue record for this book is available from the British Library

ISBN 0–415–23452–2 (hbk)
ISBN 0–415–23453–0 (pbk)

Library of Congress Cataloging-in-Publication Data
Stockwell, Peter.
  Sociolinguistics: a resource book for students / Peter Stockwell.
    p. cm. – (Routledge English language introductions series)
  Includes bibliographical references (p.) and index.
  1. Sociolinguistics. I. Title. II. Series.

  P40.S783 2002   2001040364
  306.44–dc21

HOW TO USE THIS BOOK

The Routledge English Language Introductions are 'flexi-texts' that you can use to suit your own style of study. The books are divided into four sections:-

A Introduction – sets out the key concepts for the area of study. The Units of this section take you step-by-step through the foundational terms and ideas, carefully providing you with an initial toolkit for your own study. By the end of the section, you will have a good overview of the whole field.

B Development – adds to your knowledge and builds on the key ideas already introduced. Units in this section might also draw together several areas of interest. By the end of this section, you will already have a good and fairly detailed grasp of the field, and will be ready to undertake your own exploration and thinking.

C Exploration – provides examples of language data and guides you through your own investigation of the field. The Units in this section will be more open-ended and exploratory, and you will be encouraged to try out your ideas and think for yourself, using your newly acquired knowledge.

D Extension – offers you the chance to compare your expertise with key readings in the area. These are taken from the work of important writers, and are provided with guidance and questions for your further thought.

You can read this book like a traditional text-book, 'vertically' straight through from beginning to end. This will take you comprehensively through the broad field of study. However, the Routledge English Language Introductions have been carefully designed so that you can read them in another dimension, 'horizontally' across the numbered Units. For example, Units A.1, A.2, A.3 and so on correspond with Units B.1, B.2, B.3, and with Units C.1, C.2, C.3 and D.1, D.2, D.3, and so on. Reading A5, B.5, C.5, D.5 will take you rapidly from the key concepts of a specific area, to a level of expertise in that precise area, all with a very close focus. You can match your way of reading with the best way that you work.

The glossary/index at the end, together with the suggestions for Further Reading, will help to keep you orientated. Each textbook has a supporting website with extra commentary, suggestions, additional material and support for teachers and students.

SOCIOLINGUISTICS

In this book, ten numbered sub-sections in section A introduce you to the key concepts in sociolinguistic study. Terms and ideas are introduced quickly and clearly, so that if you read this section as a whole, you can rapidly start to link together the different areas of sociolinguistic study. Then you can use the numbers for each area to follow a theme through the book. For example, Unit A2 sets out key ideas in the study of accent and dialect. In Section B, you will find that Unit 2 presents a real student's study in the same area, together with my commentary. The idea behind this is to show you in as practical a way as possible that you can achieve a high degree of detailed and sophisticated sociolinguistic study in a fairly short space of time.

The best way to learn about language and society is to investigate the area for yourself and think about your own place in it. Section C gives you a chance to do this, and following on from A2 and B2, for example, Unit C2 provides you with some genuine data of dialectal variation and some questions to consider. Finally, in Section D, Unit 2 offers some published reading and suggestions for further study, to complete your thorough understanding of the stand.

The same pattern applies for every numbered section throughout the book. In general, I have tried to increase the cumulative difficulty through each section, and in Section B I have added four extra areas to the toolkit which can be followed through to the data in Section C. If, by the end, I have encouraged you to discover more about sociolinguistics, and if you are encouraged to take issue critically with existing studies in the area, then this book will have served its purpose.

CONTENTS

CONTENTS **CROSS-REFERENCED**

CONTENTS **CROSS-REFERENCED**

C	EXPLORATION

D	EXTENSION

UNITS

LIST OF FIGURES

LIST OF TABLES

ACKNOWLEDGEMENTS

A book in sociolinguistics owes everything to the writing, thinking and talk of others. In this I am privileged to have worked with many people who have shaped my ideas and inspired me to think further about language and life. Paul Simpson, Andrew Hamer, and Kay Richardson first taught me the broad meaning of the word 'sociolinguistics'. More than any other area, I have learnt about sociolinguistics by teaching it and I am grateful to all the students who have taken my courses and especially those whose work and thinking appears directly here: James Baderman, Chris Barenberg, Virginia Barnes, Vicky Bristow, Lauren Buckland, Miranda Chadwick, Li En Chong, Joel Dothie, Sharlene Goff, Matthew Hassan, Naomi Holdstock, Judith Jones, Louise Kessler, Tim Knebel, I Ching Ng, Kate Oakley, Vicki Oliver, Lynne Senior, Joanna Shirley, Hardip Singh Amarjit Kaur, Martin Stepanek, Zoe Taylor, Kathryn Tibbs, Katherine West, Sarah Wood, and Ben Woolhead. I have benefited from discussions over the years while teaching with David Cordiner, Maureen Alam, Louise Mullany, and Rocio Montoro, and owe many of the ideas and language examples in the following pages to the conversations and hospitality of friends and colleagues around the world. It is a hazard of talking to me that you might end up as a piece of data: thanks to Michael Burke, Ron Carter, Urszula Clark, Annette Combrink, Szilvia Csabi, Zoltan Dornyei, Anthea Fraser-Gupta, Alex Gavins, Lucy Henderson, Howard Jackson, Lesley Jeffries, Carmen Llamas, Mike McCarthy, Iain MacGregor, John McRae, Yoshifumi Saito, Norbert Schmitt, Barbara Sinclair, Ismail Talib, Masanori Toyota, Peter Verdonk, Doug Yates, Sonia Zyngier and of course to my wife Joanna Gavins for living through much of the data with me.

This book is dedicated to the men and women of Teesside, who have the accent of home.

PJS
Nottingham

The author and publishers would like to thank the following for permission to reproduce copyright material:

John Edwards for extracts from *Multilingualism* (Routledge, 1995);
The Evening Gazette, Teesside for the 'Teesside Tommy' column by Anthony Vickers, from 24 July, 1999;
Norman Fairclough and Arnold Publishers for extracts from *Media Discourse* (1995);

The Guggenheim Museum, Bilbao, for extracts from the exhibition catalogue October 1999–February 2000;

Andrew Hamer for extracts from 'Early Standard English: linguistic confidence and insecurity' (1993);

Janet Holmes, Ruth Wodak and Sage Publications Ltd for extracts from 'Story-telling in New Zealand women's and men's talk' in *Gender and Discourse*, edited by Ruth Wodak (1997);

Braj Kachru and the University of Illinois Press for extracts from 'The bilingual's creativity' in *Discourse Across Cultures* (edited by Larry Smith, 1997);

Rosina Lippi-Green for extracts from *English with an Accent* (Routledge, 1997);

The Telegraph, Calcutta for the article 'Sorry, no fish 'n' chips for Mr John Major';

James Milroy for extracts from 'Some new perspectives on sound change', *Newcastle and Durham Working Papers in Linguistics* (1993);

Harvey Sacks and Emanuel Schegloff, and Mouton de Gruyter publishers for extracts from 'Opening up closings', *Semiotica* 7;

Ronald Wardhaugh and Blackwell Publishers Ltd for extracts from *Introduction to Sociolinguistics* (3rd edition, 1998);

'Women in EFL materials' for the extract from *On Balance*, 1991.

The article by Deborah Cameron, 'Respect, please!', is previously unpublished and copyright remains with Deborah Cameron. Many thanks for allowing its use here.

While every effort has been made to contact copyright holders of material used in this volume, the publishers would be happy to hear from any we have been unable to contact, and we will make the necessary amendment at the earliest opportunity.

INTRODUCTION

KEY CONCEPTS IN SOCIOLINGUISTICS

A SOCIOLINGUISTIC TOOLKIT

❑ All language events consist of a piece of language in a social context.
❑ Every different social context determines that particular form of language.
❑ The language used in particular situations determines the nature of that social event.

Given these three points, the potential scope of the discipline of sociolinguistics is enormous. Indeed, given such a broad definition of the field, it would be difficult to see any linguistic situation that did not come within the concern of sociolinguistics. Though a theoretical argument can be made along these lines, it is clearly impractical for a book on sociolinguistics to be a book on the language of everything. We can even say that accepting the three points above means that the only way of proceeding in the exploration of language is by practical investigation. So this book explores the territory and boundaries of sociolinguistics by presenting real studies and real data.

In Section B (Development), sociolinguistic case studies are presented from the work of my undergraduate students. Section C (Exploration) sets out some sociolinguistic data for your own investigation. In the last section of the book (D – Extension), excerpts from professional published studies are presented. All of these sections thus allow you the freedom to conduct practical thinking and analysis, and present you with real examples of how to go about your own study. However, you will also need a map of the area and a toolkit for investigation, and these are provided in Section A.

Awareness of theory and method

One mistake that new students of sociolinguistics often make is to run off enthusiastically with recorder in pocket to collect some data, and then examine the transcript to see what they have caught. The problem with this 'trawling' approach is that they may not know what they have in their sociolinguistic net, may not be able to recognise it, classify it, nor know what to do with it, and they will not be able to claim anything believable about their fishing trip.

The fact is that successful explorations require a bit of planning and preparation. Fundamentally, this means knowing what you want to find out, and devising a plan of action to discover it. First, then, it is important to understand the theoretical basis of the study. Some of the following might seem obvious, but you need to be absolutely clear in your mind before the investigation how you would satisfy each requirement:

❑ make sure that the thing you want to investigate is a credible area for investigation
❑ make sure it is a regular feature rather than an example of an individual's mis-cue or mistake
❑ make sure the feature is available for analysis, and that you do not affect the data in the process of investigating it
❑ make sure that the feature can be described systematically, so that your readers can verify that what you claim is testable, able to be replicated if possible, and able to be evaluated.

Many of these issues can be settled by reading around the area before you begin. This will also help you to resolve areas of investigation that are new or that you find unsatisfactory in previous work. Gaining a theoretical awareness will allow you to decide how far you can generalise your findings to wider social situations, and will allow you to discuss the consequences of your work for sociolinguistics, and for the understanding of language and society.

Your method of data collection will largely be determined by these theoretical issues. They will tell you where and how and what to investigate. For example, your methodology might comprise any one or a combination of the following:

❑ self-report: do you set up a questionnaire (spoken or written) and what questions do you ask; do you set up an empirical situation (a test) in which you try to elicit the feature you are interested in with the groups of people you are interested in; do you record a structured or open-ended interview or conversation?
❑ covert observation: do you participate in the group; do you tell the informants what you are after; do you make them aware they are being recorded; do you want them in a formal or relaxed situation?
❑ sampling method: do you choose people randomly; do you select from a specified group; do you select a representative sample; do you minimise the interference by other factors by limiting yourself to one factor; how many informants do you need?

Lastly, you must also consider your ethical responsibilities in collecting linguistic data from people who might not be aware that they are being observed and recorded. In most cases, even where the language event is public, many linguists consider it unethical to gather data completely covertly. The problem is that in warning people they are being recorded, they are likely to alter their behaviour (this is known as the **observer's paradox**). It might be possible to avoid this by telling potential informants that they are being observed, without going into the details of what you are investigating; or by sharing your findings with them afterwards and gaining their permission; or by deciding that the observer's paradox is not a significant factor in a particular case and so the observation can be open. Whatever you decide should be considered and discussed thoroughly. (See D5 for more on this.)

Variables in sociolinguistics

Armed with theoretical and methodological knowledge, you only need one more elementary tool. This is the notion of the **variable**.

There are two types of variable in social investigation. The **social variable** is the factor that determines a variation in language. Possible social factors include gender, geography, age, occupation, and so on, as set out in the areas of Section A below. The **linguistic variable** is the feature that you want to investigate. This might be a language (English, Basque, Hokkien), or a dialect (Irish Hiberno-English, Jamaican Patwa), or a style (formal, careful, casual), or a register (romantic novels, recipes, bank manager talk), or a syntactic pattern (passive, intransitive, verb agreement), or a word or phrase ('neb', 'you-all', 'you know') or a particular sound (/h/, /t/, /a/), for example. Many sociolinguistic studies use individual sounds in pronunciation as the linguistic variable, since it is a relatively easy practical matter to either set up or come across a situation in which many of them will occur.

To investigate whether the use of a linguistic feature is caused by a particular social factor, you will need to collect examples of a situation in which the feature has a chance of being used. Suppose you are investigating gender usage. You must get two groups of informants who are as alike as possible in every respect except that one group is female and the other male: otherwise the same age, education, social class, political viewpoint, and so on. In this way, you have 'controlled' for other interfering variables, and any linguistic differences you find are likely to be determined by gender alone. In effect, what you have done is focus on the dependent linguistic variable, and manipulated the independent social variable to discover social usage.

Treating the feature as the linguistic variable, you will be faced with two circumstances of its usage. Either the feature occurs or not (e.g. someone says the word 'hotel' by pronouncing the /h/ or by 'dropping' it – that is, presence or omission, or x/Ø). Alternatively, the variable is graded so a range of possibilities present themselves (e.g. people pronounce the middle 't' in 'butter' in four different ways: /t/, /d/, /ʔ/ or Ø – omitting it altogether).

This outline is the simplest way of doing sociolinguistic investigations. In the rest of this book, the procedure will be exemplified over and over, and other complicating factors gradually introduced. Other tools will also be added to the basic kit, including some precise terminology and, in the next section, an important sociolinguistic tool: the means of talking objectively about accent variation.

ACCENT AND DIALECT

In common perception, **accent** is something other people have: 'He's very broad', 'She has a lovely speaking voice', 'That's a thick accent', can be heard on innumerable occasions. Many of my students deny that they have an accent at all. These common judgements are interesting for what they tell us about people's attitudes to language, but as sociolinguists we must not share their evaluative biases. Apart from sign language, it is as impossible to speak without an accent as it is to speak without making any sound.

Describing accents

Assume a British 'BBC English' accent in the example words, unless stated otherwise.

Selected IPA (International Phonetic Alphabet) symbols

Consonants (including glides/liquids)

p	pip	ʧ	church
b	bib	ʤ	judge
t	ten	m	man
d	den	n	man
k	cat	ŋ	sing
g	get	l	let ('light l', at the front of the mouth)
f	fish	ł	pull ('dark l', at the back of the mouth)
v	van	r	ride, parrot
θ	thigh	ɾ	rubbish (Scots) ('tapped r')
ð	thy	w	wet
s	set	ʍ	which (aspirated, with breath)
z	zen	j	yet
ʃ	ship	ʔ	bu'er (glottal stop)
ʒ	leisure	x	loch (Scots)
h	hen		

Vowels

Monophthongs

ɪ	pit
ɛ	pet
æ	pat
ɒ	pot
ʌ	putt
ʊ	put
ə	patter
o	eau (French), low (Northern England)
a	calm (Scouse), farm (Teesside)
y	tu (French), school (Scouse)
ø	peu (French), boat (Geordie)
iː	bean
ɜː	burn
ɑː	barn
ɔː	born
uː	boon
eː	bait (Northern England)

Diphthongs

aɪ	bite, night
əɪ	night (Scots, Canadian)
ɛɪ	bait
ɔɪ	boy
əʊ	roe
aʊ	house
əʊ	house (Scots, Canadian)
ʊə	sewer, poor
uə	poor (Northern England)
ɪə	ear
iə	ear (Northern England)
ɛə	air

You will have noticed some familiar symbols, as well as some unusual ones (the 'tapped' /ɾ/, for example), especially among the 'pure' vowels (**monophthongs**) and complex vocalic elements (**diphthongs**). In all the example words given, I assume what used to be called a 'BBC English' accent (known properly as **Received Pronunciation** –

RP). Sometimes I have indicated a different regional accent, where RP does not use the sound. The IPA includes many notational marks – known as **diacritics** – to modify the sound represented. In the chart above, the colons (:) indicate that the vowel is lengthened.

Accent variation is often most noticeably carried in the vocalic elements of pronunciation, and in the glides (/j/, /w/) and liquids (/r/, /l/) that are sort of 'semi-vowels'. For example, a speaker who says [fɑ:rm] rather than [fɑ:m] is likely to be American or Irish rather than English: that is, their accent is said to be **rhotic** if they pronounce this sort of 'non-prevocalic /r/' (/r/ when it is not before a vowel, as in 'farm' or 'car'). Americans and most Irish people have a 'retroflex' /r/. By contrast, if they 'tap' the 'r' (by flicking the tip of their tongue against the ridge behind their front teeth), the vowel quality is likely to change slightly and they are likely to introduce a vowel between the 'r' and 'm' to make the last two letters syllabic: [færəm]. This is more likely to be a Scottish speaker, or someone influenced by Scots, such as speakers in Ulster (and the square brackets are used to write down actual realisations in speech).

Phonetic details like these can help you pinpoint the differences between accents. The crucial factor for sociolinguistics is that accent variation tends not to happen just randomly, but in relation to observable social patterns. Accent can often tell us where someone comes from, their age, gender, level of education, social class, wealth, how well-travelled they are, and whether they are emotionally attached to their home town, job or political party. All of these factors can also be carried in someone's **dialect**.

Dialectology

A2.2

Just as everyone has an accent, so every form of English (or any language) is a dialect. Where 'accent' refers to the sounds a speaker makes, 'dialect' covers the word choices, syntactic ordering and all the other grammatical choices a speaker could make. A 'language' consists of one or many dialects, all of which are more or less mutually intelligible to other speakers of the language. The most prestigious dialect in Britain is UK Standard English (UKSE), originally a southern dialect of English which has become the form used in most print media, law and education. It can, of course, be pronounced in any accent. For example, 'It's very dirty' can be pronounced in RP ([ɪts vɛri dɜ:ti]), or in a northern British accent ([ɪʔs vɛrɪ dɛ:tɪ]), but the same sense can be expressed in several dialects: UKSE (as above); Yorkshire ('Tha's right mucky'); or Teesside ('It's hacky'), and so on.

Though, in principle, any dialect can appear in any accent, in practice some accents tend to accompany certain dialects. RP almost never appears in anything but UK Standard English, though UKSE is usually pronounced in most accents. Scouse dialect always appears in a Liverpool accent, though, Tyneside dialect in a Geordie accent, West Midlands dialect in a Birmingham or a Black Country accent, and so on. So closely are accent and dialect connected in common perception, that the word for the accent (Cockney) and the dialect (Cockney) are often the same. Different groups even have different words for other groups: thus 'Brummies' in Birmingham notice the different accent in Coventry of the 'Yam-Yams' (derived from the pronunciation of 'I am . . .').

Of course, dialects do not suddenly change from area to area. Accents and dialects that are geographically close to one another tend to be similar in form, gradually varying the further you travel away from them. We can thus talk of **dialect chains** rather than discrete dialects. This applies even across national boundaries: the dialects of northern Germany are closer in form to bordering Netherlands than to Bavarian, though the latter is usually counted as the same German language and the former is the foreign language Dutch. Political allegiances have a lot to do with this attitude, of course.

Traditionally, 'dialectologists' were able to study different areas of accent and dialect use fairly easily, drawing lines on the map (**isoglosses**) to separate one form and speech community from another. This is much more difficult in an urban setting, where migration and industrialisation tend to mix up family origins. The sociolinguistic method outlined in A1 has enabled the study of **urban dialectology** in these situations.

A3   REGISTER AND STYLE

Dialect is a variety of language defined largely by its users' regional or socio-economic origins. However, much language variation is a result of differences in the social situation of use. This affects the word choices and syntactic ordering of utterances (together, the **lexicogrammar**), and has been called **register** (or sometimes, by analogy with 'dialect', it is referred to as **diatype**). One of the recent findings of **corpus linguistics** (using a large computer database of actual language examples) is that there is far more variation as a result of register than as a result of dialect. Furthermore, register differences operate within and across different dialects. For example, the lexicogrammatical composition of registers such as 'playing a computer game', 'buying a coffee', or 'writing a letter to a friend' remain constant even in different dialects. People are engaged in similar communicative acts and so tend to use similar linguistic patterns.

What is surprising is that people are far more aware of dialectal differences than diatypic differences. People are readily conscious of regional words and phrases, but will only really think about the variant patterns in different registers when they are pointed out to them in a book like this. Of course, register is socially motivated and involves social negotiation among the participants in the discourse, in order to speak or write in an appropriate way. Since these decisions involve a whole range of social perceptions to do with social rank, politeness, and appropriacy, choices of register and stylistic choices are the concern of sociolinguistics.

A3.1   Register

Register can be defined either narrowly or broadly. The narrow definition sees register simply as an occupational variety of language. So, for example, teachers, computer programmers, mechanics or sociolinguists tend to have characteristic ways of speaking which involve certain particular word choices and grammatical constructions. This is most commonly perceived as **jargon**, and most people associate it with particular word choices. However, the syntactic ordering and patterns of larger-scale linguistic organisation are also important.

A wider definition of register sees it as a sort of social genre of linguistic usage (sometimes specified as a **sociolect** to differentiate it from 'dialect'). Examples of registers under this definition would include the language of a newspaper article, the language of a conversation about the weather, academic prose, a recipe in a cookery book, and so on.

It is important that register is defined primarily by the circumstance and purpose of the communicative situation, rather than by the individual user or ethnic/social group using the variety. In other words, the definition must be a non-linguistic one, against which particular linguistic features can then be set. One way of pinpointing a register is to identify a communicative event along three dimensions:

- ❏ field
- ❏ tenor
- ❏ mode

The **field** is the social setting and purpose of the interaction. In the case of an academic article in a professional journal, for example, the field would be the subject matter of the article, and the purpose in publishing it would be to spread the argument and ideas among academic colleagues. The **tenor** refers to the relationship between the participants in the event. The writer of the article and readers including academic colleagues and students constitute the tenor here. Finally, the **mode** refers to the medium of communication (e.g. spoken, written, or e-mailed). An academic article is in the written mode. Changing this last dimension to the spoken mode would alter the register from an 'article' to a 'lecture', and there would be corresponding and predictable differences in the lexicogrammar: most simply, the sentences are likely to be shorter and contain fewer embedded clauses in speech; word choice is likely to be slightly less formal and perhaps less technical; there might be more direct interaction with the audience and direct address in the form of 'I' and 'you'; and so on.

Clearly there are further details and sub-types within each set of three dimensions. The context of use is the crucial determinant in identifying register. In this way slight differences in linguistic style can be ascribed to close differences in social function. For example, a recipe basically has the register dimensions of (field) cookery, (tenor) professional cook to amateur cook, (mode) written, as a table of ingredients followed by the method. However, I have a French cookery reference book which clearly assumes a very knowledgeable reader: this variation in tenor makes the register very technical and mainly too difficult for me to use. I also have a cookery book with sumptuous photographs and mouth-watering lyrical prose which is clearly intended as a 'coffee table' book for reading rather than cooking anything practical, and this linguistic variation is determined by the difference in field. I have also had instructions on how to make an apple and rhubarb crumble telephoned to me by my mother, and the difference in mode here (spoken rather than written) produced a very different set of linguistic patterns.

Finally, all these register distinctions have to be matched to cultural expectations. A discussion about the weather in Britain contains a very different lexicogrammatical structure from a discussion about the weather in California (as well as the content conveyed). Similarly, I have a recipe book from the Raffles Hotel in Singapore which is clearly intended as a practical cookery manual, but since in Nottingham I cannot get ingredients like green pandan leaves, I read its register as an exotic fiction rather than a cookery book. In this case, the actual tenor has changed.

Style

In the context of sociolinguistic study, **style** refers to variations within registers that can represent individual choices along social dimensions. One stylistic dimension within a register would be the scale of formality–casualness. 'Place the ingredients into a pre-pared dish' could more casually be: 'Put the mix into the bowl you've got ready'. Clearly, since the field, tenor and mode of both these utterances could be the same, stylistic variation can occur within a register. However, style is independent of register since the mode of the first utterance could be written and the second spoken. Very generally, the written mode tends to be more formal than the spoken mode, with e-mail a new sort of discourse that is not so much a midway blend of the two as a bundle of features all of its own.

Most styles are best thought of as scales or clines, for example from very formal to very casual, with many relative gradations in between. People are very adept at matching their style as appropriate to the social setting. Other stylistic scales include impersonal–intimate, monologic–dialogic, formulaic–creative, and so on. All of these can be manifest in the linguistic choices of the utterance.

With both registers and styles, most people have a far greater passive **competence** than active competence. In other words, they can understand a great many more variations than they usually perform, and if put in unfamiliar social situations will often become highly self-conscious and misjudge the pattern they should produce. Such 'errors' are an important feature of sociolinguistic behaviour.

ETHNICITY AND MULTILINGUALISM

Many English speakers living in predominantly monolingual countries such as Britain, the US or Australia, might think that it is an unusual skill to be able to speak more than one language. Indeed, English speakers in these countries have a very poor record in learning other languages, partly because the powerful influence of English worldwide makes it seem less necessary to do so. However, the ability to speak more than one language is perhaps more common in the world than monolingualism. Even in the apparently monoglot countries mentioned above, there are huge numbers of people routinely speaking not only a variety of types of English, but also many indigenous languages (Irish Gaelic, Scots Gaelic, Welsh, aboriginal languages such as Dyirbal, and native American languages) as well as community languages brought by large numbers of recent immigrants (especially Spanish in the US, Indian languages such as Punjabi, Urdu, Marathi and other Southeast Asian languages in the UK and Australia, and all the European languages in all three countries).

Language use, then, though seen as a symbol of nationalism, is also the major badge of **ethnicity** – that is, racial, cultural or family origins. An individual might choose to speak in a particular language, or dialect, or register, or accent, or style (let's use the general term **code** to cover all of these varieties) on different occasions and for different purposes. The choice of code can be used to claim in-group identity with other speakers.

Code-switching

Most individuals have a repertoire of codes available to them. Even if you only speak English, you will almost certainly be able to switch from a casual to formal style (if you employ a 'telephone voice' for example), or into different accents (as in telling a story or a joke), or even into different dialects (when moving from writing a message on a note on your fridge door to writing a letter to your bank). The main point to notice here is that these different uses of different codes are tied to different situations or **domains**. One theory of **code-switching** claims that the choice of code is determined by the domain in which speakers perceive themselves to be. This means that the choice of code itself is communicatively meaningful, as well as the actual content of what is said. For example, I recently overheard a group of three teenage boys on a bus quoting catchphrases from a popular and cultish comedy show; in doing so, they imitated the accents of the characters when incorporating the phrases into their own speech, switching back and forth from their own voices to the 'comedy' voices. This went on for some time, but when they approached their bus stop they all switched back into their 'own' voices to make final arrangements for meeting up again that evening. It was obvious that any arrangements made in 'comedy' voices would not count as real arrangements but would be taken as a joke.

The life of one of my students illustrates the 'domains theory' of code-switching very well. Melinda is studying in Britain but her ethnic origins are Straits Chinese from Singapore. She speaks Cantonese with her family in Singapore, and Hokkien to traders in the small shops, markets and food halls. In larger shops, however, and especially in multinational chains, she speaks Singaporean English and can understand the popular local blend of Chinese and English known as Singlish, though as a highly educated woman she rather looks down on it. She reads the Mandarin newspaper *Lianhe Zaobao* and the Singaporean English newspaper *The Straits Times*, and she has a good knowledge of Malay and various Indian languages. In most formal correspondence in Singapore she uses Singaporean English. In Britain, of course, she reads and writes in British Standard English, though she can now switch into a Nottingham accent and dialect but only ever for comic effect. She recently married an Italian student, Mario, and so is adding Italian to her repertoire of codes to be used in different domains.

When a speaker moves from one domain into another, and changes their code as a result, this is **situational code-switching**. Sometimes, however, a speaker can deliberately change codes in the middle of a situation, in order to indicate to the hearer that they consider a new domain to be 'in operation'. This is called **metaphorical code-switching** and can be seen in the teenage boys' usage to differentiate 'joke time' from 'serious time'. Conversations are often brought to a close by one participant code-switching into a different variety in order to signal that they want to get away. Metaphorical code-switching is thus a means of changing the perceived context.

Where a domain is not well defined or two domains could be seen to be operating (such as meeting a family friend in an expensive and unfamiliar restaurant, or having a work colleague round for a family occasion), speakers can often be heard **code-mixing**, in which the switch between languages can occur within utterances. The most chaotic code-mixing I have ever experienced was with English and Scottish friends out with colleagues from their English-language school walking from bar to bar in the Basque country near the Franco-Spanish border.

A4.2   **Multilingualism and diglossia**

When discussing an individual's ability to speak more than one language, we usually use the terms **bilingual** or **multilingual**. A person's native language, which they learnt as a baby, is their **vernacular** (or 'mother tongue'). This is sometimes referred to as L1. Many people go on to learn another language later in life, to the point at which they become fluent in this L2 language. Such people are **compound bilinguals**, since there is a definite sequence of linguistic competence. My sister-in-law Alex is a native English speaker, but is fluent in French and Spanish which she first learnt at school, and has a passive competence in Basque.

Some people, however, are born into families in which two or more languages are spoken routinely, and they develop both languages equally as vernaculars. Such people are **co-ordinate bilinguals**. My friend Urszula was born in York to Polish parents, and is a co-ordinate bilingual in English and Polish; she has never visited Poland. Many people with this ability nevertheless associate each language with different domains (such as English with work and Polish with the children's grandparents), and will then associate each code-choice with particular situations and emotions.

An individual speaking more than one language is said to be **multilingual**, but we can also use this term to talk of whole communities in which two languages are commonly spoken by most people. Thus, Switzerland is a multilingual country with French, German and Italian the main languages, and with each language predominating in different areas; though an individual will probably have one of these as a vernacular, they are likely to have a good facility in the others. Multilingual communities include French Canadians, American Hispanics, many Welsh people, the ethnic Greek community in Sydney, English-Punjabi speakers in Birmingham, Gaelic-English speakers in Connemara, South African speakers of English, Afrikaans and Shona, and so on.

In communities in which two language varieties are used by everyone, and there is a distinct and institutionalised functional divergence in usage, this is called **diglossia**. For example, Classical Arabic is the language of the Koran and is reserved for religious purposes, and a range of vernacular Arabic varieties are used for most other purposes across north Africa and the Middle East. In diglossic situations, the code which is used for writing or in prestigious or formal domains is known as the H variety, and the other code is the L variety: High German is used in books and newspapers across Germany, Switzerland and Austria, but various forms of Low German are used in regions of this area. Spoken Swiss German sounds very different from the German spoken in Dortmund, but in both areas people can read the same book or newspaper without difficulty.

SOCIAL CLASS

One of the most significant and also most complex determinants of linguistic variation is **social class**. This is not an easy concept to define precisely or measure accurately, and the stratification of class into different levels varies considerably across nations and cultures. Most language communities, however, have a hierarchy of wealth and power defined in relation to economics and prestige that can be covered by the term **class**.

Most sociolinguistic studies that have investigated the impact of social stratification on language use have employed the **variationist** method. That is, they have taken a linguistic variable and recorded its variations by placing it alongside a range of apparently independent factors: in this case, social stratification. Sociolinguistics was initially developed by William Labov's investigations of accent variation in various socially stratified situations.

Fixed variables

Perhaps the most famous sociolinguistic study of all was conducted by Labov in order to test the social stratification of rhoticity (pronunciation of /r/ when not before a vowel) in New York City. This was then used as a pilot study for a much larger investigation. In New York, rhoticity has been a prestige feature since the 1940s. Labov selected three department stores each of which served as an index of social stratification. He used non-linguistic measurements to stratify the stores (location, quality of goods, size of price tags, and so on). In each shop, he stopped people and asked a question to which he knew the answer would be 'fourth floor'. He would then pretend to mishear, in order to get the informant to repeat 'fourth floor' more emphatically. In this elegant and neat way he was able to note four occurrences of /r/ pronunciation.

Labov's findings show a clear class stratification in rhoticity, confirming its prestige value: generally, more occurrences of /r/ in the higher-class store than the lower-class one. He also found that there was a greater /r/ stress when the speaker was emphatic and relatively self-aware. The most interesting finding was that in the middle store, the emphasis on the final /r/ in both occurrences of 'floor' was much stronger than would have been expected on a steadily rising scale from lower to higher class. This group showed a heavy emphasis on /r/-pronunciation when they were aware of their own usage.

In Labov's larger New York study, this same phenomenon occurred. This time, in order to grade the scale of self-consciousness, Labov observed informants'

casual speech	(in relaxed conversation)
careful speech	(in a more formal situation)
reading style	(from a set text)
word lists	(to focus their awareness on reading out loud)
minimal pairs	(to make them particularly aware of their speech by giving them closely similar words like 'law'/'lore').

Labov noted the same prestige variation across the socio-economic classes (a more objective measurement of class than department stores), and again the same over-emphasis by the 'lower middle-class' group. He termed this over-compensation

hypercorrection, and described it as a manifestation of the linguistic insecurity of this social group.

In a similar variationist study in Norwich, Peter Trudgill investigated 16 multiple variables including the presence or absence of /h/ in words like 'happy', 'home', /n/ or /ŋ/ at the end of 'singing', and the vowels in 'bad', 'name', 'path', 'tell', 'here', 'hair', 'ride', 'bird', 'top', 'know', 'boat', 'boot', 'tune'. He divided informants into 5 social classes, and also by gender, age and local area. Like Labov, Trudgill used a range of elicitation techniques to increase the self-awareness of informants: casual style, formal style, reading passage style and word list style ('boot/boat', 'bust/burst', 'moon/moan', and so on).

Trudgill also found hypercorrection towards the prestige pronunciation amongst the middle-class group. More specifically, he found that middle-class women tended to hypercorrect the most, especially in the more self-aware styles. Most curiously, he found middle-class men actually aiming for more stigmatised pronunciations when they were aware of their own speech. This sort of 'reverse hypercorrection' is called **covert prestige**, and can be explained in this case as middle-class men wanting to identify with a more 'streetwise' and 'plain-speaking' lower-class norm.

A5.2   **Graded variables**

One of Trudgill's variables was based, not on simple presence or absence (x/Ø), but on a graded scale of possibilities. He looked at variants of /t/ pronunciation, realised with lots of breath ('aspirated'), unaspirated, glottalised (towards the back of the mouth), and as a full glottal stop ([ʔ]). These four realisations are graded from the prestige standard to the stigmatised non-standard, and showed similar social stratification in the study.

Another form of gradation is apparent in Jenny Cheshire's (1978) study of schoolchildren in Reading. Focusing on verb form agreement ('I knows', 'we has', 'they calls', and so on), she found that usage was not so much a matter of standard and non-standard as a matter of the frequency of use of the various possibilities. Everyday vernacular words were more likely to appear in non-standard form than verbs associated with authority and power which cannot operate on individual prediction but apply more generally across groups in terms of frequencies of usage.

A6   **PRESTIGE AND LANGUAGE LOYALTY**

The main social determinants of linguistic variation can be said to be:

geography   (see section A2)
gender   (see section A7)
age   (see section A7)
class   (see section A5)
race and ethnicity (see sections A4, A8 and A9)
occupation   (see section A3)
ideology and politics

The last of these means that the opinions, attitudes and self-awareness of individuals and communities can affect linguistic usage. It is noticeable, for example, that in the sharply divided politics of Northern Ireland, republican and nationalist politicians adopt some of the accent features of the Irish Republic (especially the Dublin accent) and unionist and loyalist politicians emphasise particular Ulster accents, regardless of their actual regional origins (Democratic Unionist Party members have been observed moving towards the Ballymena accent of leading figure Ian Paisley, for example). Throughout history, people have altered their own language or forced others to change their language because of their own attitudes and beliefs.

Ideological beliefs (by which I mean not only explicit political opinions but also everyday attitudes) act as modifying factors in sociolinguistic usage. Self-consciousness changes the way people speak and write. The formality of the context is another important modifying factor. Two final factors act in opposite directions: the pressure of **standardisation**, usually from elsewhere in society; and the **language loyalty** of individuals to their own local usage.

Prestige and stigmatisation

A6.1

I used to teach a Finnish student who told me that there was a community on the Sweden/Finland border whose language was neither 'proper' Finnish nor 'proper' Swedish, and he said that Finns referred to these people as 'half-linguals'. Clearly this community is not without language, and it is more likely that they speak a particular non-standard dialect. However, it is equally clear that this dialect is enormously stigmatised in the eyes of Finnish speakers like my student, to the extent that they do not even regard the dialect as a form of language at all.

Such opinions of language varieties have behavioural, educational and governmental policy consequences that can have real effects on forms of language. The sociolinguist Roger Bell (1976: 147–57) has suggested several criteria by which the prestige (or stigma) in which a code is held can be measured. These are:

❏ **standardisation** whether the variety has been approved by institutions, codified into a dictionary or grammar, or been used for prestigious texts (national newspapers, religious books, canonical literature);

❏ **vitality** whether there is a living community of speakers who use the code or whether the language is dead or dying (like Manx, Cornish, Latin, Toccharian);

❏ **historicity** whether speakers have a sense of the longevity of their code (compare Modern Greek with Modern Hebrew);

❏ **autonomy** whether speakers consider their code to be substantially different from others (compare the relative status of Standard English/German with Standard English/Scots);

❏ **reduction** whether speakers consider the code to be a sub-variety or a full code in its own right; whether it has a reduced set of social functions; for example, it might not have its own writing system (like Geordie or Scouse) or might have only a very reduced function (like a football chant accent);

❏ **mixture**   whether speakers consider their language 'pure' (as do the French) or a mixture of other languages (as are creoles);

❏ **'unofficial' norms** whether speakers have a sense of 'good' and 'bad' varieties of the code, even if there is no 'official' codification in grammars and dictionaries.

Note that it is not always straightforward to measure these. English is a 'mongrel' language of early Germanic, Norman French, Scandinavian languages, Classical Latin and Greek, and others, but instead of being stigmatised for this mixture it receives ideological spin as a 'rich' language. Similarly, institutional adoption has ensured the prestige of Classical Latin and Greek, in spite of not being the living vernacular of anyone.

A6.2 | **Standardisation**

It is common when a language community roughly corresponds with national boundaries for one dialect to be promoted above all others and attract prestige to the point at which it is regarded as the 'standard' form, even to the extent that it is seen as the 'proper' language and all other dialects 'bad' forms of the language. There are always socio-political reasons why this happens (the roots of the standardisation of UK Standard English can be seen in the domestic policy of the Tudors: see D1).

Haugen (1966) has delineated four stages in the process of standardisation:

selection	of one dialect above others;
codification	largely through the education system;
elaboration	increase in functions and range of uses of the code;
acceptance	by the community at large of the code as the 'standard' form.

The institutional emphasis on Standard English is so strong that it is illuminating to consider its grammatical peculiarities in relation to other varieties, as Peter Trudgill (1998) has done. Standard English:

❏ fails to distinguish between the forms of the auxiliary verb 'do' and its main verb forms ('I do it' vs. 'I do think so');
❏ has irregular present tense morphology (with the verb 'go', only the third person singular is marked with 's': 'he goes');
❏ lacks multiple negation ('so you ain't never able to do this');
❏ reflexive pronouns are irregularly formed (some are derived from possessive – 'myself', some from objective – 'himself');
❏ does not distinguish singular and plural pronouns in the second person ('you' for both, not 'tu/vous, thou/you, tha/yer', 'you/youse', or 'yer/yall');
❏ verb 'to be' is irregular in present ('am', 'is', 'are') and past tenses ('was', 'were');
❏ redundantly has two forms of past tense ('I saw'/'I have seen');
❏ only has two-way distinction in demonstrative system ('this'/'that', 'these'/'those').

To these could be added:

❏ redundantly adds plural 's' to words already modified by numeral ('two dogs');
❏ lacks habitual, narrative, and future tenses (unlike French or African-American English);

❑   currently developing confusion between subjunctive, conditional and declarative forms ('shall/will', 'should/would', 'if I was/were . . .').

As sociolinguists, though our analysis must be as descriptive as possible, it is important that common attitudes and perceptions that might have sociolinguistic effects are taken into account. We can distinguish various degrees of awareness in common perception:

❑   **stereotypes**   the very obvious features that all speakers are aware of in their own usage (Scottish, Irish and American rhoticity);
❑   **markers**   obvious identifiable features that are easily measurable and that speakers are aware of only when explicitly discussing their own usage (Geordie rising intonation popularly described as 'sing-song', /w/ for /l/ in a Cockney accent);
❑   **indicators**   measurable features that are useful for linguists because they are below the normal level of users' awareness (/ɪn/ for /ɪŋ/ in Norwich, glottalling /t/ in London-influenced British accents).

People commonly attach all sorts of social evaluations to variations in usage like these.

AGE AND GENDER   A7

Sociolinguistics has mainly been concerned to describe a 'freeze-frame' of society at a particular modern moment (which means it is **synchronic**). Traditionally, the disciplines of philology and etymology have been concerned with the processes of sound and word change over time, taking a **diachronic** approach to linguistic study. However, sociolinguistics has been able to develop techniques providing insights into language change by using age variation as a social variable.

Sociolinguistic insights into change   A7.1
Undertaking a **longitudinal** sociolinguistic study is possible over a few years but more difficult over longer periods. However, there are two ways in which sociolinguists can analyse change. One is to compare older studies and records of sociolinguistic features with modern studies. The other method is to investigate the variations in usage across the age ranges, since older people will manifest earlier forms of language learned in their youth. William Labov (1963 and in 1972b) employed both methods in his study on the Massachusetts island of Martha's Vineyard.

Labov compared the findings of the 1930s *Linguistic Atlas of New England* with his own study, and also investigated modern usage correlated with age (and also geography and ideology – where on the island people lived and what was their attitude to island life). Martha's Vineyard was selected for study as a linguistically unusual place: for example, people there have rhotic accents even though the rest of New England remains non-rhotic (unusually in the US). Labov was interested in a local pronunciation that **centralised** the vowel sounds in 'night' and 'house' to the middle of the tongue; so that instead of being pronounced /naɪt/ and /haʊs/ they were closer to the Scottish and Canadian-sounding /nəɪt/ and /həʊs/. This centralisation was seen as a particular feature of the local island accent.

He found that the highest 'centralisers' (that is, those who emphasised their local accent the most) were those who had the greatest loyalty to island life. This included fishermen living away from the main tourist centres (and so not dependent on it), especially men aged between 31 and 45. The most strong 'centralisers' were those who had been away to college on the mainland and then chosen to return. Not only does this show **language loyalty**, but Labov was able to use the diachronic evidence to show that the centralisation that had been dying out in the 1930s was actually being reinforced in assertion of the island's native identity.

A7.2   **The possibility of genderlects**

One of the main social changes of the last 50 years, and one which has been extensively studied by sociolinguists, is the role of gender as a determinant of linguistic usage. We have already seen (in A5) how both Trudgill and Cheshire discovered gender differences in hypercorrection and covert prestige, even within the same social class, age and region. Trudgill also asked his informants to report what they considered to be their own usage. When compared with their actual observed behaviour, he found that women claimed to use prestige features far more than they really did, and equally that men claimed to use fewer prestige features than they actually did use. This over- and under-reporting further supports the view that women hypercorrect and men aim for covert prestige, especially among the middle-class groups. However, Trudgill explains this behaviour for each gender slightly differently. Men, he says, aim for a more streetwise, 'macho' standard, whereas women are more conscious of being judged on appearance and so hypercorrect 'upwards'. Notice, though, that the scale of values and terminology here (as well as the divergent explanations) are based very much on a male-oriented value system. It is this methodological issue that much feminist linguistic work has addressed.

Sociolinguists have taken the view that it is linguistic practices and communities who use language in a sexist way, rather than the language being inherently sexist or controlled by men (largely since, it is argued, meanings are a matter of social negotiation and cannot be fixed by anyone). There is certainly evidence that we can use the term **genderlect** to refer to the different lexical and grammatical choices that are characteristically made by men and women. Robin Lakoff has pointed to certain features she identifies as 'women's talk' such as: frequency of particular colour terms ('mauve'); frequency of certain evaluative adjectives ('lovely', 'sweet'); hesitant intonation; pitch associated with surprise and questions; tag phrases ('you know', 'kind of', 'sort of'); and superpoliteness (including euphemism, less swearing, more indirectness and hedging). Many of these claims have been investigated and criticised ever since.

More recently, Deborah Cameron, Jennifer Coates and Deborah Tannen have shown that it is features at the level of discourse and interaction that mainly realise the underlying variation in the socialisation of men and women. For example, men seem to see the purpose of conversation as information gathering, whereas women see it as a support mechanism, and both groups act accordingly. All of this translates into different linguistic behaviour: in mixed groups, men tend to dominate the time and turn taking; women tend to support and reply; men explain things to women; women ask more

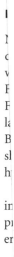

18

Ancient Greek around the Mediterranean basin, or later Latin thro... Empire, were both contact languages. They tend to vary in use in di... and there is often a great deal of local language interference. ... developed many local forms which eventually became Fre... tuguese, and so on. The contact language usually domi... speakers of that language have military or economic...

By contrast, a trade language such as Swahili ... ates a more equal relationship. This coastal Sw... whereas further west into the interior of Af... functional language, and consequently...

An international language, suc... India after independence in 194... speaker communities, and a... Other international lang... class in the eighteenth... central and north A... East Asia, and A... More recentl... influence...

pidgin
|
creole = new language —— decreolisation

basilect   mesolect   acrolect { post-creole
                                   speech
                                   continuum

⟵—————————————⟶
creole   x-isation (e.g. New English)

The evolution of pidgin languages

A8.1

In situations in which two speech communities come into prolonged contact, a **lingua franca** (common language) usually develops. This can take one of four forms: a **contact language; auxiliary language; international language;** or a **trade language**.

ghout the Roman
ferent local contexts,
atin, for example, later
nch, Italian, Spanish, Por-
ates in situations in which the
power over other language users.
n the east coast of Africa often indic-
hili is only used in commercial contexts,
rica, Reconstructed Swahili serves as a fully
is much more developed in complexity.
as English, is often used as a neutral form, as in
. Indian English did not privilege any of the native-
so gave India a linguistic access to the Western world.
ages have included French (especially amongst the ruling
nd nineteenth centuries), Spanish across large areas of south,
nerica, Chinese in both China and the headlands and islands round
rabic across the Middle East, North Africa and in Islamic countries.
y, English has ridden on the back of American economic and political
Most tellingly, 80 per cent of global internet traffic is in English.
xiliary languages include the artificial languages such as Esperanto (largely com-
d of European elements), Business English, Maritime English (Sea-Speak), and
Air-Traffic Control English. Such **Englishes for Special Purposes (ESP)** tend to have
a highly restricted and technical vocabulary, and exist in a frozen, regulated form.
It would be highly dangerous, for example, for airline pilots suddenly to develop
dialectal innovation in their expression!

When the contact between groups of people is prolonged, a hybrid language can
develop known as a pidgin. These tend to occur in situations where one language dominates, and there are two or more other languages at hand. Elements of the syntax
and lexis of each language are simplified and combined as speakers struggle to make
themselves understood by accommodating towards each speech community. Though
the pidgin might have recognisable elements of existing languages, it is not simply a
'broken' form of one of the languages: pidgins have rule systems and have to be
learnt. Nevertheless, pidgin languages tend to be restricted in vocabulary, are usually
syntactically simple, and have a limited range of functions (trade, local commerce,
marriage negotiations, land disputes, for example). Anyone who uses the pidgin will
always have their own native vernacular language, and will switch into the pidgin only
when necessary.

Pidgins tend to be found in coastal areas, generally around the equatorial belt in
former colonial locations, and have arisen typically in time of imperialism, slavery,
plantation labour migration, war and refugee situations, and around trading ports.
For these reasons, pidgins tend to be based on the languages of the European
imperial powers: French (in Louisiana, Haiti, Seychelles); Dutch (Afrikaans); Spanish
(Papiamentu); Portuguese (Guine Crioule, Macau); and English (Melanesian Tok Pisin,
West African Krio, Jamaican Patwa). Around a quarter of all pidgins and creoles have
English as an element.

A

Creolisation

A8.2

A pidgin becomes a creole as soon as it is learned as the first language of a new generation. In these circumstances, pidgins rapidly develop a wider range of phonemes, a larger vocabulary, more complex syntax and a greater range of stylistic options to the point at which the creole can be used in every context and to express every requirement of the speaker. However, not every pidgin becomes a creole, and sometimes a pidgin and a creole can co-exist in urban and rural locations.

Some creoles rapidly undergo standardisation: pronunciations and spellings are judged 'correct' or 'incorrect'; law and government administration are conducted and recorded in the creole; newspapers, books and prestigious texts are produced in it; and the creole becomes the language in which education is delivered.

Like Afrikaans, creoles can develop into fully fledged languages in their own right, with little interference from either the European parent (Dutch) or local African Bantu languages. However, many English-based creoles come under pressure from locally powerful English-speaking standards (American, Australian, or British textbooks). In these circumstances, a **post-creole speech continuum** can develop. Different forms of the creole become socially stratified: the fully fledged creole is spoken by illiterate manual workers (the **basilectal** variety), and a variety (the **acrolect**) closer to standard English is spoken by the social elites, with a range of varieties (**mesolects**) in between. As described in Section A9 below, the acrolect can evolve into a **New English**, such as Singlish or Jamaican English, for example. This is part of the wider process known as **x-isation** (for example, 'Indianisation', 'Sinicisation', 'Americanisation' and so on).

If the pressure from the powerful local standard is sufficiently strong, the creole can become **decreolised**, and the basilectal and mesolectal varieties become stigmatised and associated with illiteracy and ignorance. In such situations, local governments often proscribe the use of the creole as 'improper', and the schools and newspapers teach against it. Unless language loyalty or covert prestige sustains it, the creole can disappear and eventually lose all its speakers and die.

NEW, NATIONAL AND INTERNATIONAL ENGLISHES

A9

The English language was developed by Germanic invaders into the south and east of Britain, and spread west and north into Ireland, Wales and Scotland. From the Renaissance to the eighteenth century it was spread by the English navy and emigrants to north America and Australasia. At the height of the British Empire in the nineteenth century, English became the administrative language of large parts of Africa, the Indian subcontinent, and strategic trading outposts like Hong Kong and Singapore. The number of extraterritorial English speakers means that the language no longer belongs to any one nation, and that we must speak not of English but of 'Englishes'.

The standard Englishes

A9.1

In those countries in which English is the official, main or dominant language, we can talk of 'Standard Englishes'. Braj Kachru (1988) differentiates 'the inner circle' of standard English-speaking territories from 'the outer circle' where English is very important but does not dominate to the same extent (see A9.2 below). At the beginning of the twenty-first century, a variety of standard Englishes are spoken in:

The British Isles	(around 65 million people)
US and Caribbean	(around 300 million people)
Canada	(around 27 million people)
Australia	(around 18 million people)
New Zealand	(around 4 million people)

Thus just under half a billion people use English as their first or main language in the world.

The characteristic accents and standardised dialects of these areas derive from the time at which the main settlement from Britain occurred, and they are all founded on southern British speech variants. North American speech derives from the seventeenth and eighteenth centuries and shows an especial East Anglian influence. Australasian accents come mainly from the south-east of England and London in the eighteenth and nineteenth centuries – at which time parts of South Africa were also settled. The rest of the Commonwealth (across Africa, India and Southeast Asia) takes its English norms from the late nineteenth and early twentieth centuries. Former British colonies were garrisoned and ruled by an army largely recruited from southern England, led by public school educated officers who were upper middle class or even aristocracy, speaking RP. Caribbean accents derive from the west African origins of slave ancestors.

Later local variations entered as a result of later settlement and evolution. For example, the influx of eastern European refugees, Irish and Jews from famine and war in the late nineteenth and early twentieth centuries gave the arrival point of New York its characteristic accent. Large numbers of Scots and Irish emigrants to Canada produced Canadian English, and the Scots dialect similarly influenced New Zealand speech.

Historically, the population of English L1 speakers has been larger than the number of English L2 users in the world, with a shift of influence to the US over the twentieth century. However, the populations of the 'outer circle' are increasing at a faster rate, and the estimate is that the number of L2 users will overtake L1 users in 2007.

A9.2

The standardising Englishes

Kachru's 'outer circle' includes:

African territories (Ghana, Kenya, Nigeria, Tanzania, Zambia)	(300 million)
Indian subcontinent (India, Pakistan, Bangladesh, Sri Lanka)	(1.2 billion)
Pacific rim (Malaysia, Singapore, Philippines)	(80 million)

In total, a population of 1.5 billion live in these areas in which English has a special importance – though of course not everyone speaks English either as a vernacular or fluently.

English in these areas co-exists with many other indigenous languages. Inevitably, there is **interference** between the codes, with lexical copying and grammatical structures repositioning the English variety. We can thus talk of the x-isation of English, and x-ised forms include the Indianisation of English, the Africanisation of English, and so on, to produce New Englishes with their own lexicogrammars and rules. In effect, they are in the process of standardising.

The 'Americanisation' of English has been documented for many years, with many eighteenth-century British features (rhoticity and other variant pronunciations, verb forms like 'do you got', older meanings of words like 'mad', 'guess' and 'fag', among many others), as well as subsequent independent developments. American English has a noticeably developed spelling system, thanks to lexicographer Noah Webster and his efforts to establish 'an American language'.

The 'Indianisation' of English is also a global force. Written Indian English uses many features which would be considered very polite, formal or conservative in a British or American setting. Features of spoken Indian English include:

omission of articles	'I borrowed book from library.'
Subject-Object-Verb word order	'I door open.'
prepositional variation	'I my aunt to visited.'
comparative/superlative	'good, more good, most good/good of all'
itself/only	'Can I meet with you tomorrow itself?'
adverbial for dummy 'there'	'Meat is there, vegetables are there.'
politeness markers	'These mistakes may please be corrected.'
tense and aspect variation	'I am having a cold.'
question non-inversion	'Who you have come to see?'
undifferentiated tag question	'You are going home soon, isn't it?'
lexical variation	bandh (regional labour strike)
	crore (10 million)
	lathi (bamboo iron-clad police truncheon)
	biodata (CV)
	co-brother (wife's sister's husband)

Other New Englishes show similar interference patterns and characteristic features.

Finally, English is an increasingly important L2 in the rest of the world, which Kachru calls 'the expanding circle':

Far East (China, Indonesia, Japan, Korea, Nepal, Taiwan)	(1.7 billion)
Middle East (Egypt, Israel, Saudi Arabia)	(70 million)
Africa (Zimbabwe)	(10 million)

Thus, around 20 per cent of the world's population have English as L1 or L2, and a further 45 per cent have English as an important language in their lives: this amounts in total to nearly two-thirds of the human race.

POLITENESS AND ACCOMMODATION   **A10**

Much of this section has focused on 'macro-sociolinguistic' dimensions of language. However, social negotiation also has an individual, micro-sociolinguistic aspect.

Language choice is motivated by **recipient design** – that is, users aim for an effective communicative purpose, bearing in mind the target of the utterance. All languages have a range of features available that encode very subtle social and individual relationships, and many areas of sociolinguistics are concerned with encoding power. This suggests perhaps that power is a super-determinant in sociolinguistics.

A10.1

Name and address

Many languages, including some varieties of English, differentiate singular and plural second person. This is known as the T/V system:

French	tu/vous
Latin	tu/vos
Russian	ty/vy
Italian	tu/Lei
German	du/Sie
Greek	esi/esis
Swedish	du/ni
Old English	þe/ge
Middle English	thou/you
Yorkshire English	tha/you
Liverpool and Dublin English	you/youse
Appalachian English	you/yall

These forms can have a variety of functions:

- ❏ **number** differentiating singular (T) and plural (V);
- ❏ **politeness** to mark intimate and familiar (T) or respect (V);
- ❏ **social rank** V used to superiors, T used to inferiors;
- ❏ **solidarity** V used outside the group, T used as an in-group marker.

English developed its T/V through number to include politeness by the early Middle Ages. It developed as a marker of social rank during the Renaissance, but then became non-differentiated in many dialects (including the dialect that was to become Standard English) beginning around the time of the English Civil War (seventeenth century). In modern times, it is only heard in some dialects, in frozen utterances such as the traditional wedding service, prayers from the Authorised Version of the Bible, Quaker language, and in productions of Shakespeare plays.

In other languages, speakers are aware of the choice to be made: French signals it with the verbs *vousvoyer* and *tutoyer*; German with *duzen* and *siezen* and a little ceremony to mark the shift in the relationship. Speakers have the choice of:

- ❏ reciprocal T usage to show equality and familiarity (used by French revolutionaries in 1789 and modern communists);
- ❏ reciprocal V usage to show mutual respect or formality (French aristocrats such as former president Valéry Giscard d'Estaing use V to everyone, including, it is reported, to voters, ministers, his wife and passing dogs. Apparently Jean-Paul Sartre and Simone de Beauvoir addressed each other using V);
- ❏ asymmetrical T/V usage to show power difference (based on age and youth, serving staff and customers, boss and worker, professor and student, for example).

There are cultural variations within this, of course. The rigid asymmetrical T/V usage is loosening, especially amongst young French speakers. French and Italian speakers are more likely to use T to friends than Germans, but Germans are more likely than them to use T to distant relatives. Norwegian schoolchildren can use T to teachers, but German and Dutch tend not to do so. Male Italian students are likely to use T to female students, but then in general Italians use more T than French or Germans. Speakers who are politically conservative tend also to be linguistically conservative and preserve the T/V asymmetry.

This system is echoed in the title and address options which are also available to all English speakers without a T/V system. Politeness is encoded by use of title, first name, last name, by combinations of these (TLN, TFN, FNLN), or by avoidance (Ø). Again, asymmetrical usage indicates a power inequality, and a switch from a more polite to less polite form must always be initiated by the most powerful person ('Dr Stockwell?' 'Please, call me Peter'). Breaking these norms generates certain social effects: consider, on meeting the Queen of England, 'Alright Betty!'

English has to use title and address options very subtly, since it lacks the complex verb-ending system of, for example, Korean:

intimate	-na	polite	-e yo
familiar	-e	deferential	-supnita
plain	-ta	authoritative	-so

The pragmatics of politeness affects all linguistic choices, including accent and intonation selection and choice of register: consider the real 'Customers are reminded that New Street is a no smoking station. Please extinguish all smoking materials', with a possible alternative, 'Oi you, stop bloody smoking – get that fag out'.

One model of politeness (Brown and Levinson 1987) is based on the notion of **face**. This is the social role that you present to the world. **Negative face** is your desire to be unimpeded in your actions; **positive face** is your desire for identification with the community. Any interpersonal event is potentially a **face threatening act (FTA)** which needs to be negotiated with particular politeness strategies:

positive politeness	appealing to positive face ('You look fit and healthy – any chance you could help me push the car?');
negative politeness	hedge ('Could I, er, just, sort of do this . . .');
	indicate pessimism ('I don't suppose you have the time on you?');
	minimise the imposition ('Do you mind if I borrow it for a second?');
	indicate deference ('I'm an idiot – forgotten my keys again! Any chance of borrowing yours?');
	apologise ('Sorry about this, but could I . . .');
	impersonalise ('The management reserve the right to refuse admission . . .')
	use politeness tag ('please').

Of course, it is important to match the politeness strategy to the force of the imposition: you would not require much politeness to ask the time, but you would need a lot to borrow a car. Mismatching the expected norm will be seen as rudeness, over-familiarity, aggression, or over-formality, obsequiousness or sarcasm. Of course, you always have the option of just asking, plainly and baldly, without any redressive politeness, for the thing you want, but usually only those with either extreme power or extreme intimacy can get away with this.

A10.2 **Phatics**

Phatic tokens are the parts of conversation whose primary function is social rather than content bearing. They are used typically at the beginning and end of exchanges, and to repair a conversation when it collapses. Examples include 'Good morning', 'How are you?' 'Nice weather we're having', and so on. According to Laver (1975), phatic tokens are normatively:

> emotionally uncontroversial;
> expect a positive response;
> expect a non-committal response.

So, the normative response to 'Nice weather we're having' would be 'Hmm, lovely isn't it'. It would be very strange to reply with 'Rubbish. Any fool can see it's going to rain. What are you, an idiot?' Again, non-normative choices will generate particular sociolinguistic effects.

Laver distinguishes three types of token:

❏ neutral token – refers to the context of situation (the weather, the view, the news);
❏ self-oriented token – is personal to the speaker ('My, I'm hot today');
❏ other-oriented token – is personal to the addressee ('How are you?').

He claims that the normative pattern is that when a superior (e.g. a baron) initiates a conversation with an inferior (e.g. a peasant building a wall), he will use an other-oriented token ('That looks like hard work'). When an inferior begins the conversation, he will use a self-oriented token ('Hard work, this'). Though this example is extreme, the same pattern can be observed where the 'superior' is socially more powerful, chairing a meeting, in authority in a situation, seated higher than the other, sitting in their room and interrupted, answering the door or phone in 'their' territory, and so on. Phatic and politeness mitigation is also required when a person in motion encounters a stationary person – since they have intruded on their personal space (an FTA, in effect).

All of these linguistic facilities are available for social negotiation. Participants also evolve their strategies and choices in the process of interaction. The most interesting is the phenomenon of **accommodation**, in which participants converge their speech styles. This can mean that people with different accents alter their vowel quality towards each other, or begin to echo certain words or phrases used by the other person, or adopt similar discourse and politeness strategies over time.

As always, there are cultural differences here of course. For example, in mixed sex conversations, men and women tend to use fewer features of their genderlects and tend to move towards a common norm. In Britain, however, men tend to accommodate more towards women, whereas in the US, women tend to move further towards the male norm.

DEVELOPMENT

STUDIES IN LANGUAGE AND SOCIETY

HOW TO USE THESE STUDIES

The key concepts set out so far in this book are the product of many discussions by many researchers in sociolinguistics. Some of these professional studies are represented in Section D. Students setting out to investigate language and society use the published work and concepts to structure their own explorations, and to provide a disciplined framework within which to conduct and present their study. In this section, I will outline the work of my own recent undergraduate students in sociolinguistics. The intention in doing this is to encourage you, if you are new to the area, to have confidence in your own skills and thinking.

Each study is linked to the corresponding numbered area in Section A. The students who conducted each study also read theoretical work and case studies in their area of investigation. In contextualising their work for this book, I have added my own comments, and each section has a set of references to further reading. Some of the data for your own analysis in Section C also comes from fieldwork studies collected by my students.

Finding an area for study

The most successful studies tend to be those that are done by students with a direct interest in the area of investigation. This can arise in two different ways: **theory-driven** or **data-driven**.

In the former case, students are introduced to key ideas and debates within an area, and are led to further reading of published material. As they read and engage with the subject, I encourage them to 'read with a pencil', to think critically about their reading. A useful way of doing this is to assume a sceptical attitude towards every claim made in a book or article, unless direct evidence or reasoning is provided. Students are encouraged to examine closely every detail of the presentation, and also to think in general about what theoretical assumptions and positions underpin the writing. Often, what might at first glance appear to be minor details of difference between different studies can turn out to be examples where the writer 'buys into' a set of associated frameworks and positions that are highly contentious. Encouraging students to seek out these frameworks and discuss them directly is often a successful way of getting them to the heart of a discussion, and to engage seriously with the research. Theory-driven work is often the only practical way a British-based student can investigate, for example, African or Pacific pidgins and creoles, or diglossia, or cross-cultural politeness norms, and so on.

The contrary way of approaching an area of sociolinguistics is to discover the personal sociolinguistics in a student's life and develop that in a systematic way within the discipline. For example, many of my international students choose to investigate community multilingualism, personal bilingualism and code-switching, or examples of language loyalty towards new Englishes, and so on. By far the most popular area for study amongst English students at the moment is language and gender. The danger in exploring a familiar area, of course, is that the work becomes anecdotal and over-subjective. The way of avoiding this is to send students off to read published material in the area, and to develop very rigorous and transparent empirical procedures. They should also be encouraged to apply the same sort of sceptical rigour to their own draft work as they would apply to published studies.

It is also part of the learning process in sociolinguistics that students develop their skills in academic writing. Though it is possible to set out the linguistics of academic prose and teach it, selecting the most appropriate conventional register is best learned by reading lots of professional sociolinguistic studies. The key to ensuring both this and a high level of rigour in evidence is to insist upon accurate and thorough referencing of all material read for the study. The model for setting this out is used in this book. I refer simply to the author's name and date of publication in the text, and all references are collected together at the end.

ATTITUDES TO ACCENT VARIATION   B2

The reason why accent variation is so important in sociolinguistics is because of the significance people attach to different accents. The case study below is partly a **replication study** of original work in informants' subjective evaluations of accent.

Evaluative reactions to accents   B2.1

Sarah Wood researched original work done by Giles and Powesland (1975) and others which used a method of data elicitation known as the **matched-guise** technique. Briefly, this involves playing a recording of the same speaker imitating a variety of different accents, and then asking listeners to rate each 'speaker' on a range of different dimensions. These might include their sense of the attractiveness of the speaker, how communicative they were, what their social status seems to be, and so on. In this way, a pattern of common stereotypical associations in attitude to accents is built up. The original studies used a range of British accents (northern, southern, rural, urban and RP) and some foreign-accented English (American, Italian, Indian, German, French, and so on), and used informants from south Wales and the southwest of England.

The findings were that, for many people, standard accents (such as RP) were more likely to be considered as belonging to prestigious, aesthetically pleasing and intelligible articulate speakers. The 'broadest' accents and those associated with urban and industrial areas, by contrast, were considered to be used by low-status speakers and were regarded as unattractive. Rural accents were considered aesthetically pleasing, but subordinate to RP on the dimensions of social status and intelligibility.

Much of this work was conducted in the 1970s, and Sarah Wood was concerned with discovering the current situation. In general, she replicated Giles's (1970) study but made a few adjustments to improve the analysis. She restricted the recordings to 8 native British accents (RP, west London, Norwich, north-east England, Nottingham, Cheshire, Burnley, and Sheffield), and she used genuine native speakers of these accents in the recordings. All speakers read a passage which was specially written to contain many accent-variant features (this 'Goldilocks' passage appears in C2). All speakers and informants were female students in their early 20s, to control for gender, age and some class variation, and the informants included 2 northern speakers, 2 southern speakers, and a Midlands speaker.

Sarah ensured an easy comparability of data by setting a written, multiple-choice questionnaire, as follows:

Q1   Please name the accent you have just heard.

Q2   Please circle the description you most agree with based on your view of the pleasantness/unpleasantness of this accent:

1 extremely pleasant   2 pleasant   3 neutral
4 unpleasant   5 extremely unpleasant

Q3   Please circle the prestige rating you would give this accent:

1 very prestigious   2 prestigious   3 neutral
4 unprestigious   5 very unprestigious

Q4   Please circle the intelligence rating you would give this speaker:

1 very intelligent   2 intelligent   3 neutral
4 unintelligent   5 very unintelligent

Q5   Please circle the type of house you would expect this person to live in:

1 homeless
2 council/housing association rented
3 council/housing association owner-occupied
4 rented private housing
5 terraced owner-occupied
6 average-sized owner-occupied
7 large owner-occupied
8 'mansion'-size owner-occupied

Q6   Please circle the type of job you would expect this speaker to have (examples are simply guidelines):

1 unemployed
2 unskilled manual (rubbish collector)
3 semi-skilled manual (factory worker)
4 skilled manual (engineer)

> 5 routine non-manual (clerical, sales)
> 6 low professional (civil servant)
> 7 self-employed (own business)
> 8 management
> 9 higher professional (doctor, lawyer)

Sarah presented her detailed results as a table, and then contrasted her findings with those of 30 years previously. She found that the 'southern' accents (RP, west London and Norwich) attracted the highest and most prestigious overall ratings in most categories, across all informants. Though the RP speaker was judged more intelligent than the others, they were judged equal in social status, and the RP accent was judged as being less pleasing. The northern accents came out worst in the prestige judgements, with the urban accents more stigmatised than the rural ones.

It is interesting that there was largely a consensus across informants, which suggests that language loyalty was a small factor in this study (though the northern informants did rate the northern accents slightly higher). Furthermore, judgements tended to parallel each other across the dimensions: so an accent tended to be judged consistently either prestigious or stigmatised across all the questions. Sarah also conjectured that the status of RP was changing so that it was becoming seen as 'too posh' and thus untrustworthy, and she discussed other reading which supported this view. Finally, she discussed the consequences of such accent stereotypes for non-standard speakers in relation to their social standing, job opportunities and educational access.

There are all sorts of connections to be made from Sarah's study. First of all, replication studies are a very useful means of investigating **language change**: in this case, changes in attitude to accents. It is largely as a consequence of such attitudinal changes that the use of RP seems to be diminishing in Britain (it is certainly less commonly heard in universities and on the BBC), and in many cases is being 'toned down' by being casualised in the direction of local urban vernaculars like Mancunian, Geordie and Cockney. This process produces the sort of hybrid 'posh Geordie', and so on, that can be heard on regional television news programmes, and has been characterised in relation to Cockney as 'Estuary English'.

Second, Sarah's study could lead into a discussion of the prestige and stigmatisation of accents and dialects in general. When people are aware of their own accent and its prestige value, they will often adjust it either towards a more standardised form (this is hypercorrection if it is overdone) or even towards a more stigmatised form (if they want to sound 'less posh', this is covert prestige).

Finally, Sarah's study offers a refinement of sociolinguistic methodology along the lines of using naturalistic elicitation procedures to generate naturalistic and reliable data. It is thus a contribution to the methodological discussion of the field.

Further reading ➤➤➤➤   B2.2

❑   Accent and dialect studies are the foundation of sociolinguistics, so there is a mass of material in almost every sociolinguistics book.

❏   The classic accounts of accent varieties are the three volumes of Wells (1982), and Trudgill and
     Hannah (1982); see also Lippi-Green (1997 and D2).

❏   On dialect, see Hughes and Trudgill (1979), Chambers and Trudgill (1980), Davis (1983, 1990),
     Petyt (1980), Francis (1983), Downes (1984), Trudgill (1986a, 1990).

❏   The original studies of attitude to accent are: Addington (1968); Ellis (1967); Giles (1970); Hopper
     and Williams (1973); Giles and Powesland (1975); Lambert, Frankel and Tucker (1966); Seligman,
     Tucker and Lambert (1972); Eiser (1984).

❏   The area has been revisited by Andersson and Trudgill (1990); Edwards (1989); Giles and
     Coupland (1991).

B3   EUPHEMISM AND REGISTER

Register and style are both means of marking out social groups and establishing solidarity. In general, the sort of lexicogrammatical choices made at this level are based
on selection of words and sequencing them in particular ways. Selection can be seen
as a sort of metaphorical system, since one word is chosen to fill a linguistic slot in
place of another word. **Idioms** (the individual words and phrases peculiar to a language variety – see B14) often rely for their meaning on metaphorical interpretations.
'Kick the bucket', for example, has a metaphorical meaning of 'to die' (rather grue-
somely originating in the method of hanging criminals by kicking an upturned
bucket away from their feet). Conversely, **euphemism** can be seen not so much as a
lexical replacement by a dissimilar word as a replacement by a closely associated word
(a **metonymy** rather than a metaphor). 'The rest room' is not a metaphor; rather it
conveys slightly different, more pleasant associations than other possibilities ('bog',
'crapper', 'thunderbox', 'shithouse', and many others). Many terms take polite cover
under foreign languages ('toilet', 'lavatory', 'netty' all mean 'washroom' in French, Latin
and Italian, and the French 'loo' – the place – is the most vague of all). Euphemisms
for taboo areas (sex, death, war, defecation, and all manner of social unpleasantnesses)
are a useful area for mapping social relationships and attitudes.

B3.1   Euphemism and death

Vicki Oliver examined ways of presenting death in 100 obituaries from *The Times* and
the *Daily Telegraph* on the same day. She noted that *Roget's Thesaurus* lists 115 terms
for the verb 'to die', and a further 65 noun phrases for the word 'dead'. Not surprisingly, the newspaper obituaries only used a tiny proportion of these (excluding, for
example, 'croaked', 'snuffed it', 'bit the dust' and so on). The main linguistic strategy
was euphemism – 'the saying of something innocuous that either hints at, or establishes a precondition of some previous offensive intended act' (Ortony 1993: 43).
Otherwise, the only conceptual metaphor used was the notion that 'Life is a battle',
as in the baby who 'bravely fought but sadly lost her battle', and the cancer patient
who 'died suddenly after a courageous fight'. This was only applied in the case of ill-
nesses, however, and not in the case of old people who have 'had a good innings',
relying on a different conceptual metaphor, 'Life is a game of cricket'.

What was immediately noticeable in this small corpus of data was that the word
for death was often omitted entirely (omission is itself a form of euphemism). Only

25 of the 100 obituaries used the word 'died' at all, and of these, 12 were qualified by the adverbs 'peacefully' or 'quietly'. In fact, many obituaries simply began with the adverb, omitting the verbal element: 'Mitchell, Eric James, peacefully at Bognor War Memorial hospital'. These elliptical forms are not simply the result of space saving in newspapers; the 'Forthcoming marriages' section nearby often begins, 'The engagement is announced between . . .'. Vicki points out that it would be unthinkable to begin an obituary, 'The death is announced of . . .'.

The standard form, then, is: 'Name > adverb > prepositional phrase denoting location > details of funeral service time and place'. Variations on the adverb include 'joins Arthur after a long illness', and 'reunited with Vic'. Deviations from this pattern are thus foregrounded: only one obituary used the word 'killed', in relation to a 19-year-old student who 'died tragically after a fall at university'.

Vicki discusses her data using work done by Paul Chilton (1986), in which he identifies in the ideological field a point similar to the notion of a face threatening act (see A10). He calls such moments, when the dominant ideology is potentially transparent, a **critical discourse moment (CDM)**. Talking about death is a CDM, a taboo area that needs to be linguistically negotiated. Euphemism, argues Vicki Oliver, is a form of verbal avoidance designed to preserve negative face, or the reader's right to be ideologically unperturbed.

Chilton (1986: 15) defines two 'functional poles of ideological discourse', as follows:

twin poles of ideological discourse:	metaphor	euphemism
methods:	coercive	suppressive
	legitimising	dissimulating
typical linguistic strategies:	replacement	omission
	framing	passivisation
	modalisation	nominalisation
	narrative . . .	lexical replacement . . .

In these ways, ideologically problematic areas can be negotiated and fitted into the speaker's (or, more typically, the writer's) worldview. Chilton analyses the discourses of war and the nuclear arms race ('nukespeak') in order to illustrate how governments use metaphor to coerce people into thinking in a particular way, and euphemism to avoid facing up to the harsh realities of war. In Vicki Oliver's study of death notices (and notice how 'obituary' is itself a euphemistic shift into a word from Latin), euphemism as opposed to metaphor is the preferred approach, because the intent is to repress rather than broaden the meaning. The result, claims Vicki, is a prototypical form of discourse (a naturalised register for announcing deaths in newspapers) that is designed to comfort rather than confront social concepts of death. She asserts that the obituaries simultaneously evade its reality, respect its significance, and conform to an accepted but implicit social format.

Further reading ➤➤➤➤

❑ The area of investigation of ideological discourse strategies has come to be called **critical linguistics** or **critical discourse analysis**.

❑ Chilton's (1986) article appears in revised form in Chilton (1988), and his work on nuclear discourse appears in Chilton (1985).

❑ Examples of critical linguistics appear in Fowler (1986, 1991), Fowler, Hodge, Kress and Trew (1979), Kress and Hodge (1979) and Hodge and Kress (1988).

❑ Critical discourse analysis receives its theoretical foundations from Fairclough (1989, 1995a, 1995b, see C3), and examples can be seen in the reader edited by Caldas-Coulthard and Coulthard (1986).

❑ Register has been investigated by Ventola (1987), Swales (1990) and Biber and Finegan (1994).

B4   **CODE-SWITCHING IN GERMAN**

There are many permanent multilingual communities around me in Nottingham. The university sits in a park with Polish and Ukrainian bilinguals on one side, and bilingual speakers of Punjabi and English, and Patwa and English on the other, living alongside the main student areas in the city. Within the campus there are many more temporary multilingual communities, as international and exchange students form their own groups. In the city and university, then, there are many opportunities for students to investigate multilingualism.

B4.1

Code-switching

Christopher Barenberg was chatting in English outside the library to a German friend who suddenly said: 'I think the essay will be alright, *aber Du weisst ja wie das ist*' ('but you know what it's like'). This is code-switching as defined by Gumperz (1982: 59): 'the juxtaposition within the same speech exchange of passages belonging to two different grammatical systems or subsystems'. The essay in question would have been written in English, and the two Germans were standing in an English university. This domain is shifted onto the level of intimacy and familiarity: both speakers are German exchange students facing the uncertainty of submitting an essay in a different university culture.

Since Chris is a part of the speech community under investigation, the method employed is one of **participant observation** (see B5). He recorded several exchanges within the German student community – previously all living in monolingual Germany but now living as a bilingual minority in a predominantly English-speaking culture. Only he was aware that the conversations were being recorded for a sociolinguistic study.

Using Romaine's (1989: 112) descriptive terms, he provides examples of the different types of code-switching used within his speech community, and he discusses the motivations behind each usage in the light of the domains underlying the utterances:

- ❏ **tag-switching** – 'I'm pleased to see you're getting a *Bewegungsmelder, ja*' ('security light, yes'). Chris surmises this tag-switch might simply be because the speaker lacked the necessary vocabulary in English for the previous word.
- ❏ **intersentential switch** – 'We're going to Nicki's house at nine and maybe to the Bomb [a nightclub] afterwards. (Short pause). *Kristina bleibt allerdings zu Hause sie muss noch arbeiten*' ('Unfortunately Kristina is staying at home because she still has to do some work'). This telephone conversation switches at a sentence boundary, marked with a short pause, at the point where the topic changes to refer to the speaker's German housemate.
- ❏ **intrasentential switch** – though there were many examples of the first two types recorded, the only example of a shift within a sentence was the conversation outside the library given above. Even this occurs at a clause boundary rather than mid clause. Chris points out that this sort of switch is the most 'risky', requiring the greatest degree of mutual bilingual proficiency which might not have existed in this temporary speech community.

The German students manifested the use of German as an 'in-group' marker, using it in the domains of 'home' and 'socialising', and illustrated their code loyalty by greeting each other in German while on campus. However, they also showed their sensitivity to both the domain and to the 'out-group' by switching back into English whenever the domain became 'academic work' or when monolingual English speakers were to be included.

Du and *Sie*   B4.2

Martin Stepanek used a questionnaire to determine the domains in which a German speaker today would use the familiar *Du* and the plural, respectful *Sie* (see A10). He found that the published studies did not match up to his intuitions as a native German speaker, and he suggests that the sociolinguistic situation in this area is changing very rapidly.

He talked through 18 questionnaires with German-speaking students studying in Britain. All were 19–25 years old, 13 from Germany (including 5 from the eastern part of the country), 4 Austrians and 1 of Swiss origin but living in Germany. On the age dimension, this 19–25 year old group are at the boundary of asymmetrical T/V usage, and are thus most likely to show up changes in progress. The questionnaire (in German) firstly established the social background of the informants' age, gender, origins, vernacular, education and attitude. Informants were encouraged to give details and examples in addition to their 'yes/no' answers.

The questionnaire asked a series of **open-ended questions** such as:

- ❏ Can you think of situations in which you aren't sure which form to use?
- ❏ Has there ever been a situation in which you felt uncomfortable being addressed with *Du* or with *Sie*?
- ❏ Do you ever address someone with *Sie*, being addressed by this person with *Du* in return?

Then a series of 'yes/no' questions, with boxes to tick:

❏ Do you find it OK to be addressed with *Du*?
   in a furniture shop   11 yes, 7 no, 0 don't know
   in advertisements   14y, 3n, 1dk
   on national election posters   6y, 12n
   on student union election posters   18y
   by professors   7y, 7n, 4dk
   by students   18y
   in a student magazine   18y
   in a newspaper/weekly magazine   4y, 14n

❏ Do you find it OK to be addressed with *Sie*?
   by professors   14y, 1n, 3dk
   by younger people (−18)   1y, 14n, 3dk
   by older students (40+)   2y, 15n, 1dk
   by students of the same age   1y, 17n
   by an acquaintance of your parents   3y, 14n, 1dk
   by a former teacher   6y, 9n, 3dk

❏ With which form are you normally addressed?
   by parents   18 *Du*
   by grandparents   17 *Du*, 1 *Sie*
   in primary school   18 *Du*
   in lower school (10–14)   15 *Du*, 1 *Sie*, 2 both
   in upper school (15–19)   11 *Du*, 3 *Sie*, 4 both
   by professors   14 *Sie*, 4 both
   by students   18 *Du*
   by people over 50   3 *Du*, 11 *Sie*, 4 both
   by unfamiliar children   4 *Du*, 9 *Sie*, 5 both
   by youngsters   9 *Du*, 3 *Sie*, 6 both
   on the street   12 *Sie*, 6 both
   in a pub (i.e. bar)   13 *Du*, 2 *Sie*, 2 both
   in a café   7 *Du*, 9 *Sie*, 2 both
   in a club   7 *Du*, 9 *Sie*, 2 both

❏ Which form do (did) you normally use?
   as a primary school pupil to teachers   1 *Du*, 17 *Sie*
   in lower school to teachers   18 *Sie*
   to university professors   17 *Sie*, 1 both
   to students over 40   10 *Du*, 5 *Sie*, 3 both
   to youngsters   18 *Du*
   to a former teacher who has not explicitly offered you *Du*   18 *Sie*

Having heightened the informants' self-awareness, the questionnaire then asks some
more open-ended questions designed to elicit anecdotes and opinions. It ends by

asking whether the informants find it acceptable that the questionnaire uses *Du* throughout! All 18 approved.

In both these quantitative findings, as well as in the qualitative data from his discussions, Martin found that although younger Germans use mutual *Du* more with each other, it seems that these young adults are moving towards *Sie* as a neutral option, especially in traditionally asymmetric T/V domains. They do not like the use of *Du* when it denotes disrespect, in a service setting where it shows undue familiarity, or when used by older people to frame them as having child status.

Martin discusses his findings in relation to the published literature, identifying the dimensions of power and solidarity, especially in terms of age, in his data. He also uses the background information to speculate on possible differences between these informants' reports of their usage with their actual observed usage. Finally, he also considers the situation within his own dialect of Vorarlberg in Austria. Here, an additional pronoun *Ihr* is used. Originally a second person plural, Martin notes how his 75-year-old grandmother's generation use it as the neutral option to refer to people singularly without the deference and formality of *Sie*. She only uses *Sie* with people she does not know '(and probably does not like), and to people who she thinks are to be highly respected, like architects, and people who studied at university'. *Du* is then reserved for very close family and children.

However, Martin notes that neither he nor his parents' generation seem to use *Ihr* in this way, and he claims that the standardisation pressure of High German in schools and the media is causing it to die out.

Further reading ➤➤➤➤   **B4.3**

❑   Edwards (1995) is recommended for discussion of multilingualism.

❑   On pronoun usage and terms of address, see Mühlhäusler and Harré (1990), Braun (1988) and Adler (1978).

❑   The classic works on bilingualism and code-switching are Fishman (1972, 1974, 1978), Beardsmore (1982), Heller (1988), Romaine (1989), Myers-Scotton (1993a, 1993b) and Milroy and Muysken (1995).

❑   The classic case studies can be found in the following collections: Fishman (1968), Whiteley (1971), Gumperz and Hymes (1972), Giglioli (1972), and Pride and Holmes (1972).

ON THE FOOTBALL TERRACE   **B5**

Not all sociolinguistic situations are amenable to careful control of the variables to link specific linguistic features with specific social determinants (this is the 'variationist' method – see A5). Alternative methods of accessing and eliciting sociolinguistic data have been developed which place more emphasis on more complex causes and effects. One of the first and most famous examples of this is Lesley Milroy's (1978, 1987a, 1987b) study of **social networks** in Belfast.

Social networks   **B5.1**
Recognising problems in the application of a social stratification model (see A5) to local communities, Lesley Milroy applied the notion of social networks to the study

of three inner-city speech communities in Belfast. The advantages of a social network approach are: it is a useful tool for studying small, self-contained groups in detail; it is useful in situations (such as immigrant communities, or amongst schoolchildren) where the concept of social class is either irrelevant or not clear cut; and it is based on the relationships between individuals rather than subsuming individuals into group averages, and so it is fundamentally inter-subjective.

Milroy developed a 'network strength score' based on the nature of social network connections within a group of people. This had two main dimensions:

❑ a **dense** social network results when all the people in a group are linked to each other, so that everyone knows everyone else;
❑ a **multiplex** social network results when individuals in the group are related to each other in a number of different ways (such as being neighbours, drinking in the pub together, working together, having children at the same school, and so on).

A very close-knit community will be both dense and multiplex and thus have a high network strength score.

Milroy was interested in how stigmatised vernacular norms (mainly accent variants) were maintained in local communities. She collected her data by being introduced to the communities as 'the friend of a friend', a method known as **participant observation**. She found that the highest incidence of the vernacular norms occurred in those communities with the highest network strength scores (in the Belfast communities studied, this was among Protestant men in Ballymacarrett who both worked together and lived in the same neighbourhood, and young Catholic women in the Clonard whose partners were mainly unemployed, isolating the community even more).

It seems that a close-knit social network operates as a 'norm reinforcement mechanism' – encouraging innovative linguistic features and helping to maintain and diffuse them into the wider society. Furthermore, close-knit networks are very common in low-status communities, and this partly offers an explanation for language loyalty as resistance to the pressure from standardisation.

| B5.2 |

The sociolinguistics of football crowds

James Baderman applied a range of sociolinguistic methods, including Milroy's study of social networks, in his analysis of football crowd discourse. His participant observation technique involved attending Tottenham Hotspur games and making covert recordings amongst the crowd at both home and away matches. His findings and analysis are as follows.

Club loyalty as language loyalty

'Spurs' is a football club based in London, and James found that when inside the ground the supporters used songs and chants that accentuated the most covertly prestigious elements of the Cockney accent. This meant that particularly stereotypical accent features were adopted, even by speakers who were observed outside the ground with more standardised accents. For example, the cry, 'Come on you lily whites', aside from displaying a close cultural knowledge of an antiquated nickname for the team, was always uttered in an exaggerated, even cartoonised Cockney accent: [kam ɔn ju: lɪliwɔɪtsɑ], with a forceful final vowel added for extra emphasis.

James suggests that many of the most familiar chants were deliberately phrased or owed their success to the fact that they used stereotypical Cockney features. Furthermore, it seems that the language loyalty effect was even more emphatic when the team were playing away, with even more emphasis placed on the Cockney stereotype. Most surprisingly, the emphasis was most strong when playing Spurs' close London rivals Arsenal, whose stadium, barely two miles away, is nevertheless perceived as being in 'south London' and their supporters thus as an 'out-group'.

In relation to the segregation of rival supporters that is a characteristic of the policing of British football crowds, the aisles and lines of stewards can be seen as isoglosses marking out different areas on a dialect map. These areas are also linguistically maintained to preserve group identification. Rival fans' chants, in other, perfectly clear accents, are likely to be met by feigned misunderstanding: 'You what, you what, you what you what you what?' Where a linguistic structure crosses these boundaries (as in certain songs that are common in tune and general lyrics), it will undergo assimilation and x-isation in the new speech community (such as the insertion of the local team name and nickname into generic songs in order to make them the fans' own).

Code-switching at the turnstile

Entering the highly-specified domain of a football ground renders many registers inappropriate, and limits the sociolect of the crowd. James adopts Platt and Platt's (1975: 35–6) distinction between the group's **speech repertoire** and an individual's **verbal repertoire**. Unusually, the crowd repertoire is smaller than the repertoire of individual people. James notes that unlike in society at large, there is no prestige to be gained by exhibiting a large repertoire; prestige lies in conformity to and knowledge of the group codes. All lexicogrammatical choices must reflect the register of 'football talk'.

Furthermore, the 'football' code is reserved exclusively for the domain inside the stadium, or closely related domains such as pubs on match days and the area immediately around the ground. The accent features of football chants, for example, are never considered appropriate in any other context. Equally, register which in any other domain would be perceived as aggressive and hostile is downgraded to the level of normative discourse in the ritualised code of the stadium.

James notes that, in Milroy's (1987a: 35–6) social network application, vernacular norms 'are perceived as symbolising values of solidarity and reciprocity rather than status'. This applies to football fans though, curiously, the crowd could well be composed of non-dense and uniplex social network groups: people whose only relationship is attendance at the match. It seems that a further dimension is needed to add to density and complexity in social network texture, and this is the perceived value of the network link. Although football fans' links are loose and simplex, the passionate value they place on their support serves to make the norm reinforcement function operate in any case. This is a strong consequence of solidarity and reciprocity.

The segmentary structure of fan groups

Applying Brown and Levinson's (1979) notion of segmentary structure to account for the different identifications felt by supporters relative to other groups, James points out that someone is a Spurs fan in relation to an Arsenal fan, but an England supporter (even when England includes Arsenal players) in relation to an Italian supporter, and a football fan in contrast with a rugby fan. All of these social roles are linguistically encoded. Not only this, but the detailed communicative competence diminishes upwards on this scale. That is, there are fewer linguistic discontinuities at the national level, whereas the sub-cultures of different clubs are marked with very specific chants. A smaller number and variety of chants are heard at national games. And at a recent international tournament, all nationalities were observed singing the same 'official' song.

All of these findings illustrate that even an apparently highly codified speech community can reveal sociolinguistic complexities on closer examination.

B5.3

Further reading ➤➤➤➤

❑ The classic method in sociolinguistics is exemplified by Labov (1966, 1972a, 1972b, 1994), and Trudgill (1972, 1974, 1984, 1988).

❑ A critique of the classic 'variationist' paradigm in sociolinguistics has been made by Cameron (1990, 1992), Coates (1993), Fasold (1990), Bickerton (1981, 1990), and Chambers (1997).

B6

THE CHANGING PRESTIGE OF RP

The prestige dialect Standard English is spoken by around 15 per cent of the population of Britain; the prestige accent Received Pronunciation (RP) is spoken by no more than 5 per cent of the population (Holmes 1992: 144). This means that many people are speaking Standard English using a regional accent, and also that there is a different perception in status between the standardised and codified dialectal form and the accent that was once known as 'BBC English'.

B6.1

Changes in RP

Two studies by my students show the prestige value of RP today. Judith Jones took a random sample of 64 television advertisements and analysed them along Hymes's (1974) dimensions of a communicative event (using the acronym 'speaking'):

❑ setting: daytime 81%; evening 11%; night-time 8%;
❑ scene: home 34%; countryside 30%; office 8%; shop 9%; bar/restaurant 5%; other 6%;
❑ participants: monologue/voice-over 61%; dialogue 30%; multiple people 9%;
❑ ends: the framing purpose or objective was, of course, to sell the product, but most ads drew mainly on narrative structures and 'mini-soap' formats;

❏   act sequence: (the actual linguistic content, register and style used) this was
                         always appropriate to the setting – formal in the office, casual
                         in the bar, for example;
❏   key: (the tone of the event) 75% light hearted; 23% serious; 2%
                         (i.e. 1 ad) mock pompous;
❏   instrumentalities: (choice of speech style) RP 70%; other accents 20%; music
                         only 10%;
❏   norms: all choice of language was non-deviant and appropriate to the
                         setting;
❏   genre: advertising.

Analysing the accents in the adverts, Judith found that RP was generally used to adver-
tise expensive products, electrical goods and financial services, and regional accents
were used for natural products, especially food. Furthermore, 63 per cent of voices
were male, against 37 per cent female; and women tended to have RP accents, with
men showing the regional variation.

A similar analysis of 7 hours of television advertisements over one week, conducted
by Lynne Senior, also revealed a bias towards RP usage. RP was used in 60 per cent
of the adverts, with Scottish, Irish, Yorkshire, American and Cockney accounting in
almost equal part for another 25 per cent. These are also mainly prestigious accents.
The remaining 15 per cent consisted of other accents such as Mancunian, Scouse,
Lancashire, Black English and 'cartoon' French, all used in humorous contexts. Lynne
discussed the claims made by Wilkinson (1965) and Giles and Powesland (1975) that
there are three bands of prestige in British accents: RP; rural regional accents and educated Irish, Welsh and Scottish; and finally the modern urban accents.

The prestige of the Oxford/Cambridge, educated middle-class London and home
counties accent that became RP owes much to its recommendation by phonetician
Daniel Jones and its adoption by Lord Reith as the appropriate 'voice' of the early
BBC on radio in the 1920s and 1930s. Since then, like every other linguistic code, RP
has changed along with changes in the social environment of its speakers. We can track
historical change by looking across the age ranges (see A7) to see an older form of
conservative RP retained from the 1930s by older people: markers of this accent include
the pronunciation of 'off' and 'lost' as /ɔːf/ and /lɔːst/ rather than /ɒf/ and /lɒst/, for
example. RP users between age 35 and 65 tend to speak general RP, while younger
users speak a more casualised advanced RP. This last change (recorded by Trudgill
and Hannah 1982) has since then developed even further.

Casualisation of RP

B6.2

It seems that by the early twenty-first century, general RP has come to be seen by
many people as being 'too posh'. Trudgill (1974, 1988) found that as early as the
1970s, middle-class men tended to aim for the covert prestige of a non-RP form
(see A5.1), seeing the RP usage as being somehow unmanly. More recently, advanced
RP forms have been heard more often on nationally broadcast media, with conservative RP almost never heard now except in historical archive material or in comic
situations.

Many younger adults in the greater London area whose social and educational background might traditionally have meant that they used RP have begun using an accent called **Estuary English (EE)** or the **New London Voice**. First observed by David Rosewarne (1994) around the Thames estuary, east of London, Estuary English is described as being 'mid way' between RP and Cockney. It manifests some Cockney features such as /w/ for word-final and medial /l/ (in 'real' and 'always', though not the first /l/ in 'little'), use of /d/ and fronting of /t/ in words like 'little', 'gateway', 'Gatwick', and 'seatbelt', and 'yod dropping' (/j/ loss) in words like 'tune' and 'news'. What makes EE a mid way accent is that speakers will sometimes pronounce the Cockney variant of these features and sometimes the RP variant. They will also code-shift from RP to EE when they are sensitive to and aware of their own usage.

Rosewarne claims that EE has spread across the south-east of England and can now be heard from the river Avon to The Wash, and is spreading north and west to become, in effect, the new RP. It is perceived as a classless, regionless accent that has prestige value, especially among younger men in their 20s and 30s. Of course, EE can be seen as a local manifestation of a global trend in the post-standardisation process: x-isation (see A8.2). EE is an example of the **casualisation** of RP towards the local vernacular – in this case, Cockney. While there are some Cockney elements observable in northern English (such as /t/ fronting), other regions of Britain have manifested their own casualisations of RP towards the local vernaculars. So people talk of 'posh Geordie', 'posh Brummy', 'posh Scouse', 'posh Yorkshire Leeds' and so on.

Kathryn Tibbs studied regional BBC news programmes with local presenters to identify this casualisation process across the country. In all cases, newsreaders from Manchester, Nottingham, and Newcastle all displayed a blend of RP and local accent features. This is the new BBC English.

A corresponding change is rapidly affecting the pronunciation of younger women. If you are female, middle-class, under 35 and live in the south or east of England, you will probably use a rising intonation (which has traditionally marked questions) even on declarative sentences. This **uptalk** or **upspeak** spread rapidly during the 1990s amongst young women in London enjoying high-earning careers in the media and public-relations. It is rapidly spreading geographically, so that it can now be heard being used by women in the north and west, by age as its original users move into their 30s and 40s, and even by gender as the male middle-class partners of uptalking women adopt their speech patterns.

Traditionally associated with a questioning or uncertain tone, uptalk is now so common that it seems to represent a default norm of female discourse, corresponding better with the greater use women make of backchannel noise and co-operative feedback in conversation (see B13). Perhaps this too can be seen as a new, gendered response to the casualisation of RP.

Meanwhile, Kathryn Tibbs argues, RP maintains its status mainly outside the British Isles. Through the BBC World Service and old textbooks, wherever English is not taught with an American or Australian accent, it is learned in an RP accent. In Japan, Indonesia, Saudi Arabia, Argentina, Chile, and many other places, general RP retains a prestige value that it is rapidly losing in Britain.

Further reading ➤➤➤➤

❑ There is a great deal of work on RP, Standard English, their prestige values and people's attitudes to speakers of these and more stigmatised varieties.

❑ Peter Trudgill (1974, 1975, 1978, 1983, 1984, 1986a, 1990 and 1995) is a major figure.

❑ See also Honey (1989), Giles and Powesland (1975), Giles and Coupland (1991), Wilkinson (1995), and Bex and Watts (1999).

❑ Bell (1976) and Hymes (1974) remain useful sources.

❑ Joseph (1987) and Milroy and Milroy (1993, 1999) address the whole issue of 'correctness' in dialect.

❑ Discussion of Estuary English and related accent shifts in Britain can be found in Rosewarne (1994, 1996), Coggle (1993), Wells (1994, 1997), and Mugglestone (1995).

THE REALITY OF GENDERLECTS

Linguistic studies in this area tend to be concerned either with the reality/mythology of genderlect, or the sexist use of language in general. One particular issue is the notion of common gender: words which might be assumed to be sex-neutral turn out to be used in very specific and exclusive ways. Examples from Cameron (1992) and Coates (1993) include: 'fourteen <u>survivors</u>, three of them women . . . ,' '<u>people</u> are much more likely to be influenced by their wives than by opinion polls,' where the underlined element is clearly not gender-neutral in the succeeding context. In a similar way, women are often named in newspaper articles only in relation to men ('wife', 'sister') or in evaluative ways ('Mrs Hall, a blonde 45-year old') that are almost never used for men.

Corresponding with this is the feature of semantic non-equivalence between gendered pairs of words. Consider the differences in connotation and the register where you are likely to find the following pairs used: 'waiter – waitress', 'master – mistress', 'bachelor – spinster', 'patron – matron', and try other collocations such as 'head waiter' or 'old master'. Similarly, if a man has a 'client', he is a businessman, but if a woman has a 'client' (especially in inverted commas), she is a prostitute. A man who is a 'pro' is highly competent or a golfer, a woman is a prostitute. A 'tramp' is a homeless scruff if a man, but not if a woman. These distinctions also show up in collocations such as the comparison between: 'She's John's widow', 'He's Sally's widower.' Many terms of abuse are female-based, and there are still no real male equivalents for 'tart', 'harlot', 'slut', and so on, when spoken seriously.

The semantics of gender

Lauren Buckland conducted a study to discover whether men and women instinctively preferred to express themselves in characteristic semantic domains. She asked 5 men and 5 women to write down the first 50 words that occurred to them as fast as possible on a piece of paper. Folding over the name on each sheet (thus 'marking' them without reference to gender) she then analysed the lists to see whether there were any discernible semantic trains of thought characterising each informant.

This economical and neat study showed that words tended to cluster along the features of: rhyming, alliteration, abstract, particular/response to surroundings, and swearing/innuendo. Cross-referencing the lists for gender revealed the following frequencies of words:

rhyming	women 1	men 14
alliteration	women 13	men 25
abstract	women 10	men 13
particular/response to surroundings	women 90	men 24
swearing/innuendo	women 4	men 20

Most noticeably, the women overwhelmingly tended to produce words that referred to their immediate concrete surroundings ('table', 'chair', 'carpet', 'badge', 'laundry basket'). Men tended to favour abstract words ('speed', 'music', 'fellowship') and were much more likely to produce sequences by word play ('night', 'fright', 'kite', 'bin', 'brown', 'blue') than women. Far more men relied on sexual swear words to fill out their 50 words. Lauren used this analysis to discuss the published work in the area and argue that many stereotypes were based on real usage.

B7.2 Colour terms and evaluation

Louise Kessler wanted to test the ability of two groups of men and women to give verbal descriptions of pictorial stimuli. Since it is still the case that there is a gender imbalance in subject areas at university, she chose 3 male and 3 female physicists, and 3 male and 3 female art historians as her informants. She gave them a series of photographs taken from magazines and the university promotional material: all in full colour, realistic and not explicitly 'artistic'. Each person was invited to 'describe and discuss the images, spending no longer than one minute on each'. The responses were recorded and transcribed.

The proportions of the total number of words used was interesting:

male art student:	33% of the total
female art student:	30%
male physicist:	24%
female physicist:	13%

Louise pointed out that this supports Coates' (1993) claim that men are more verbose than women, though it is women who 'chatter', in stereotypical mythology.

She also found that the men, of both groups, used the most colour terms (see A7 for contrast). However, a closer analysis revealed that men tended to use modifiers with their colour terms: 'very green', 'unusually green', 'rather green', 'slightly green'. The women tended to use adjectives as intensifiers instead: 'bold reds', 'vibrant colour'. Furthermore, women used far more evaluative adjectives ('nice', 'beautiful', 'rather bizarre') in general than men; even the female physicists used these more than the male art historians. It seems that genderlect considerations outweighed academic discipline in this respect.

B7.3 Men, women and prestige

One problem in using a variationist method to pin down gender as a linguistic determinant is that so many other factors interfere. Matthew Hassan tried to control for these by setting up a microsociolinguistic qualitative study of the language of a brother and sister (thus assuring parity of geography, age, class, education and social background). In order to minimise non-verbal factors, he recorded a telephone conversation between the two, and analysed the transcript for the phonetic variables /h/-dropping and use of the glottal stop for medial /t/ – both stigmatised features. After the conversation, Matthew revealed the purpose of the study, and got the brother and sister separately to read out a list of words: 'better', 'getting', 'butter', 'water', 'have', 'horse', 'has', 'horn'.

Matthew found a marked difference between the sister's higher use of the prestige variant, both in casual conversation and in continual usage in the word list, and the brother's speech. By contrast, he always glottalised the /t/ in conversation and dropped the /h/ in the majority of cases. In the word list, he glottalised 'getting' and 'water', but not 'better' or 'butter', and he pronounced the /h/ in 'horse' and 'horn' but omitted it in the grammatical words 'have' and 'has'.

Having reproduced the findings of Trudgill and others, Matthew discussed possible reasons for the disparity. He dismissed as sexist the notions that women are intuitively more concerned with prestige or being conservative or with social status or ambition, and instead focused on the speech patterns as examples of solidarity. He noted that the brother had a more close-knit social network and thus was more likely to have his vernacular norms reinforced. Moreover, the sister tended only to use the stigmatised features when talking about the 'male' domain of football and hooligans, so it seems that a semantic field element is also pertinent. Even in such a carefully controlled study, there are problems of interference.

Further reading ►►►►   **B7.4**

❏   The classic work in sociolinguistics from a feminist perspective is in Cameron (1990, 1992 and 1995).

❏   See also Coates (1993), Coates and Cameron (1986), Graddol and Swann (1989), Tannen (1992) and Johnson and Meinhof (1997).

❏   Older studies include Thorne and Henley (1975), Thorne (1983), Poynton (1985), Spender (1985), and the original study by Lakoff (1975), updated in Lakoff (1990).

❏   With specific reference to the educational and classroom context, see Mahony (1985) and Mahony and Jones (1989).

❏   For a perspective from sociolinguistics into literature, see Mills (1995a).

PATWA AND POST-CREOLISATION   **B8**

One of the most influential and widespread creoles is Jamaican Patwa. It is obvious from the history of the slave trade why it shares many of the features of West African creoles and the African-American vernacular English (AAVE) spoken across the US. The third point of the slave trade triangle first brought the language to Britain, and twentieth-century immigration to the UK consolidated the Caribbean roots of British Black English.

Jamaican Patwa and Jamaican English

Patwa and Jamaican English stand in a post-creole continuum relationship with each other, as basilect and acrolect respectively. The following is a brief description of the basilectal form; Jamaican English features some of the pronunciation patterns and lexical choices, but is otherwise closer to UK Standard English.

Phonology

The following vowel sounds appear in the words given:

/ɪ/	pit	/ɛ/	pet	/a/	pat, pot, one, father
/ʊ/	put	/o/	putt, run	/iː/	bee
/uː/	boot	/aː/	bard, law	/oː/	board, bird

(The last two words are pronounced without the /r/ – Jamaican English, unlike some other Caribbean Englishes, is non-rhotic.)

/ie/	bay, beer, bear	/ai/	buy, boy

These sets of words are all pronounced the same. In order to make some distinctions not allowed by vocalic variation, Patwa introduces glides to distinguish

/kjat/	cat	/bwail/	boil
/kat/	cot	/bail/	bile

There tends to be no /t - θ/ or /d - ð/ distinction, making /wɪt/ ('with') and /dɪs/ ('this').

As in AAVE, final consonant clusters tend to be devoiced (/d/ becomes /t/), reduced, or deleted altogether. So 'child', 'tact', 'wind' are pronounced /tʃaɪl/, /tak/, /wɪn/.

Most difficult of all for non-native speakers is the fact that Patwa is not stress-timed (as General American English and most native British accents), but is syllable-timed. In the following words, for example, each syllable receives almost equal emphasis: /dʒamieka/ ('Jamaica'), /daːta/ ('daughter'), /wandaful/ ('wonderful').

Lexicogrammar

variant plurality marker on nouns – 'five dog', 'all di cat';
variant possessive marker on nouns – 'dis man son' (this man's son);
variant pronouns – 'me' (I), 'im' (he), 'dem' (they, their);
variant third person verb concord – 'im like it' (he likes it);
copula deletion/variation – 'di boy sad' (the boy is sad), 'im a come' (he is coming);
variant negative formation – 'di woman no see dat' (the woman does not see that);
tense is marked lexically rather than morphologically:

'he walk home last night'
'he did walk home last night'
'he bin walk home last night'.

Many lexical items are specific to Patwa, and have been codified in the *Dictionary of Jamaican English* (Cassidy and Le Page 1980).

B8.2

Patwa and its influence in the UK

Virginia Barnes designed a study to investigate claims by Hewitt (1986) that Patwa was becoming highly influential in Britain beyond the traditional base of its native speaker community. Specifically, Hewitt noticed that elements of Patwa were being borrowed by young white and Asian people in east London youth clubs. Virginia was surprised that, as a white woman, she was able to recognise and even used some features of Patwa herself. These features tended to be lexical items rather than grammatical or pronunciation patterns.

She based her study on Hewitt's written test, and chose subjects at random but who were in their early 20s and thus had grown up in the 15 years since the original observations. These subjects were divided into a northern, Midlands and southern group, in order to provide some guide as to the degree of diffusion of the linguistic features geographically. Using Hewitt's work, and the contemporaneous glossary from Sutcliffe's (1982) *British Black English*, Virginia compiled a lexical list of 20 words. She printed these in a questionnaire with two possible meanings for each item, and invited the informants to tick what they thought the word meant. (Correct answers, a or b, are marked here on the right).

bad-mouth ((*a*) to insult; (*b*) ear-hole; don't know)	a
bahty (exclamation of annoyance; buttocks; don't know)	b
chip (to take one's leave; to enrage; don't know)	a
cruff (untidy, rough, ugly; yapping dog; don't know)	a
cuss (tin can; mock aggressive use of language; don't know)	b
go deh/there (disbelief; exclamation of encouragement; don't know)	b
hard (excellent, admirable; very bad; don't know)	a
juba (unflattering term for a woman, busybody; extravagance; don't know)	a
kenge (puny; shed; don't know)	a
labrish (gossip, relaxed lively talk amongst friends; laziness; don't know)	a
renk (superior; impudent, cheeky, wild; don't know)	b
ress (stop; untidy; don't know)	a
sad (sorrowful; pathetic; don't know)	b
soff (clumsy; weak, ineffective; don't know)	b
stylin (showing good style; wrapping in paper; don't know)	a
star (annoyance; close friend; don't know)	b
sweet (complete; pleasing, satisfying; don't know)	b
tracing match (quarrel; fire-lighter; don't know)	a
wicked (excellent; old-fashioned; don't know)	a
wickedness (mischief; excellence; don't know)	a

In her findings, Virginia discovered a marked increase overall in the correct scores for the group. She suggested that many of these terms, originally Patwa words, had diffused into general British youth usage and were even beginning to lose their sense as markers of Caribbean ethnicity. Many of her informants were unaware of the origins of the words. More strikingly, the Midlands group scored highest, followed by the southern group, with the northern group least accurate of all. If generalisable, this could suggest two possibilities. It could be that the words were innovative borrowings into young white speech in London in the 1980s, and have since spread out across the country. They have then become less used (or replaced by other words) in London. The study is thus a 'snapshot' of geographical diffusion away from London. Alternatively, Virginia suggests that the high numbers and integration of multi-ethnic communities in the Midlands compared with both London and the north have made the terms more current and longer-lasting amongst young people in the Midlands than elsewhere. She optimistically suggests that this indicates the potential for the development of a modern vernacular that borrows freely from different ethnic origins and better reflects the multiracial nature of Britain.

B8.3

Further reading ➤➤➤➤

❏ There is an enormous amount of literature on pidgins, creoles, and post-creole forms of English, including Todd (1974), Romaine (1988), Aitchison (1991), Morgan (1994), Holm (1988, 1989), Sebba (1997) and the *Journal of Pidgin and Creole Languages.*

❏ Edwards (1986) and Sutcliffe (1982) remain the classic accounts of British Black English, supported by Sutcliffe and Wong (1986) and Sutcliffe and Figueroa (1992).

❏ Wells (1973), Hewitt (1986) and Sebba (1993) record Jamaican English in London.

❏ There is an *International Journal of Bilingual Education and Bilingualism.*

B9

SINGLISH AND NEW ENGLISHES

New Englishes have developed all over the world, but just as with indigenous Englishes in Britain, the US, Canada, and Australia, for example, these codes also show sociolinguistic variation. Many of the New Englishes have similar features in terms of accent and grammar, as a result of similar conditions of origin (typically having made contact with English through colonialism and trade). Most are distinguishable from each other at these levels and especially at the level of lexis, as a result of interference patterns in contact with the indigenous languages. Patterns of intonation, 'straight' translations of local language syntactic ordering, and lots of copied words create a blended New English with its own form and sound.

B9.1

Singaporean English and Singlish

Singapore has a population of just over 3½ million, of which 76 per cent are Chinese, 15 per cent Malay, 7 per cent Indian, and 2 per cent other. There are four official languages: Chinese, Malay, Tamil and English, and a 92 per cent literacy rate. Because the island is so small, there is no regional variation in Singaporean English. Sociolinguistic variation occurs solely along the scale of education, which confers social status. So, using the terms of Fraser-Gupta (1991) and Pakir (1994), it is possible to talk of an acrolectal 'Singaporean English' that is close to the standard Englishes of Britain, America and Australia; a 'Singapore Dialect English' that forms a mesolectal continuum; and an x-ised version of English that is popularly known as 'Singlish', as a basilect (see A8 for definitions of these terms). The process of x-isation in the last of these can be divided further into Indianised, Sinicised and Malayanised influences.

Pronunciation

Singaporean English speakers tend to reduce final consonant clusters, so that 'next' becomes /nɛks/, 'just' becomes /jʌs/, 'recent' becomes /risən/, and so on. This feature is also found in various Caribbean New Englishes, African-American English and the Patwa spoken in English cities; in Singapore it is further distinguished by word-final stops being glottalised and unreleased. So, for example, 'rope', 'dog', and 'pick' become /rəʊpʔ/, /dɒkʔ/ and /pɪkʔ/. In basilectal varieties of 'Singlish', all word-final clusters are reduced to the unreleased glottal: /rəʊʔ/, /dɒʔ/ and /pɪʔ/.

Acrolectal Singaporean English speakers tend to aim for a general RP accent on the British model, and the emphasis across an utterance is 'stress-timed': that is, <u>con</u>trastive <u>em</u>phasis falls on <u>diff</u>erent parts of the word (<u>e</u>very poly<u>syll</u>abic word in this <u>sen</u>tence would take its stress – <u>un</u>derlined – on the first <u>syll</u>able in an <u>RP</u> voice). However, most Singaporean speakers' accents are rather 'syllable-timed', with a much more even emphasis in intonation. Where there is a contrastive stress, it tends to occur later in the word than in RP: 'assoc<u>ia</u>ted', 'educ<u>a</u>ted', 'ex<u>pert</u>', 'lite<u>ra</u>ture', 'op<u>por</u>tunity', 'ac<u>a</u>demic', 'in<u>div</u>idual', 'distri<u>bu</u>tor', and so on.

All of these phonological features produce a 'staccato' effect, which is further reinforced by the fact that Singaporeans tend not to elide words together. In fluent RP, for example, there is no break across the underlined words in, 'I'll ha<u>ve an</u> apple'. Singaporean speakers tend to insert a very brief break between these words.

Grammar

'Got' is used very commonly for possessive 'have' and existential 'there are':

> I got very good cabinets here.
> Here got many restaurants.
> Got very good beach on Sentosa.

'Can or not' is often used as an interrogative tag, as is 'isn't it':

> You will come, can or not?

> They'll hit him, isn't it?

The indefinite article is used less frequently than in other Englishes:

> She is computer programmer.

'Would' is used for 'will', perceived as being more polite (in general, Singaporean English uses register that would be considered formal or polite by British or American speakers):

> We hope you would return to teach us next year.

Aspectual variation reveals most interference from other languages:

Completive 'already':

> My son was born already two years (i.e. two years ago).

Habitual 'use to':

> She use to shop in Takashimaya (i.e. and still does today).

Lexis

Many Singaporean words are copied from the indigenous and neighbouring languages. A stereotypical feature is the insertion of 'la' as a marker of informality and solidarity, deriving from Hokkien Chinese (it also corresponds to the Malay 'lah'). Similarly, the Chinese 'ah' is used as an intimacy marker by inserting it between the two parts of a Chinese name. In Singapore, this is also used around first names. Other Singlish words include:

hepch	often used by sales assistants as 'help', showing a variant of the cluster /lp/;
kena	Malay for 'receive' or 'get';
chope	'reserve', also used in the children's game of 'tag' in Singapore to denote the player who has been 'got' or 'tagged'; in Malay, 'cap' is a stamp or seal trademark, deriving from Chinese printing in which a 'chop' was a seal or stamp (also, in Hindi, *chhap*);
chin chye	Hokkien, 'it doesn't matter';
dowan	a common form reduced from 'I don't want';
botak	Malay, 'bald', also used to refer to a 'crew-cut' hairstyle;
keen	Hokkien, 'quick', often repeated (or **reduplicated**) for emphasis or intensification;
alamak	an exclamation, from the mild Malay curse 'mother of Allah';
kiasu	someone who does not want to lose out, from a popular comic strip character, Mr Kiasu;
hup-ply	half price;
kenna ketok	Malay, 'to get a knock', metaphor for 'being cheated'.

All of these words can be used to translate the passage in B9.2 below.

B9.2

A Singlish haircut

In times past, foreign visitors with long hair would be asked to have a haircut at the airport before being allowed into Singapore. These days, immigration is more tolerant of scruffy Westerners. The following exchange is reproduced from the work of Li En Chong, one of my Singaporean students, from a barber's in the Takashimaya department store on Singapore's Orchard Road. The store has been renamed in Singlish from the original Japanese into the Mandarin 'Da Jia Qu Mai Ya'.

Hairdresser:	hello ah-John-ah long time no see. how can I hepch you?
John:	okay I want to cut my hair
Hairdresser:	sorry lah cannot sit here. after I kena scolding. another client chope the seat already. so how do you wan me to cut your hair?
John:	chin chye but dowan botak okay? also keen keen I got a meeting soon
Hairdresser:	so long never see you. you frequent another hairdressers ah?
John:	yah lah you so expensive since you move here to Da Jia Qu Mai Ya
Hairdresser:	alamak don so kiasu lah. I give you hup-ply discoun. you go to another stylist sure kenna ketok

Both Li En Chong and another student, Hardip Singh Amarjit Kaur, discussed the features of Singaporean English and Singlish, and related the variants to the government policy of promoting a standardised Singaporean English. Their essays focused on the formation of New Englishes and on language planning respectively.

Further reading ►►►►   B9.3

❑   The features and sociopolitical situation of Singaporean English are described by Crewe (1977), Platt and Weber (1980), Fraser-Gupta (1991, 1992), Pakir (1994), and in the articles in Foley *et al.* (1998).

❑   More generally, there is a mass of recent work on the formation and status of the New Englishes, including Kachru (1983, 1988, 1992), Smith (1983, 1987), Bailey and Gorlach (1984), Platt, Weber and Ho (1984), Quirk and Widdowson (1985), Ashcroft, Griffiths and Tiffin (1989), Sajavaara, Marsh and Keto (1991), Cheshire (1991), Mohanan (1992), Pennycook (1994), Crystal (1995) and McArthur (1998).

POLITENESS IN MIXED-SEX CONVERSATION   B10

In many sociolinguistic studies, the language of men and women is observably different. Whether this is a result of innate 'hard-wiring', different processes of gendered socialisation or merely men and women acting to their domain roles and expectations is a matter of ongoing debate. Gender certainly seems to affect every different level, from accent variation to lexical choice and syntactic preference. One of the most interesting areas of research has been in studying gender differences at the level of discursive strategies: how men and women perceive spoken discourse differently and so behave differently in conversation. This is most apparent in the discursive politeness markers used by the different genders.

The difference between men and women   B10.1
In a range of studies, the following characteristics have been observed:

❑   men are more likely to interrupt others;
❑   when they interrupt, men are more likely not to wait for a pause or clause boundary;
❑   women are more likely to make backchannel noise and support;
❑   men are more likely to use backchannel noise as a means of entering the conversation;
❑   women are more likely to frame their turns as questions;
❑   men speak more than women, both in terms of word total and number of turns;
❑   men's turns tend to last longer than women's turns;
❑   men keep their turn by avoiding pauses at clause boundaries, by using utterance incompletors ('firstly . . . ', 'but . . . ', 'and so . . .'), by fillers ('mmm', 'er'), by raising their voices, speeding up, and avoiding 'nominating' eye contact;
❑   women pass on their turns by nominating by name, by eye contact, by open-hand gesture, and by signalling their turn is over (by falling intonation and pausing);

❑ women reply to men;
❑ men make jokes and women laugh at them;
❑ men and women accommodate through a conversation towards each other's norms;
❑ women are more likely to use polite forms of register and indirectness;
❑ women use more hedges ('kind of', 'sort of', 'I think . . . ', 'maybe');
❑ women use more hedges and fillers as embarrassment markers before using technical or over-fluent words or phrases;
❑ women perceive men's conversation as aggressive and unsubtle;
❑ women are more likely to repair the conversation after a silence;
❑ women are more likely to personalise, using a range of personal pronouns;
❑ men are more likely to generalise, only using 'I' and using nominalised and passive verb forms;
❑ men tend to end a conversation by summarising its content or end point;
❑ women are less likely to initiate the close of a conversation.

Of course, the reality of all of these has been hotly debated, as well as the complexities arising in single-sex or mixed-sex groups, and because of age differences, social class and education differences, and topic differences.

B10.2 **A gender-comparison study**

Sharlene Goff recorded different groups in conversation:

> mixed conversation between 4 friends (see C7);
> single-sex conversation between 2 male friends;
> single-sex conversation between 2 female friends;
> mixed conversation between 4 people unfamiliar with each other.

She minimised the awareness of the recording equipment by using the Labovian technique of getting the informants emotionally involved in the topic, setting them questions that she knew they cared about: fox hunting, the abolition of the monarchy, and genetic experimentation. Using some of the features she had studied in the published research, she examined her transcripts for evidence of gender polarisation at the level of politeness strategies. Her conclusion was that there does seem to be a 'dominant' style of discourse, but this could not necessarily be equated with gender. She argued that factors such as familiarity seemed to exert a strong modifying influence on gender as a factor in discursive behaviour.

Single-sex conversation between male friends

Q: what are your opinions on the monarchy – are they still important to society?
M1: absolutely. mmm – I think history's a terribly important thing and the monarchy's
      been around for a long time and there's something – they're a body and an
      institution and. they might not have as much meaning as they used to. as much
      power or authority but – nevertheless they're a figurehead and they symbolise our
      nation and therefore they should stay put

M2: well I fully concur – well it's easy to be an idealist and say there's no place for a monarchy in a truly democratic society but. looking at it objectively what can the monarchy offer us right? it's unreasonable to expect them to be perfect fucking citizens but – what we can say is what can they bring to this country and they bring millions upon millions of tourists into this country – okay. get all the monarchy's money and give it to everybody in the country and everyone will have a mars bar – millions and millions of pounds in like. revenue in the tourist industry

M1: people think of England they think of the Queen

M2: exactly –

M1: keep the Queen.

M2: keep the Queen.

Single-sex conversation between female friends

Q: what are your opinions on the monarchy – do you think they should be perfect role models for society?

(2.5)

F1: it's a very difficult thing – but. personally. I think that. mmm. that. they should be allowed to do whatever they want – they're just people. I mean –

F2: yeah. you can't expect people to be perfect – and it's quite rare for royal families to even exist at all so=

F1: but then they are – mmm – in the public eye all the time – so if they're [-   ]

F2:   [yeah]

F1: if they're giving a bad impression then. it's surely going to reflect on the rest of society

F2: I think as well that we have to bear in mind that the Queen's head of the church – and having affairs is going against the ten commandments [-   ]

F1:   [yeah – sure]

F2:   so I'm not sure they should be having – if they have that sort of responsibility. they should take it seriously –

F1: but then do you think that Charles should be allowed to remarry?

F2: mmm well. I think I agree – I mean it's only fair enough cos they're people – but I think it's. mmm. contradictory of their roles to claim to be head of one thing and not of the other. but I guess that shows that they're just normal people

F1: yeah definitely

Mixed-sex conversation between people unfamiliar with each other

Q: what are your opinions on choosing your own baby – selecting attractive genes for engineering?

M1: I've got opinions – mmm – I mean. based on what I know. I don't know a great deal but – mmm. I sort of learnt a little bit and I reckon that – mmm – that

       although they've – well. they're trying to put ethical stops on it – mmm. but I still
       don't see how – mmm – they're gonna stop scientists doing whatever cos they'll
       pursue it to the limit won't they=

F1:   yeah

M1:   they'll try and get as far as they can. mmm – and. yeah I think it's bad wrong to.
       to. mmm. have the choice of the perfect baby and stuff

F2:   I think there are some cases where it's acceptable. for instance – mmm – there's
       lots of – mmm – hereditary diseases which can be avoided if they just look at the
       embryo and test it and find one that doesn't have a certain – disease that's going
       to be fatal to [them then]

F1:   [mmm   ]

F2:   I think it's acceptable – I mean. do you agree?

M1:   yeah yeah I mean. I know they're doing stuff with – mmm. cystic fibrosis you
       know? having inhalers with – mmm. like. genetic inhalers – but at the same time
       they could stop it completely [-   ]

F1:   [mmm]

M1:   by looking. like you say. at the [embryos]=

F2:   [yeah]=

F1:   haven't they got some kind of law though stopping it?

M1:   yeah they're not allowed to stop it before it's born

F1:   no but I mean. not allowed to use it for like. choosing hair colour

F2:   yeah

F1:   mmm

F2:   there's obviously going to be some kind of black market. I mean – I should think=

F1:   yeah

F2:   that there's a black market being set up [where]

F1:   [yeah]

F2:   I mean – it's probably already
       happening we just don't know about it

M1:   mmm

F2:   I think it's sort of in theory but they're definitely thinking about it and sort of
       bidding for the best genes and=

M1:   what happens to all the ugly babies?

F2:   I don't know

((laughter))

M2:   I mean – what – mmm=

F2:   it's like the film Gattaca. has anyone seen it?

All: no

F2:   it's all about that

F1:   really?

F2:   and the sort of reality – its. like. a futuristic. sort of – science fiction all about the
       reality of that sort of situation

F1:   yeah

F2:   it's quite interesting

F1:   it's scary isn't it

B10.3

Further reading ►►►►

❑ On politeness norms and the address system see the original research by Brown and Gilman (1960), and also Adler (1978), Brown and Levinson (1987), Braun (1988), Mühlhäusler and Harré (1990) and Watts, Ide and Ehlich (1999).

❑ Key texts in pragmatics include Leech (1983), Levinson (1983) and Grundy (2000).

❑ The analysis of gendered discourse is addressed in Mills (1995b), Crawford (1995) and Wodak (1997).

STANDARDISATION AND LANGUAGE CHANGE

B11

Sociolinguistics is the modern counterpart of historical language study, focusing on a synchronic view of current linguistic usage. However, historical or diachronic study has been an important element in sociolinguistics, and the insights of the modern discipline can be used to illuminate and explain changes in the past. In turn, these insights can be further usefully applied to understand the language of the present.

Principles of language change

B11.1

Ancient commentators on language change assumed that languages only changed when a country was invaded by foreign speakers, and so change was associated with degeneracy or mongrelisation. Of course, though invasion often affects language, specific changes reflect existing trends or newly required features. For example, the loss of inflectional suffixes in Old English words was an existing process that was accelerated by both Viking and Norman French invasions in the tenth and eleventh centuries. As an international language, with many cultural varieties, English as a whole is now uninvadable. Changes in World English can be said to fall into two areas: a general realignment to reflect social and technological evolution (this largely involves creation and innovation in language); and a local realignment in contact with other languages (this involves borrowing or copying). Aitchison (1991: 120–3) has codified the principles of copying:

❑ detachable elements are most easily copied;
  (for example, Middle English copied words from French but not its future tense inflectional system);
❑ copied elements are x-ised
  (Russian or Japanese copies from English are rendered into Russian or Japanese phonology; English copies from Spanish, French, Latin or Greek are anglicised);
❑ copied elements have an existing superficial similarity
  (for example, words which already 'fit' the English phonological system are copied);
❑ changes happen a small step at a time – the principle of 'minimal adjustment'
  (for example, the loss of rhoticity in most English accents has taken over 500 years and is still ongoing).

Labov (1994: 21) points out that long-term stability is in fact more puzzling than linguistic change. He claims a continuity between the past and current sociolinguistic study by quoting Christy's (1983) **uniformitarian principle**: 'knowledge of processes that operated in the past can be inferred by observing ongoing processes in the present'. This notion of a continuity of linguistic principles is fundamental to sociolinguistics, which must not treat language as a 'random fluctuation system' (that is, as simply being at the whim of fashion) but as a system governed by discoverable patterns and conventions.

The difficulty of studying language change is a consequence of the complexity of the past, and the fact that evidence and data are always incomplete. This is the **historical paradox**: studying the past demonstrates the extent to which it is not absolutely recoverable. Labov's solution is a sort of 'triangulation' method:

> Solutions to the Historical Paradox must be analogous to solutions to the Observer's Paradox. Particular problems must be approached from several different directions, by different methods with complementary sources of error. The solution to the problem can then be located somewhere between the answers given by the different methods. In this way, we can know the limits of the errors introduced by the Historical Paradox, even if we cannot eliminate them entirely.
>
> (Labov 1994: 25)

Claiming a uniformitarian link with the past does not entail a commitment to seeing history either as catastrophes nor gradualness. Labov points out that catastrophic changes (large political and population disjunctions) tend to generate external change that is properly sociolinguistic; gradual change tends to generate change internal to the language system (strictly linguistic). Language change, then, seems to happen in both rapid shifts interspersed with gradual adjustments, analogous to 'punctuated equilibrium' in evolutionary science (sudden change between long periods of stability).

| B11.2 | **Golden age-ism** |

Even in ancient Athens, writers looked back to a previous age when the language was more 'pure' and 'elegant' than their own. This nostalgic delusion occurs throughout the ages: fifteenth- and sixteenth-century English writers looked to ancient Latin as having more prestige than English; seventeenth- and eighteenth-century English writers compared their own 'corrupt' English with the language of Chaucer, Shakespeare and Milton; in the nineteenth century they looked back to the previous 'Augustan' age; and politicians in the twentieth century have longed for Victorian values. In all of these, there is often a linkage made between linguistic 'purity' and national 'purity', and it is then a short step from merely describing language to setting out prescriptive rules by which you would like it to change.

The notion of 'correctness' emerged in the late sixteenth century, and this golden age notion was applied to produce 'standardisation'. In the late seventeenth and eighteenth centuries, it was taken up by influential people including Dryden, Swift, Addison, Johnson, Priestley, Sheridan and especially Bishop Lowth, whose *Short Introduction to English Grammar* (1762) pontificated the following, mainly by (false) analogy with Latin:

❑ he condemned 'had rather', 'had better' for 'would rather';
❑ condemned the use of the double negative, previously perfectly respectable;

- ❏ condemned ending a sentence with a preposition;
- ❏ condemned splitting an infinitive;
- ❏ condemned 'between you and I' and 'it is me', on the basis of Old English grammar;
- ❏ arbitrarily preferred 'different from' to 'different to';
- ❏ preferred 'larger' when the comparison was only for two items (not 'largest');
- ❏ preferred 'you were' not 'you was', even when the 'you' was singular;
- ❏ distinguished 'shall/will' and 'should/would' though there had been little agreed distinction across the country for 500 years.

These prescriptions from the great age of dictionary and grammar writing still find their counterparts in modern prescriptivism. Applying a descriptive but analytical sociolinguistics to these attitudes in the past can also provide critical insight into the ignorance of the present.

Sociolinguistic re-evaluation   B11.3

Tim Knebel re-examined the situation in the Middle Ages using a modern socio-linguistic framework. Adapting Ferguson's (1964) classic study of diglossia (see A4 and B4), he discussed the linguistic situation of Middle English with French as the H variety and native English as the L variety. The following characteristics of diglossia from Ferguson were applied convincingly to medieval society:

- ❏ H is written;
- ❏ H is the medium of education;
- ❏ diglossia is a socially stable pattern;
- ❏ H has greater prestige than L;
- ❏ H vocabulary is often copied into L;
- ❏ repeated vocabulary ('doublets') often diverge in meaning and connotation.

French was the dominant written and literary form in the twelfth and thirteenth centuries, and was taught alongside Latin and Greek. This situation lasted almost 500 years, with Francified English maintaining its prestige in parliament, government, law, administration, ecclesiastical and culinary domains. Many French words passed into English, with divergences between, for example, 'lamb'/'mutton', 'beef'/'cow', 'pig'/'pork', and so on.

Tim pointed out that modern diglossic situations have been shown to come to an end in the same way as did medieval diglossia. Ferguson (1964: 436) gives the following reasons:

- ❏ the expansion of literacy;
- ❏ broader communication and social mobility;
- ❏ standardisation as a mark of national sovereignty.

All three of these can be discerned in fourteenth- and fifteenth-century English life. Furthermore, Tim used the model of the late medieval collapse of diglossia in order to predict a similar H/L assimilation in modern Arabic, and explain the pressure from dominant standardised languages on modern pidgins and creoles.

B11.4

Further reading ➤➤➤➤

❑ Language change in general is addressed by Aitchison (1991), Hock (1986) and Labov (1994).

❑ The historical development of English is described in the classic texts by McCrum, Cran and MacNeil (1992), Baugh and Cable (1993), Pyles and Algeo (1993), Graddol, Leith and Swann (1996), and from a social perspective by Leith (1997).

❑ On authority, correctness and standardisation, see Crowley (1989), Bex and Watts (1999), and Milroy and Milroy (1999).

B12

LANGUAGE AND EDUCATION

One of the reasons sociolinguistic study is so important is that thinking about the link between language and society is also the ground for language planning by governments largely through the education system. Performance in linguistic skills (literacy in reading and writing, oracy in listening and speaking) is taken as an indicator of educational level and intelligence, and provides access to the whole range of education in the first place. The way that the links between language, education, social class, wealth, family background and gender are made involve theoretical and ideological frameworks that can be made explicit by sociolinguists. The discipline is inescapably bound up with political thinking in this respect. I also believe it is our responsibility to use this special training and knowledge to influence current thinking and policy.

B12.1

Linguistic codes, education and social stratification

The most influential work in the area of educational linguistics has been done by Basil Bernstein and his colleagues. Observing the difference in educational attainment by middle-class and lower working-class schoolchildren, Bernstein set out to establish a connection between their school experience and their characteristic language usage. He distinguished two types of linguistic patterns used by schoolchildren: **restricted code** and **elaborated code**.

Restricted code features	*Elaborated code features*
unfinished and short sentences	accurate grammatical order
simple clauses	complex sentences: co-ordinacy/
commands and questions	superordinacy
categoric statements	frequent use of prepositions
repetition of conjunctions	impersonal pronouns
hesitancy	passive constructions
confusion of reasons and conclusions	unusual adjectives and adverbs
rigid and limited use of adjectives and adverbs	
sympathetic circularity ('you know')	
language of implicit meaning	

Elaborated code is explicit and can be communicated without gesturing to the immediate context: it is thus **universalistic**. Restricted code is implicit and requires participants who share assumptions and a local context: it is **particularistic**. Bernstein claimed that middle-class children have access to both codes, whereas lower working-class children only had access to restricted code. Since school life and education generally is 'predicated upon elaborated code', Bernstein asserts that exclusive users of restricted code are likely to do less well at school.

Bernstein's work is primarily sociological rather than sociolinguistic, as you might guess from some of the impressionistic and evaluative terms in the lists above. Nevertheless, his approach presents a linguistic explanation for educational attainment and failure. Though Bernstein has denied the label, his approach is clearly a **deprivation theory** in that it claims to offer a linguistic indicator for cognitive ability. This would need to be balanced by 'compensatory' education schemes such as special literacy programmes, teaching the prestige value of standardisation and so on.

There have been many criticisms both of Bernstein's experimental methodology and his theoretical reasoning. However, the linguistic choices characterised by 'restricted' and 'elaborated' codes do seem to represent the reality of some children's performance. The features of restricted and elaborated code look very like the difference between spoken and written discourse, and it may well be that middle-class children are socialised more readily into literacy and understanding the rules and conventions of the middle-class school system. Bernstein has gone on to suggest that these respective linguistic choices are dependent on family background. He differentiates **positional family** types (in which everyone has a distinct and fixed role) and **person-oriented** family types (in which familial roles are shared and individual characteristics are more prominent), and connects them respectively to restricted and elaborated codes.

Social class and language use

B12.2

Vicky Bristow devised a classroom-based experiment with two groups of 10-year-old boys, one from a fee-paying school (F) and one from a state school (S), in neighbouring areas of Nottingham. She used the sensitivity to social status and readiness and ability to pay for education as an index of social class. In the experiment, she discussed a moral beast fable with the two groups, and transcribed the discussion. Her aim was twofold: to determine whether the features characterised as restricted and elaborated code could be differentiated in the data; and to evaluate whether there was any perceivable cognitive or communicative difference between the groups.

Along most of the dimensions listed above, there was very little difference between the groups. Noticeable differences were in self-aware references and pronoun usage. In order to compare similar functions, Vicky examined all the utterances which were concerned explicitly with the indication of turn-taking (including nominations of who was to talk next, reference to the speaker's own talk and explicit instructions such as 'shut up you'). She found that group F produced this sort of 'meta-talk' on 33 occasions, compared with the 20 occurrences of group S. Furthermore, group F used only 28 pronouns, compared with the 40 pronouns used by group S. In the work of Bernstein and his colleagues, pronominalisation represents limited possibilities for modification, since pronouns unlike nouns cannot take adjectives. High pronoun usage, then, is treated as part of the implicit, context-bound restricted code, with an implication that it is also cognitively limiting.

However, in Vicky's data, group S also used proper names 16 times, compared with only 1 direct nomination by group F. This would seem to be a universalistic feature more associated with elaborated code. Vicky points out that all these linguistic performances could simply represent different ways of negotiating the context. After all (as Stubbs 1983 also points out), in a face-to-face interactive discussion, a usage of implicit and particularistic meaning is entirely appropriate, and elaborated code is rather redundant. One explanation could be that group F saw the task as a test-situation and group S as a simple discussion, and each acted accordingly.

Finally, to illustrate the complexities of trying to equate form with function too inflexibly, compare the following two utterances in which children summarise the moral of the fable:

Group F

Child 2: follow your destinies whatever whatever it takes try. and because if you if you try and do something and finally – you got this chance. take it. and no matter what happens try try and achieve it

Group S

Child 6: try – I'd try because if you try you never knew. if you try you could do it

The first example is syntactically more complex and indeed is longer, but the propositional content is simply a repetition of the injunction to 'try'. The second example, though shorter, completes the conditional clause and gives a reason for the proposition. The problem, as Vicky ends by pointing out, is that qualitative evaluations of this type cannot measure cognitive ability simply by a surface linguistic analysis. Studies in educational linguistics need to be theoretically aware and sophisticated if the consequences in educational policy and pedagogic practice are to have any value.

B12.3

Further reading ➤➤➤➤
- ❏ The original work of Bernstein (1971) and his associates, and more educational linguistics, is discussed by Stubbs (1976, 1980, 1983, 1986), Trudgill (1975) and Perera (1984).
- ❏ Bernstein (1990) is a re-evaluation.
- ❏ Recent discussions on language and education appear in Carter (1990, 1995, 1997), Carter and McRae (1996), Bain, Fitzgerald and Taylor (1992), and McCarthy and Carter (1994).

B13 **CONVERSATION AND SPOKEN DISCOURSE**

B13.1 **Transcription conventions**

If you are collecting spoken data, you might need to use a systematic set of notational conventions when transcribing speech, as set out below. The level of detail depends on what you are investigating: you will need the IPA for accent variation; you will need to note pause lengths and overlaps to study politeness and conversational 'turns'; you might only need the barest annotation if you are investigating features such as a word or idiom occurrence, or discoursal features across the whole transcript, for example.

You should bear in mind that transcription will take you a lot longer than you will imagine, and certainly a lot longer than the recording took to make. You should be selective and only transcribe those parts of the discourse that you need to examine closely.

→	utterance continues without a break onto the next line of text
←	line of text is a continued utterance from the last arrow
=	next speaker's turn begins with no break after current speaker
↑	point at which heavy emphasis by rise in pitch begins
↓	point at which lowering of pitch begins
?	intonation marking a question
word	indicates heavy contrastive emphasis on a single word
WORD	indicates shouting
( )	indecipherable word
(word)	indecipherable word, containing best guess as to what was said
((smiles))	contains note on non-verbal interaction
(2.3)	indicates pause, with length in seconds
.	indicates significant pause below measurable length
–	indicates very brief pause
[	point at which overlap between speakers begins
]	point at which overlap between speakers ends

You might want to develop your own notes to signal features you are particularly interested in.

An example

S1:   ↑WHAT do you think you're doing. look at the *mess*
      (0.7)
S2:   it wasn't me – ↓it was (Clare)=
S1:   *don't* lie to me. you clear it up ↑right now ((points)). she's not even here – I just
      saw her in the garden [and she could hardly be   ] in two places at once→
S2:   [but it was her ((starts to cry))]
S1:   ←now could she
      (2.0)
S2:   ((continuous crying))
      ((S3 comes into room))
S3:   what's all this noise then. shush shush ↓shush ok that's alright (0.5) ↑what have
      you said to her=
S1:   *look* at the mess she's made – and. and *I'll* be the one who has to clear it up
      ((begins to clear up))
S3:   look. you go and find Clare and we'll all (   ) together. that's a good girl
      ((S2 leaves))
      (7.0)

S1:   give me a hand then
S3:   here. let me do it. go and have a coffee
       ((S1 leaves room))

This passage represents about 45 seconds of recording, but it would take anything up to half an hour to transcribe. There is no punctuation or capitalisation in the passage, since these are features of written language. The dots and dashes have a fixed value. This passage could be used for various investigative purposes, such as turn-taking between child–adult or between mother–father. It could not be used for accent investigation – for this you would need a closer phonetic transcription. Similarly, the passage is useless if you are investigating inter-language code-switching, creolisation, dialectal markers, metaphoric usage, and so on. The point here is that you need to decide in advance what you are studying, in order to go somewhere that you are likely to find it. Data is never just data – all data collection is theory-driven. You should take this into account when planning your project.

B13.2

A study of conversational endings

Joanna Shirley wanted to investigate how conversations were closed and how the participants 'escaped' from the exchange. She noticed that conversations often ended with phatic tokens, farewells, and idiomatic expressions, and set up an experiment to focus on the last of these: **idioms**.

Idioms are 'ready-made phrases that communicate a clear, agreed meaning' (Carter 1997: 99). They are fixed and cannot be replaced in part by a synonym: thus 'over the moon' but not 'over the satellite' (Wood and Hill 1989). Makkai (1972) claims that idioms can work even with two lexemes, as in phrasal verbs such as 'give in', 'run up (a bill)', or as in 'take-away (food)'.

With a colleague, Joanna covertly recorded (in a notebook) the ends of 30 conversations held in public places (because she was not interested in the content, and the informants were not identifiable, she did not regard this as an ethical problem), in a variety of randomly chosen locations. They noted the gender and rough age of the participants.

Joanna distinguished between **escapable** and **non-escapable** conversations. The first is when both participants are free to signal the end of the talk and move away physically without breaking any social norm. A non-escapable conversation is when neither is free to move away (because of being 'trapped' on a bus or train journey, in a lecture, and so on). Of course, this distinction only works prototypically where the power relations are symmetrical. In an asymmetrical exchange, the conversation is more escapable for the powerful participant (who has 'licence' to end the exchange) than for the less powerful person (who has to remain there until 'released'). Disruption of these norms constitutes rudeness.

The results revealed that escapable conversations ended with phatics and a farewell (such as 'bye', 'see you later'). However, the signal for the ending occurred just previously in the conversation. These idiomatic signals fell into four types:

❑   the excuse ('better go', 'I've gotta go to the shops', 'I'd better be going now')
❑   the single-word signal ('well', 'so', 'anyway', 'right')

B

❑ the future-phatic ('have a nice evening', 'hope it goes well')
❑ the rendezvous strategy ('meet you outside the shop at 6').

These were often also combined, especially the 'single-word signal', with the others. The 'single-word' was used in 65 per cent of escapable conversations.

By contrast, non-escapable conversations ended with silence. Where escapable conversations are oriented towards the end of the interaction (and thus require social markers such as phatics and farewells), non-escapable conversations end when the topic ends. The silence signals the end of topic, and is broken only by the resumption of a new topic. Alternatively, the conversation can be moved by one of the participants into an escapable mode. An example concerned two people on a bus who had not spoken for a minute, but who got off the bus together, and had an escapable closing conversation on the pavement before going their separate ways.

Further reading ➤➤➤➤

B13.3

❑ The area of conversation analysis is growing rapidly.
❑ Classic models for the analysis of discourse include the 'turn-taking' model of Sacks, Schegloff and Jefferson (1974 and see C10), Sacks (1992), Ochs, Schegloff and Thompson (1996) and the initially classroom-based discourse analysis model of Sinclair and Coulthard (1975), developed by Stenström (1994).
❑ See also Schiffrin (1987, 1994), Burton (1980), Boden and Zimmerman (1991), Hoey (1983), Sinclair, Hoey and Fox (1993), McCarthy (1991, 1998).
❑ The use of computers to analyse spoken discourse transcriptions (**corpus linguistics**) is also a fast developing field: see Barnbrook (1996), Greenbaum (1996), Stubbs (1996), Biber, Conrad and Reppen (1998), Aston and Burnard (1998), and Biber *et al*. (1999).

LANGUAGE AND IDEOLOGY

B14

It will have become clear by now that sociolinguistics has come a long way from being a straightforwardly descriptive discipline. Sociolinguists do not live outside society but are an integral and even privileged part of it. Developing sociolinguistic theory has demonstrated that people's attitudes and perceptions towards language help to shape their usage, and these perceptions shape governmental and educational policy and language planning. All studies are undertaken, not in a vacuum, but for a social and individual purpose: methods of data collection, deciding what even counts as data, as well as the analytical approach to take, all rely on an ideological awareness. **Ideology** here does not just mean political ideology, but the particular system of beliefs and assumptions that underlies every linguistic analysis and every social event. The only way of investigating these assumptions and understanding their workings is by an exploration of the language that represents them. Ideology, then, is also a sociolinguistic matter.

The linguistics of ideology

B14.1

The sub-disciplines of critical linguistics and critical discourse analysis (CDA) have emerged with a specific concern for the ideological investigation of linguistic representation. Central to their approach is the notion that language is only meaningful in its social setting. The method of analysis, however, is different from traditional socio-linguistic studies. CDA uses close linguistic analysis mainly of written texts such as newspaper reports, political speeches, institutional regulations, advertising, contracts, romantic fiction, graffiti, and other public announcements. Its objective is to reveal, through analysis rather than experimentation, the underlying ideological discursive practices involved in the production of the text. In the work of Norman Fairclough, CDA has relied on the **systemic-functional grammar** of Halliday as its main linguistic framework. This is an approach to the analysis of language that categorises the parts of language in terms of their function in the world. Halliday differentiates three dimensions of language:

❑   textual – the actual organisation of language features to appear grammatical;
❑   interpersonal – the relations between the participants in a communicative event;
❑   ideational – the content and belief-system involved.

These dimensions are all involved in any single text or utterance. The classic example of the relation of linguistic form and function lies in the two alternative headlines:

> Demonstrators are shot.
> Police shoot demonstrators.

The second of these places the agents of the action ('police') in the prime position and the active verb attributes the action clearly. In the first example, the agents have been deleted by the passivisation of the verb form. Here, it is the 'demonstrators' who are the focus and appear almost to be responsible for events.

At the centre of CDA is a treatment of language as **discourse**: that is, as a social process involving participants in a specific social situation with particular aims and objectives and beliefs. Practitioners of CDA claim to be interventionist; they want to create an explicit awareness of the linguistic forces of social control and manipulation, in order to resist these forces.

The area of metaphor and euphemism (see B3) can be seen as an example of CDA interest in the linguistics of coercion in media representation. Fairclough has argued:

> Metaphor is a means of representing one aspect of experience in terms of another, and is by no means restricted to the sort of discourse it tends to be stereotypically associated with – poetry and literary discourse. But any aspect of experience can be represented in any number of metaphors, and it is the relationship between alternative metaphors that is of particular interest here, for different metaphors have different ideological attachments.
>
> (Fairclough 1989: 119)

For example, in newspaper reports he distinguishes between metaphorical and congruent orders of discourse. The latter consists of the register you would ordinarily expect: medical register for a medical story; formal style for a parliamentary story; less formal style for a political sketch, and so on. Metaphorical orders of discourse are often used to 'spin' a controversial or sensational story, such as a war report. For example, where a broadsheet newspaper might report an air strike using journalistic attribution and citing evidence of eye witnesses, a tabloid newspaper might blend the

lexicogrammatical choices usually associated with playground bullying, sport, sensational war fiction, fairy tales and fables, and so on. Fairclough points out that when
such blends are habitually used, they become **naturalised** forms of discourse: we no
longer see them as ideological 'spin' but as the natural way of talking about war and
conflict.

Studying the news

Katherine West recorded and transcribed two radio news reports from the upmarket,
serious BBC Radio 4 and the youth music-oriented BBC Radio 1. She was particularly interested in Fairclough's notion of the 'conversationalisation' of news, by
which informal features of style and register are adopted. This forces a political story
into the evaluation of an everyday conversation. While this may appear to appropriate politicians' discourse in favour of ordinary people, Katherine argues that it makes
it much more difficult to disentangle the reporter's opinions from those of the other
participants (in this case, politicians). Having two news reports of the same story allowed
her to see what had been edited out from each story. She focused on several different
linguistic features, including the representation of the politicians and public through
naming strategies and direct address, the framing of the story of an election as a fairy
tale with a hero and villain, and the placing of the participants in grammatically foregrounded or backgrounded positions.

Ben Woolhead investigated television news, focusing on how identities and relations of participants are linguistically represented. He recorded six different channels'
news programmes on the same day, and examined the transcripts for the same story,
looking particularly at the lexical and syntactic levels. His aim was to construct a scale
of apparent 'authority', in terms of the claims to truth and certainty and rejection of
arguability in the news discourse. Specific linguistic choices which encode these different points of view can be seen in a selection from Ben's data:

The battle of Seattle (BBC Nine O'clock News)

siege conditions (ITN News)

thugs invaded the city (BBC News)

protestors hijacked the agenda (BBC News)

rentamob (Channel 5 News)

Protesters without gas masks fell victim to police pepper spray (Channel 4 News)

Police used tear gas against protesters (Channel 4 News)

The police used tear gas, pepper spray and rubber bullets to try and keep the
crowd under control (BBC Newsround – news programme for children).

All of these represent different versions of the story.

It is important to remember that none of the versions can be the 'true' form, against
which all the others are 'distortions' or 'biased'. All representations encode a viewpoint and an ideology, even if their linguistic patterns claim an apparent certainty,

truth value or neutrality. To return to a sociolinguistic principle: it is as impossible to say anything without an ideological dimension as it is to say anything without an accent.

B14.3   **Further reading ➤➤➤➤**

❏   The area of critical linguistics is represented in Fowler (1981, 1986, 1991), Fowler, Hodge, Kress and Trew (1979), Kress and Hodge (1993), Hodge and Kress (1988), and is evaluated by Pateman (1981) and Richardson (1987).

❏   Its successor, CDA, is contained in the work of Fairclough (1989, 1995a, 1995b) and Caldas-Coulthard and Coulthard (1996).

❏   See also Birch (1989), Chilton (1985, 1988, 1996), Chilton, Ilyin and Mey (1998), Meinhof and Richardson (1994), and Richardson and Meinhof (1999).

EXPLORATION

DATA FOR INVESTIGATION

HOW TO USE THE DATA IN THIS SECTION

This section presents real examples of language that have been collected for the purpose of sociolinguistic analysis. For each, I provide some details of the original naturally occurring social context. Some of the data are from students' fieldwork and some are from my own notes. Of course, no piece of language is one-dimensional, and although each passage appears under a heading, there are often insights to be gained by examining the data with a different concern in mind.

Each area corresponds roughly with the similarly numbered sub-sections in A and B above. For each, I have suggested some analytical questions, discussion points, and issues to consider, though of course the whole point of engaging with data like this is to apply your own analytical methods and thinking and develop your own ideas and conclusions.

Statistics, logic and correlations

As a way into thinking about practical methodology, consider some of the following (comments at the end in C1.2).

a Chickens and eggs and Mozart

According to *The Farmer's Guardian*, chickens lay more eggs when they listen to Mozart. Researchers suggest it is the intricate modulation of the notes which stimulates the hens and makes them less stressed. It has also been suggested that the same applies to children, whose learning shows an improvement if they are played classical music both pre-birth and in the first couple of years. Can you explain why stories such as these are nonsense?

b Sofa: so good

In one advertising campaign, the furniture shop Ikea used the results of a survey that said: people with green sofas are more likely to be adventurous in bed; people with flowery wallpaper were more likely to gossip about their friends and neighbours; people who kept cacti as domestic plants were likely to be cold and unemotional. What conceptual step has been leapt over in the logic of these findings?

c Shooting the milkman

A few years ago in Belfast, a French TV news crew filming an item on the 'troubles' persuaded a gang of children to throw some stones and a few petrol bombs for the cameras. When the trouble escalated, a local milkman was killed in the rioting. Which rule of social science had the film crew broken?

d Not being beastly to fascists

Especially during general election campaigns, the BBC tries to abide by its regulations for equal coverage given to the political parties. In 1997, there was an outcry at the right-wing British National Party being allowed a party political broadcast. Similarly, Conservative politicians – virtually extinct as a political force in Scotland – are allowed equal TV time as Labour, Liberal Democrat and Scottish Nationalist politicians. What sort of sampling method is being used here?

e Test-drive your date

'Test-drive your date. Behind the wheel, does your prospective partner regularly . . .

- ❏ jump red lights?
- ❏ clip kerbs?
- ❏ cut up other cars?
- ❏ use his horn?

If you answered "yes" to more than one, he could be a bad lover. A report by Cris Burgess, for the AA, says so-called "wilful offenders" are selfish lovers as well as being a menace on the roads. "If they don't get what they want, they're not interested and won't make an effort," explains Burgess. "They tend to have poor sex lives because they find it hard to maintain close relationships. They won't give – they only take"' (*Cosmopolitan*, September 1998: 81). What do you think of the linkages between cause and effect going on here?

f The message is the medium

In order to have a discussion on whether seances work, the researchers of the *Kilroy* BBC TV programme placed an ad in newspapers asking for people to participate in the studio talkshow. Is this alright as a sampling method?

g Is there anybody out there?

In the mid-West of the US, there are many reported cases of unidentified flying objects, lights in the sky, electricity power cuts, mutilated cattle, and crop circles. These have been attributed to the activities of extra-terrestrial intelligences. Why is this feeble-minded?

h Who you gonna call?

A recent TV advert for an insurance company features a man walking past a burnt out building, with the line: 'You'd go to the fire service to put out the fire, but they can't arrange your insurance for you.' What is the false logic involved here?

i Hey kids, just say no

A recent billboard 'drugs awareness' campaign featured the line: '80% of children will try drugs', over the large image of a hypodermic needle. Why is this ad unnecessarily alarmist in its statistical claims?

j The one about the taxi driver

An urban myth: if the Sultan of Brunei took a taxi through London, the average wealth of the two occupants of the taxi would be several billion pounds. Why is this true fact of little comfort to the taxi driver?

k Good God

In 1999 BBC web-page news reported a study that said people from the Afro-Caribbean community who went to church regularly were likely to be healthier and wealthier than their more secular counterparts. So, is God good for you?

l Dead good

The town with the highest mortality rate in the UK is Torquay. Why is it so unhealthy there?

m Cats/dogs

When it is raining, will you be drier if you run through the rain or if you walk? What are the variables to consider?

Comment   C1.2

a There is a problem here with uncontrolled independent variables. That is, there could be a whole range of other factors that explain why hens lay more eggs: perhaps farmers who play their chickens Mozart also feed their stock better? So Mozart is not a causal factor but is an index of the cause. Furthermore, the explanation presented means there is no reason why any intricate sound should not work, but no one has yet claimed that productivity goes up with the music of Jimi Hendrix.

b Ikea are deliberately missing an intermediate step here. These examples present *x* as causing *y*, whereas actually both factors are independently caused by another factor *z*. A comparison would be trying to decide whether working-class children tend to fail at school because their language is different, or whether both these phenomena are caused by a different attitude to the middle-class codes in which schools tend to operate.

c Interfering with the data you are there to record is the observer's paradox, which the film crew have seriously misjudged. Sociolinguists have tried to minimise the observer's paradox with a range of elicitation methods to collect naturalistic data.

d The sample represents all opinion equally but it does not weight the relative popularity of the parties. Of course, doing this would then preserve either the results of the previous election or the *status quo*. All of these options thus represent an ideological choice, and this illustrates that 'balance' is impossible and even statistics have an ideological dimension.

e This is similar to the Ikea ad (b above). Factor *x* (bad driving) does not cause *y* (being a bad lover); instead both are results of factor *z* (selfishness). Notice also how the ambiguous word choices reinforce the suggestion ('jump', 'red lights', 'use his horn') and how the syntactic form moves from possibility ('if . . . could') to assertion. You should look out for such rhetorical sleight-of-hand when statistical evidence is presented.

f This is **circularity**. The sampling method is set up to produce a self-selecting group of people who will already have extreme views. In sociolinguistics, circularity would be involved if a linguistic means were used to select a group for a linguistic analysis: for example, investigating the accent of working-class people, but using the presence or absence of non-standard verb agreement partly to determine whether they are working class or not.

g The explanation selected here is possible but the least likely. Of the range of possible causes of *a*, such as *b* (military test flights), *c* (weather patterns), *d* (psychotic local people), you decide that factor *z* (slobbery beings from planet Zog) must be to blame. In sociolinguistics, there is usually a range of possibilities that can be ordered into a sequence of probable to improbable, and it is useful to do this in discussion, in order to keep your conclusions in touch with the rest of the discipline.

h Chronological cause and effect are reversed here. Many people find this sentence acceptable until they think about it. The reason might be that both clauses in the sentence are stylistically connected ('but') and both belong to a similar semantic domain (fire and insurance). However, the two parts of the sentence do not logically follow: this is a *non-sequitur*.

i 'Drugs' might mean anything from heroin, to cannabis, to ecstasy, to alcohol or caffeine, though the image strongly suggests 'hard' drugs. More misleadingly, the assertion is an (unproven) prediction ('will') that also hides the less emotive fact that '100% of children will die' (eventually), and all drug users were once children.

j This illustrates the problem with group means in statistics. Taking a mean average when the population (that is, the elements) of the group are very disparate misrepresents the reality. The taxi driver's income has not actually risen (unless he gets a good tip). A calculation of **standard deviation** (how far most elements are away from the mean average) would help here.

k Like *a* above, church going might be an index of your social class, supportive community network, close extended family, all of which might influence your wealth and health. Of course, this takes another ideological slant: perhaps religious faith makes you calmer, which makes you better off; or even some might argue that better 'luck' accompanies religious belief. An empirical test or examination of social and census information might shed light on the first of these hypotheses, but the last is probably beyond the scope of sociolinguistics.

l Be careful with terms. The measure of environmental healthiness is *infant* mortality rate. Torquay is a popular retirement resort for older people.

m This raises all the complexity of controlling for possible relevant factors: distance, speed, rate of rainfall, balance of water on your head or chest, what clothes you are wearing, what sort of rain it is, what sort of haircut is optimal, and so on. Think of an experiment to decide the matter, and how you would control for all of these factors.

DIALECTAL VARIATION

An accent-elicitation reading passage

The following passage has been specially written to contain many of the linguistic features that have multiple variants in different accents of English. It is, of course, one of the advantages of having a standardised written dialect (Standard English) and a frozen medieval spelling system that written English can be read and written by anyone in their own accent.

> Once upon a time there were three bears: a Daddy bear, a Mummy bear and a little baby bear. They lived in a cottage deep in the woods. One morning, Mummy bear had made some porridge for breakfast, but it was too hot to eat at once. 'Let's go for a walk while it cools down,' said Daddy bear. 'What a good idea!' exclaimed Mummy bear, and, with their bear coats and bear shoes on, they all set off for a short walk in the woods.
>
> That morning a little girl called Goldilocks was also walking in the woods. She was picking flowers and had wandered deeper in among the trees than her parents allowed her to go. After a while of being completely lost, she came into a clearing and saw the pretty little cottage. 'I wonder who lives there?' she thought to herself, and walked up to the door. When she knocked, there was no answer, so she pushed the door. It swung open, and she went in.

Can you identify some of the particular items (letters, words or links between words) in this passage that are likely to elicit a range of variant phonetic features when read aloud in different accents? It might help if you try out different accents while reading the passage: New York, Glasgow, Dublin, Birmingham; or think of ways that men, women, boys, girls, bus drivers, mechanics, professors, sales assistants and others might pronounce the text.

Word pairs and variant pronunciations

You could use the Goldilocks passage to elicit informants' speech patterns. The familiarity of the story and the ease of its vocabulary will minimise disfluency and hesitancy, and it is likely to produce a natural accent. Of course, it is still a reading passage. You can get even more relaxed data with casual conversation, informal interview, covert recording, and so on. You can increase informants' self-consciousness and 'carefulness' by openly recording them, interviewing them formally, telling them you are interested in their speech, or by using minimal pairs or groups of words like these:

bear	beer	bier	bare			
oil	air	ear	moor	poor	pore	paw
bag	beg	big				
bad	bard	board	bored	bawd		
cot	caught	cat				
blue	blew					
moan	mown	moan	moon			
plaster	master	grass	laugh			

which	witch	weather	whether	whither	wither
butter	mother	brother	parrot	Paris	
farm	bird	lore	law	law and order	
lamp post	pen knife	bread tin	crisp packet		
Cuba	news	Tuesday	tissue	sexual	
missile	tile	leisure	tomato	either	
spear	actually	constitution			
bath	run	put	putt	pot	pat	pet
hotel	happy	house			
Mary	merry	marry	Murray		
letter 'a'	letter 'i'				

How do you pronounce these words? Do you think you pronounce them the same in these small groups as you would in normal conversation? Which accents would make differentiations between some of the words in ways that you do not? Try saying each of these words in the accents of America, northern England, southern England, Birmingham, Norfolk, Wales, Jamaica, Belfast, white South Africa, black South Africa, Glasgow, Australia, and any others you can manage. Can you outline the differences using the phonetic notation of the IPA?

C2.3

Regional variation

In different parts of Britain, these words are all used to refer to the same thing:

bun	bap	barm	batch
cob	roll	cake	flat
loaf	fadgie	stotty	

Do you recognise all of these? Do you use any of them? Do you have a different word?

Consider the dialectal differences in these sentences:

I haven't spoken to him.
I've not spoken to him.

Is John at home?
Is John home?

I live in Nottingham, on Lenton Boulevard, at number 23.
She lives on our street.
She lives in our street.
On the street where you live.
They play in the street.

Give me it.
Give it me.
Give it to me.
Give us it.
Give it.

I should like to thank you.
I would like to thank you.
I'd like to thank you.

I'll be here while 10.
I'll be here 'til 10.

Is that you?
Are you through?
Have you finished?
Are you done?

drive-through
drive-in
drive-by
drive-way

lie-in
over-lay
sleep-over
over-sleep

off-licence
off-sales
offie
beer-off
liquor store
bottle store
bottle bank

Who would use each of these? What contexts would they be used in?

Literary dialect   C2.4

Here is a song that my mother sang to me in a mock Cockney accent when I was a
baby:

> *A muvver was barfin' 'er biby one night,*
> *The youngest of ten and a tiny young mite,*
> *The muvver was pore and the biby was fin,*
> *Only a skellington covered in skin;*
> *The muvver turned rahnd for the soap orf the rack,*
> *She was but a moment, but when she turned back,*
> *The biby was gorn; and in anguish she cried,*
> *'Oh, where is my biby?' – the Angels replied:*
> *'Your biby 'as fell dahn the plug'ole,*
> *Your biby 'as gorn dahn the plug;*
> *The poor little fing was so skinny and fin*
> *'E oughter been barfed in a jug;*

> *Your biby is perfectly 'appy,*
> *'E shan't need a barf any more,*
> *Your biby 'as fell dahn the plug'ole,*
> *Not lorst, but gorn before!'*

> (Traditional; written version adapted from *The Rattle Bag*, edited by
> Seamus Heaney and Ted Hughes (1982), Faber and Faber)

Clearly, this picks up on many of the stereotypical features of the Cockney accent as well as some dialect features. As a piece of popular (oral) 'literature' rather than sociolinguistics it can present such a cartoon-like version of Cockney. There are many examples of literary uses of non-standard accent and dialect which you could investigate as a means of exploring prestige/stigmatisation and the attitudes and stereotypes which are popularly held. Some examples include:

- ❏ the speech of Joseph in Emily Brontë's *Wuthering Heights*
- ❏ the speech of Stephen Blackpool in Charles Dickens' *Hard Times*
- ❏ Mrs Durbeyfield in Thomas Hardy's *Tess of the d'Urbevilles*
- ❏ the speech of Morel in D.H. Lawrence's *Sons and Lovers*
- ❏ Scots in the poetry of Hugh McDiarmid
- ❏ the poetry of Barnsley poet Ian McMillan
- ❏ the poetry of Glasgow poet Tom Leonard
- ❏ the narrative style of Irvine Welsh's *Trainspotting*
- ❏ Irish English in the novels of Roddy Doyle
- ❏ Indian English in Salman Rushdie's fiction

and many others. You could measure these versions against an actual sociolinguistic account of the variety, in order to understand what is being foregrounded in the literature and how the traits of the accents and dialects are used to build the characterisation.

C3 REGISTER

C3.1

The art of writing

Here is an extract from the exhibition catalogue from the Guggenheim museum in Bilbao (English version), part of the International Currents in Contemporary Art exhibition:

Gallery 303 and corridor:

Gillian Wearing (Birmingham, United Kingdom, 1963), **Pipilotti Rist** (Rheintal, Switzerland, 1962), **Andreas Slominski** (Meppen, Germany, 1959)

British artist Gillian Wearing is particularly interested in the fears, fantasies, and secrets of ordinary people and in the processes of identification set up with the viewer. In *Sacha and Mum*, 1996, Wearing attempts to unmask the ambivalent emotions surrounding the complex personal relationships between a mother and her daughter. The warmth of an embrace becomes transformed into a confrontation

---

bordering on violence. The palpable tension in Wearing's work is in sharp contrast to the sensual celebration of the body in Swiss-artist Pipilotto Rist's video
installation *Sip My Ocean*, 1996. Rist has created a magic submarine dream world
in this video, which was filmed almost entirely under water and is accompanied by
her own cover of Chris Isaak's love song "Wicked Games." Her entire aesthetic
borrows from pop music and the vast area of mass culture. Double screens and
spectacular effects suggest an ideal region of unadulterated pre-Oedipal pleasure.
The work is Rist's personal invitation to take part in the eternal dance of desire
and satisfaction. For more than fifteen years, German conceptual artist Andreas
Slominski has been reinterpreting the concept of the trap. Slominski, who designs
his own functional traps for all kinds of animals (foxes, birds, insects), has found
a perfect metaphor for art: like art, the trap seduces and deceives. Hermetic and
humorous, the work lures its viewers, asking them to ponder the very limits of
what constitutes the absurd and, hence, to contemplate the boundaries of art.

What is it that linguistically characterises this as an art exhibition catalogue? You might
look particularly at the syntactic arrangement of the sentences, and especially at the
complexity of noun phrases.

Could you rewrite this for a different audience: for children on a school trip, for
a group of people on their first ever visit to an art gallery, for the use of people whose
first language is not English? Could you reframe it as speech? In each case, decide exactly
what you would need to change in order to switch registers.

A registered nurse

C3.2

Kate Oakley was interested in shifts in register amongst nursing staff in a large city
hospital, in order to identify their occupational language code.

The following is from the operation notes to treat a 'slipped disc':

PR Exploration Of L. Spine. – Operative procedure.
Patient prone on Toronto frame.
Previous incision used and extended.
L3 to S1 Vertebrae exposed.
L3 Laminectomy performed.
Normal Dura was identified at that level and traced Caudally, by careful
dissection, all the scar tissue was dissected off.
The Dura was exposed fully at all the levels from L3 to S1.
Laminectomy widened to effect better decompression.
No obvious Dural tear seen.
At the end of the procedure, standard closure in layers with Vicryl. Continuous
Prolene to skin.

Make a systematic list of the stylistic features that identify this as, respectively: a piece
of writing rather than speech, a report rather than a narrative fiction, a medical report
rather than a report of a football match.

Here is an exchange from Kate's data:

(consultant, senior nurse and junior doctor, away from the bed of a patient with tuberculosis and another long-term chest complaint)

Consultant: we'll stop Mrs Pxxxx's A [drug's pharmaceutical name] – it's done bugger all to help her. just made her more vulnerable to infection

(moving to the patient's bedside and addressing her)

Consultant: well it is TB – as long as you take the tablets to fight the infection there will be no problem – we are going to stop your breathing tablets as it's just not helping

(She turns to the junior doctor.)

Consultant: it should show up on microexamination. we need to inform the P.H.D. – forms are in the office

(moving back to the ward station away from the patient)

Consultant: unfortunately her emphysema masked the underlying tuberculosis – I've actually seen at PM widespread milliary infection that was not picked up by either CT scan or PA view on x-ray

Identify the code-switching points here, and compare the different linguistic choices of the different codes in operation.

The following written nursing notes also show a marked code-switch:

R. Leg no movement. NBM. from midnight. S/B Mr G.
For IV. Dexamethasone. T. = 37.4C. IVI. in progress.
Unable to PU. catheterised. 10mls. H20 in balloon.
CBD. good volumes. Vital signs normal. PA's intact.
Apyrexial. Feeling really fed up.
Ensure TED's are in situ.

Here is a written 'ward report' list of patients with notes for the nursing staff on duty:

Mrs S: Not coping. TIA's. # of R. Radius. G.I. bleed.
Mrs F: Not for 2's. Ascites, tapped. Ca. of pancreas. I.V. down. T.L.C.
Mrs J: MI.
Mrs P: Ca. Colostomy. Oromorph given.
Mr T: SOB. A/F. Digoxin. 02 PRN.
Mr G: NIDDM. Actrapid if over 27. 6 hrly. BM stix.
Mr P: COAD. Cont. 02. Nebs. 4 hrly.
Mr G: Haematuria. R.B.K.A. and CVA. Multi-infarct dementia.
Mrs N: For FOB.

If you can understand all of the terms used in these, you are probably a nurse, and the 'face' you present to the world as a nurse is in large part a result of this sort of linguistic competence and performance. Can you decide which other occupations and professions have a similarly exclusive register (or jargon)? For each, either list some of the characteristic features, or you could go and collect some real data like that used above, and analyse it. Comparing the registers of closely associated groups is illuminating: teachers and lecturers, checkout operators at different supermarkets, bar staff in different types of bar, decorative designers and decorators, professional engineers and mechanics, journalists and reporters, senior managers and middle managers, and so on.

Here are two letters written by a consultant surgeon. This first one was sent to the patient's General Practitioner:

> Dear Dr H,
> As you know I sent M.R.I. scans and clinical details of Mr L to a very good friend of mine, Mr Q in Cardiff, who recommended a Thoracic Spine M.R.I. scan to be performed and this has shown a very significant lower Thoracic spinal stenosis especially at TH/12. Changes do extend to higher up but it is the lower three Thoracic levels which are most significant. His Cervical spine M.R.I. scan is really not too bad and I think consideration for a lower Thoracic Laminectomy is worthwhile. He could walk 4 miles just over a year ago, but now his performance is considerably less.
>
> Mr L is going to think about it and let me know.
>
> Yours sincerely,
>
> Mr N, FRCS

The second letter was sent to the patient:

> Dear Mr L,
> There is one part of your spine that does not show up on the M.R.I. scan and that is at the low Thoracic level. My colleague Mr Q in Cardiff has recommended we do an M.R.I. scan at this level, and if you are agreeable we will do this as soon as possible and then I will see you again.
>
> Yours sincerely,
>
> Mr N.

Identify and list the differences between these. Can you imagine the same information expressed in a conversation between the consultant Mr N and the GP Dr H, or between Mr N and the patient Mr L, or how Mr L might recount what has happened to his friend in the pub who enquires about his health?

Some medical acronyms and terms:

#	fracture
02	oxygen

Actrapid	a quick-acting insulin
A/F	atrial fibrillation
Apyrexial	not feverish
Ascites	fluid accumulation in the peritoneal cavity
BM stix	trade name for blood glucose monitoring
B/P	blood pressure
Ca.	cancer
CBD	catheter bag drainage
COAD	chronic obstructive airways disease
Colostomy	surgery to bring bowel out to body surface
cont.	continuous
CT	computerised tomography
CVA	cerebral vascular accident (stroke)
CXR	chest x-ray
dexamethasone	a steroid
Digoxin	heart medication
emphysema	a lung disease
FOB	faecal occult blood – a test for blood in the stools
GI	gastro-intestinal
H20 in balloon	catheter is kept in bladder by a water-filled balloon
haematuria	blood in urine
IV(I)	intra-venous (injection)
MI	myocardial infarction (heart attack)
microexamination	microbiological investigation of tissue samples
NBM	nil by mouth
Nebs	nebuliser
NIDDM	non-insulin dependent diabetic
not for 2s	222 is the telephone number of the heart resuscitation team. So 'not for 222' means 'not for resuscitation'
OE	on examination
Oromorph	form of morphine
PA	posterior anterior
PHD	public health department
PM	post mortem / autopsy
PMH	previous medical history
PU	pass urine
PRN	pro re nata – as required
S/B	seen by
SOB	shortness of breath
T	temperature
TB	tuberculosis
TED	thrombo-embolic disease stocking
TIA	trans-ischaemic attacks – small strokes
TLC	tender loving care

ETHNOLOGY

East Asian languages and prestige

The following article formed part of a special debate in *The Straits Times* 'Life!' supplement (Saturday 12 June 1999), published in Singapore. The newspaper was discussing the relative statuses of British and American English, Singaporean English, Singlish, and the different views of Chinese languages.

Actually, Chinese May Not Be The Mother Tongue
by Sunny Goh

[. . .] Does Mandarin deserve such an unqualified position?

Two other translators, Larry Teo and Dai Shiyan, both steeped in the understanding of the Chinese language, offer contrasting views.

In my explanation on the differences between Chinese language (*huawen*) and Mandarin (*huayu*), I had made the point that in Singapore, Mandarin is deemed the only exclusive spoken form, as Teochew, Cantonese, etc are referred to as dialects (*fangyan*).

That is why in Singapore, we refer to the Chinese language as *huawen* and Mandarin exclusively and interchangeably as *huayu*. This is not exactly correct, as *huayu* is defined, strictly in most international Chinese dictionaries, as spoken Chinese. It may or may not be Mandarin.

To the global Chinese community, Mandarin, which is equivalent to *putonghua*, is "a common or standard spoken form of the Chinese language".

In short, Mandarin is *huayu* but *huayu* is more than just Mandarin.

Dai disagreed with me, saying that Mandarin can be used interchangeably with *huayu* because it has been recognised internationally as the standard spoken form.

Shanghainese, Ningbo and the southern dialects such as Hokkien and Teochew are all sub-standard representations of the Chinese language.

"Mandarin is the pure form and should be regarded as such," he said, just as Received Pronunciation in Britain has been regarded as the standard spoken form of the English language. (Linguists are more diplomatic when they refer to English variants such as Cockney English, by using the neutral term "non-standard form" rather than the emotional term "sub-standard form" to refer to them).

Teo disagreed with Dai, saying that Mandarin is not the natural acquisition of Singapore students, who are required to learn to speak a tongue that has always been considered "alien" by many Chinese in China itself, especially those from the south, where the ancestors of most Chinese-Singaporeans hailed from.

In the final analysis, it is evident that where a language is used, and by whom, plays a vital role in determining how it is being defined.

The communists in China called Mandarin *putonghua*, which fits in well with their idea that it should be the language of the masses.

> Interestingly, the Hong-kongers call it *zhongwen*, which means Chinese language, while the Taiwanese call it *guo-yu*, meaning national language.
>
> Only South-east Asians, including Singaporeans, call it *huayu*, which might have stemmed from the emphasis that they are *huaqiao*, meaning Overseas Chinese.
>
> *Huaren* (Chinese people) is another, more significant, derivative of *huawen/huayu* to describe Singaporeans.
>
> "Singaporeans who are *huaren*" is certainly a more detached term to describe Chinese-Singaporeans in a multi-racial country, as it gives the connotations that we are Singaporeans first, Chinese second.
>
> *Huaren* is also not as politically-charged as some older terms which had been used to describe overseas Chinese, such as *tongbao* (Chinese compatriots) or, worse, *zhongguo ren* (people from China).
>
> So if you think about it, *huawen*, *huayu* and *huaren* do make sense for Singaporeans after all.

Try to discern the different language loyalties in evidence here. You will also be able to use your knowledge of sociolinguistics to take issue with the comparison with RP. Applying a knowledge of the socio-political alignments of east Asian nations will also help here.

C4.2

Hong Kong chat: 'Mix'

This is an extract from I Ching Ng's data, used as part of her investigation into 'Mix', the blend of English and Cantonese heard in Hong Kong. The script is from an Internet chatroom run by a local radio station. In the original, the text in square brackets was entered in Chinese characters; I Ching provides a translation here.

Occupants:	little kit – popcorn – pp – smiling – [sara] – [granny number 8]
smiling:	[wrong spelling. shit]
granny no.8:	i am super 8
little kit:	logged on.
pp:	logged off.
smiling:	HAHAHA...............SERA, [so you make fun of him]!
granny no.8:	smile~
popcorn:	smiling, [you want to spoil the whole thing]? [Ha]
smiling:	not too GER? [So, must be pretty cool]???[You're pretty confident No.8]
[sara]:	popcorn, u too ar! don't play me next time!!
popcorn:	[sara], bye bye! take care!
pp:	logged on.
smiling:	[I'm no good. So, you are good]
[sara]:	But i go la! bye all again!!!!
popcorn:	little kit, hello!
popcorn:	[grin]:[You think I can't] put u in invisible? [You idiot]!
smiling:	[Oh]!!!!!![How dare you]!!!![Put me in invisible]!!!!!!!!

little kit:	hello~~~~~~~~~~~~~~~~
granny no.8:	go lar ~~ bye bye
granny no.8:	i am boring ar
granny no.8:	logged off.
smiling:	[yes obviously so stupid.........don't know where to escape]
smiling:	kitkit [did somebody] kick [you]??? [Because you didn't] online
	for ages [of course don't see you, you idiot]
popcorn:	smiling, u shooting arrows?

There is obviously a great deal of code-switching here, and the electronic medium makes the blending even more fluid and non-standard (to 'put in invisible' is to wipe a speaker from the screen, thus freezing them out). Exchanges are initiated in English: 'popcorn' uses mainly English with 'sara' who uses English Mix all the time, but 'popcorn' uses Chinese for 'smiling' who uses Chinese entirely. These uses (supported by the friendly 'la/lar') are also marked for solidarity by the text being posted in a purple colour. There are some direct interferences from Chinese: 'granny number 8' denotes a 'nosy' person, as '8' and 'nosy' are homophones in Chinese; 'shooting arrows' is a Chinese idiom for a personal attack; and 'GER' is an English spelling of the Chinese word for 'only'.

The common grammatical 'errors' are frequent in fast electronic posting, but also reflect the fact that only about 30 per cent of people in Hong Kong speak English – and then, most of them as an L2. English is only used in public domains: high-status financial jobs, media and entertainment. Thus, English and Cantonese in Hong Kong can be regarded as being on a cline of bilingualism, with 'Mix' being a stigmatised form gaining in popularity among young people.

SOCIOLOGICAL VARIATION

C5

Written dialect

C5.1

The following passage is an attempt to imitate the local spoken vernacular of Teesside, in the sports comment column of a local newspaper. The article is about a new player bought by Middlesbrough Football Club.

Shelling out a lot of dough

SIXTY thousand quid a week for this Leonardo gadgie, eh? Sixty bloody thousand? Yer joking aren't yer?

Looka, I don't care if he is a Brazilian – it's bloody nuts! I'll tell yer that for nowt!

I mean, that fat waste of space Branco – or Lardarso as he was known in our house – he was Brazilian wasn't he, eh? And he wasn't even worth 60p a week was he, eh?

And I don't care if this Leonardo gadgie did used to be one of them Teenage Mutant Ginger Turtles.

For one thing, he must be getting on a bit by now and for another them Turtles are bloody has-beens now aren't they, eh? Eh?

I mean, that Darth Maul gadgie might be worth 60 grand coz you'd shift loads of face paint and club crested light sabres and replica cowls and that in the club shop, but this Turtle lad can whistle for his bloody money, I reckon.

I mean, no-one that matters has ever even heard of him! Honest.

Hey, when I asked the lads on The Streetfighters Arms Punters' Panel what they knew about him two of them said straight away that he was crap in that film Titanic, y'know the one what Our Lass was always going on at me to take her to see. . . . I'll get her a video for Christmas, eh?

If I can find it on that stall on Doggy Market that is.

Anyroad, this Leonardo gadgie. Fat Stan's little brother Stevo reckoned he used to be a painter and decorator in Normanby what did a famous drawing of some whingy lass called Moaner Lisa, like.

Worth a fortune it is Stevo sez, like, but Leo still won't sell. He's got it hung in his loo. Or something like that.

(Teesside *Evening Gazette*, 24 July 1999)

Can you identify features that are dialectal here? You will have to decide whether a non-standard item is a result of dialect, or simply a spelling-form to signify accent, or whether it is an example of imitating spoken discourse and casual style, or whether the feature is simply part of the writer's individual and idiosyncratic **idiolect**. Can you write a similar passage in your own local vernacular?

C5.2 | **Working like a canine in translation**

The following interview with Madonna was conducted in English while she was in Hungary filming *Evita*. It was then translated into Hungarian and published in the magazine *Blikk*, and then translated back into English. This version appeared in *The Daily Mail* (Thursday 16 May 1996):

Blikk: Madonna, Budapest says hello with arms that are spread-eagled. Are you in good odour? You are the biggest fan of our young people who hear your musical productions and like to move their bodies in response.

Madonna: Thank you for saying these compliments. Stop with taking sensationalist photographs until I have removed my garments for all to see. This is a joke I have made.

Blikk: Let's cut towards the hunt. Are you a bold hussy woman that feasts on men who are tops?

Madonna: This is certainly something which brings to the surface my longings. In America it is not considered to be mentally ill when a woman advances on her prey in a disco setting with hardy

	cocktails present. And there is a more normal attitude towards leather play toys that also makes my day.
Blikk:	Is this how you met Carlos, your love servant who is reputed? Did you know he was heaven sent right off the stick? Or were you dating many other people in your bed at the same time?
Madonna:	No, he was the only one in my bed then so it is a scientific fact that the baby was made in my womb using him. But as regards these questions, enough. I am a woman not a test mouse. Carlos is an everyday person who is in the orbit of a star who is being muscle-trained by him, not a sex machine.
Blikk:	May we talk about your other 'baby', your movie. Do not be denying the similarities between you and the real Evita are grounded in basis. Power, money, tasty food and Grammys – all these elements are afoot.
Madonna:	What is up in the air with you? Evita was never winning a Grammy.
Blikk:	Perhaps not. But as to your film, in trying to bring your reputation along a rocky road, can you make people forget the bad explosions of Who's That Girl and Shanghai Surprise?
Madonna:	I am a tip-top starlet. That is something I am paid to do.
Blikk:	OK. Here is a question from left space. What was your book Slut about?
Madonna:	It was called Sex.
Blikk:	Not in Hungary. Here it was called Slut. How did it come to publish? Were you lovemaking with a man-about-town printer? Do you prefer making suggestive literature to fast selling CDs?
Madonna:	These are different facets to my career highway. I am preferring to become respected all over the map as a 100 per cent artist.
Blikk:	How many Hungarian men have you dated in bed. How are they comparing to Argentine men who are famous for being tip-top?
Madonna:	To avoid aggravated global tension, I would say it is a tie. See here, I am working like a canine all the way around my clock. I have been too busy even to try the goulash that makes your country one for the record books.

Most of the miscues that give this text its special flavour are a result of mismatched idioms and register, as well as direct translations of Hungarian grammar. Try to translate it back into the fluent English that Madonna might recognise as her own words. Can you work out for each alteration what has gone wrong and what difference the shift in choice of register would make?

PRESTIGE

C6

As a result of their colonial history, the main European languages have influenced the speech of millions of people around the world. English, Spanish, Portuguese, French,

Dutch, Italian and German exist in a range of varieties. The histories of the native countries of these languages have largely been ones of suppressing the other indigenous languages, either by official prohibition (Basque in Spain and France) or by official indifference and lack of support (Scots/Lallans and Cornish/Kernewek in the UK). The status of these languages is a consequence of their history of stigmatisation. In this section, several brief case studies of minority European languages are given (using data from *Contact*, the bulletin of the European Bureau for Lesser Used Languages). You could investigate these further, and evaluate their prestige value and the language loyalty felt by their speakers, using Bell's criteria (set out in detail in A6):

❏ standardisation;
❏ vitality;
❏ historicity;
❏ autonomy;
❏ reduction;
❏ mixture;
❏ 'unofficial' norms.

C6.1 Some European linguistic minorities

Scots/Lallans

Scots is the modern English descendant of the Old English Northumbrian dialect, now spoken in southern Scotland. About 80 per cent of Scotland's 6 million population have access to it, and it is a vernacular for many. It is under extreme pressure of standardisation from Standard English, though there is a Scottish National Dictionary and a version of the New Testament of the Bible in Scots. It is mostly encountered in written form in the poetry of Robert Burns, Hugh McDiarmid and Tom Leonard.

Cornish/Kernewek

Cornish is a Celtic language with no surviving native speakers (the last died 200 years ago). Evident mainly only in written form in place names and geographical features, it survives only as a learned second language. It is possible to take school examinations in Cornish, and although there is no regional Cornish-language newspaper, a learner's magazine *An Gannas* is circulated. The language has no legal or official status.

Welsh/Cymraeg

Around 20 per cent of Wales's 3 million population speak the Celtic language of **Welsh**, almost all of them as bilingual Welsh/English speakers. Welsh was largely kept alive against encroaching English from the east by its non-conformist religious tradition, a version of the Bible in Welsh, and the success of the Circulating Schools. After centuries of suppression and prohibition, the Welsh Courts Act (1942) and the Welsh Language Act (1967) provided for official recognition of Welsh. Some local councils operate a policy of bilingualism in administration, and all official documents and public notices are produced bilingually. A predominantly Welsh television channel (Sianel Pedwar Cymru), radio station (Radio Cymru), a strong nationalist political party (Plaid Cymru), several newspapers and magazines and community newspapers (papurau bro) have supported the language recently. School examinations can be taken in Welsh as a subject, and in other subjects through the medium of Welsh.

Scottish Gaelic/Gaidhlig

This Celtic language is spoken by up to 80 per cent of the population of the Outer Hebrides, with fewer speakers in the islands of the Inner Hebrides and nearby mainland, as well as an exile community in the Glasgow area. In total, around 2 per cent of the Scottish population speak **Scottish Gaelic** fluently. It is not used officially either in the Scottish Parliament or in routine government publications, and is not exclusively associated with Scottish nationalist politics. In the Gaelic-speaking areas, bilingual school provision exists, and there are bilingual schools in Glasgow and Inverness. A variety of radio stations broadcast mainly to the islands and highlands in Gaelic, and there is a children's language programme, 'Ceredigion', but no large-circulation newspaper.

Irish/Gaeilge

Around a third of the population of the Republic of Ireland can speak **Irish Gaelic**, with a further 60,000 Gaelic speakers in Northern Ireland. However, for many of these people, Gaelic is a poor L2 or an aspiration. Vernacular Gaelic speakers are mainly restricted to the Gaeltacht areas of the north-west and west, and a part of County Louth in the east, and number no more than 10,000. Officially, Irish Gaelic is the 'national language' and 'first official language', with English being the 'second official language'. In practice, most administration and publication is conducted in English and subsequently translated into Irish, though a facility in Irish is an advantage for civil servants and university staff. The Bord na Gaeilge promotes Irish across Ireland, but especially in the west. Only about 2 per cent of the state television (RTE) output is regularly in Irish, though there is an Irish-language channel and regional radio.

Basque/Euskera

The territory of the 'Basque Country' is defined largely by the presence of **Basque** speakers: Euskal Herria. It straddles the border of Spain and France. In the Spanish-governed area, Basque is now an official language, with 700,000 speakers. All of these are bi- or multilingual in Basque, Spanish and French. The language is pre-Indo-European and is not related to any other European language. Basque has only been allowed to be taught since the 1980s. Prior to that it was suppressed under Franco, with schoolteachers punishing children caught speaking their vernacular. Regional radio, television and a daily newspaper *Gara*, as well as a number of both parliamentary and extremist political parties support the use of Basque as part of a campaign for independence from Spain (and France).

Galician

The area of Galego in the part of Spain just north of Portugal contains a population with 80 per cent speakers of **Galician**. This is a Latin language closer to Portuguese than Spanish. Up until the 1930s, there was a strong development of Galician literature, but the language was suppressed under Franco and Spanish imposed on administration, education, the media and the Church. More recently it has again become the permitted common language of the area.

Catalan

Spoken by 60 per cent of the population of Catalonia along the eastern coast and Balearic islands of Spain, **Catalan** is also understood by a further 20 per cent of the people. After suppression under Franco, it has since been recognised as an official language of the region alongside Spanish, in line with the political process of 'linguistic normalisation'. This has meant that administration in the region is bilingual. There is a Catalan television channel, and several local radio stations and newspapers, though Spanish remains the dominant force in the mass media and in schools.

Luxembourgeois

This variety of German – Moselle Frankish or **Luxembourgeois** – is the vernacular language of the independent Grand Duchy of Luxembourg (population just under 400,000), as well as of the area around Arlon/Arel in Belgium, the Germanic part of the French Moselle, and areas in Germany around Bitburg and Plum (totalling a further 40,000 speakers). In Luxembourg itself, the language is encouraged though French is the official language of written administration, and German dominates in newspapers and magazines. Most of the population is therefore trilingual.

Frisian

Spoken as a vernacular by 60 per cent of the 600,000 population of Friesland, **Frisian** is the official second language of the Netherlands. After centuries of standardisation pressure from Dutch, it is now compulsorily taught in primary schools. It is not broadcast on television except as a curiosity, though there are Frisian 'slots' on local radio and news bulletins given hourly in the language. Only about 5 per cent of the content of the two regional newspapers is in Frisian. The scientific journal of the Frisian Academy has half its articles in the language.

Other codes

There are many other minority languages and dialects in Europe: Friuli, Ladin, Occitan, Sardinian, Franco-Provençal, Slovene and Romany just within the borders of Italy, for example. Try to apply a measurement of prestige and status to these and to local dialects that you know. Notice, too, that the sense of prestige and value of a code varies depending on which group is making the evaluation.

C7

GENDER

C7.1

Writing gender

The following is taken from the leaflet *On Balance: Guidelines for the Representation of Women and Men in English Language Teaching Materials*, produced by the group 'Women in EFL Materials' in 1991:

These guidelines have been compiled as a reminder to people involved in all aspects of ELT publishing to be aware of discriminatory language and stereotypical images and, wherever possible, to use inclusive language and images which reflect a more balanced and accurate view of the world and of the present state of English [. . .]

Avoiding stereotypes
Much can be done to *avoid* presenting people in a stereotyped way. [. . .]

Character
Are both women and men shown in texts, dialogues, recordings and illustrations:

– being bold and assertive?
– being weak, vulnerable or scared?
– instructing, leading, rescuing?
– being instructed, led, rescued?
– displaying self-control?
– responding emotionally?
– being strong, capable and logical?
– being uncertain and in need of reassurance?
– being powerful and able to deal with problems?
– being inept and defeated by problems?
– belonging to a range of emotional types?
– starting dialogues?
– making arrangements?
[. . .]

Women in language
As with stereotypes, language which excludes women can be dealt with 1) by avoiding its use and 2) by dealing sensitively with exclusive language that comes up in, for example, authentic recordings. In the second case it is often enough to suggest that teachers point out that a particular usage may offend many women, and to ensure that other authentic recordings demonstrate inclusive language.

False generics
Studies of native English-speaking college students and school children have shown that the generic use of words like *man* (ostensibly to include all humans), does not elicit mental images of both sexes. [. . .]

Avoiding false generic 'man'

Instead of	*Use*
mankind	people, humans, humanity
manpower	work force, staff
man-made	artificial, synthetic, manufactured
man-to-man	person-to-person
prehistoric man	prehistoric people
manned by	staffed by

[. . .]

Instead of generic	Use
businessman	executive
cameraman	camera operator
chairman	chairperson, chair
fireman	fire fighter
foreman	supervisor
policemen	police officer
statesman	leader, politician

The leaflet goes on to give guidelines on how to avoid the false generic 'he', advises not using female diminutives in job titles ('actress', 'manageress', 'poetess'), and suggests appropriate situations for using 'girl' and 'lady'.

You will probably not have to look too far in newspaper and magazine articles, and especially in advertising language to find examples of such non-PC language. (Note that PC – 'political correctness' – was a term originally coined by right-wing commentators in America to refer to the efforts of some people to avoid being racist and sexist.)

C7.2

A mixed-sex argument

The following transcript is taken from Sharlene Goff's data (see B10). It records a discussion between 2 men and 2 women who are all friends:

Q: do you have strong opinions on fox-hunting?
F1:   yeah I do. I'm for it – but you all know that anyway
Q: why?
F1:   why? because – the foxes need – to be killed because they destroy other
       animals [and]
F2:   [but.] can they not be killed in a more humane way?=
F1:   like=
F2:   than by chasing them and making a sport of it
F1:   but – [yeah]
M1:   [no]
F1:   I can see that point that they're making [a sport] of it – I *can* see your
       point but→
F2:   [yeah]
F1:   ←otherwise it's not – mmm – you've *still* got to kill them – it's
       statistically proven that fox-hunting is the best way to kill them. I mean –
       shooting – how can they ever find them?
M1:   poisoning them you kill the wildlife as well
F1:   yeah. gassing is just hideous=
F2:   I know but – I can't understand how you can go and think I'm gonna enjoy
       [myself –   ] I can see the whole sport of it and I see can the – mmm→
M1:   [yeah definitely]
F2:   ←dragging thing=
F1:   drag hunting. yeah=

F2:   yeah I can see that and I know that's different but – I just can't see how you can enjoy going out and doing something you *know* is going to hurt something so much

F1:   yeah definitely – and I understand that but what *I'm* saying is that it is a [necessity –   ] it's like shooting fishing. anything→

M1:   [it is a necessity but=]

F1:   ←like that

M1:   yeah but basically you're saying they're vermin and you need to get rid of them like rats you don't glamorise rat-hunting [and get out your   ] poncy red coats→

F1:   [no of course you don't]

M1:   ←and black hats to do it – so I think it's a necessity but they go about it in entirely the wrong way. glamorising it

F2:   [yeah]

F1:   [mmm] but it has been a tradition for hundreds and hundreds of years

F2:   tradition can't be kept up just because it's tradition when. [when it's – like   ] inhumane

M2:   [it can be kept up just for tradition's sake]

M1:   [what. like the monarchy?]

M2:   [of course it can   ]

F1:   yeah. like the monarchy

M2:   yeah

M1:   yeah but like a monarchy that rules everything cos traditions are there to be changed for the better=

F2:   yeah

M1:   you know what I mean. we=

F2:   we're trying to change society to make it better

M2:   it's people like you who live in towns that come in [and you just don't know] you→

M1:   [no no no   ]

M2:   ←you just [don't understand]

M1:   [no I'm an *advoc*]ate of fox-hunting I'm an *advocate* of it=

F1:   and also=

M1:   I honestly am but I. think they go about it the wrong way=

F1:   and also. if you take away the whole sport around it which I can see is wrong. you're also taking away a lot of employment=

F2:   I don't agree with that=

M1:   okay okay okay. people are from. you know. going to watch bear-fighting cock-fighting. shit like that. pitbull-fighting. shit like that. you don't glamorise stuff and say come and see this do you know what I mean – you don't say come and see hounds tearing apart a fox you shouldn't need to do that. you shouldn't need to glamourise=

M2:   it shouldn't be glamourised=

M1:   they shouldn't glamourise it

M2:   it shouldn't. no

C

Can you characterise the language and discourse strategies of these participants along gender lines? You might like to compare this transcript with those reproduced in B10, and any of your own recorded discussions, to see if you can come to any conclusions about gendered discourse in spoken language.

Can you apply the recommendations from the *On Balance* guidelines (in C7.1 above) to the style in which this book is written? Have I avoided gender stereotyping? Do the transcripts of real language use in this book present men and women along the lines set out under 'character' in the guidelines? Can you find examples of other texts which break these aspirations? It is easy to find newspaper and advertising language that presents a cartoon-like image of men and women, but what about recipes, car manuals, computer manuals, nightclub flyers, music lyrics and reviews, and other texts?

C8 **CREOLE**

Collecting examples of pidgin and creole if you do not live in an area where it is used is not necessarily as difficult as you might think. There is a mass of published resources on the Internet, and of course you can find communities who use Patwa, creolised African-American English, or pidginised aboriginal languages in Britain, North America and Australia too. For example, Hamish Crombie was able to investigate the identification of Afro-Caribbean teenagers in Nottingham with Patwa-based song lyrics played in his local club. He noticed the code-switch by his local kebab-seller, which he transcribes as follows (non-phonetically):

| To Hamish: | would y'like some chilli sauce wit' dat. it's pretty dry |
| To a black customer: | WILLY – wan sam sauce onit or ya wantit drai |

Joel Dothie revisited Labov's studies into African-American English and used Milroy's notion of social networks to re-interpret his data. Hannah Neale used the published work on Jamaican Creole and Tok Pisin, a creole used in Papua New Guinea, to try to identify common processes of lexical formation.

C8.1 **A crash course in Tok Pisin**

Papua New Guinea contains over 800 languages, with three forms of common contact:

❑ English – used in writing and for international business communication;
❑ Hiri Motu (Police Motu) – used around Port Moresby, a pidgin spread by Sir William MacGregor's police force in the late nineteenth century;
❑ Tok Pisin (Neo-Melanesian) – a creolised language used in speech and writing, in the process of standardisation and codification.

The features of Tok Pisin include:

❑ consonant assimilation: so no distinction is made between /p/f/, /g/k/, or /s/ʃ/ʧ/;
❑ simplified consonant clusters ('sol' = salt, 'kol' = cold, 'sikis' = six);
❑ few vowel categories: Tok Pisin uses /a, e, i, o, u/ for all vowel sounds;

❏   reduplification for emphasis ('look' = look, 'looklook' = stare);
❏   2 forms of 'we': 'mipela' = I and others not here, 'yumi' = I and others here;
❏   plural suffix '-pela';
❏   English-based lexicon ('bagarap' = break/destroy, 'hangre' = hungry);
❏   local borrowings in lexicon (Polynesian 'kaikai' = food, Malay 'susu' = milk);
❏   compounding in word-formation ('plantihan' = plenty hands: centipede, 'pikini pik' = piglet);
❏   metaphor in word-formation ('haus pepa' = house paper: office, 'haus bilong spaida' = spider's house: web);
❏   circumlocution ('singsing bilong haus lotu' (worship) = hymn);
❏   3 basic prepositions: 'long' (to, for, from), 'bilong' (of), 'wantaim' (with);
❏   tense markers by auxiliary: 'bin' (past), 'baimbai' or 'bai' (future).

A short story

C8.2

This is a story for children (which has drawn illustrations in the original) in Tok Pisin. Try to translate it into Standard English without looking at the gloss below it.

I am a crocodile
by Steve Simpson

Mi wanpela pukpuk.
Mi hangre nogut tru.

Ooo, mi laik kaikai pis. Swit moa!

Mi laik kaikai kuka.
Em tu swit moa.

Narapela samting mi laik kaikai, em pik!
Mi laik gris bilong pik tumas. Em swit moa!

Rokrok, i namba wan! Mi laik kaikai rokrok nau tasol.
Na em swit moa yet!

Olaman! Mi laik kaikai trausel ya! I gutpela tumas. Na em swit moa yet!

Dok tu em i gutpela tru. Mi laik kaikai dok tude! Swit moa ya!

Na, wanem samting moa mi laik kaikai?
YU YET!

(British English version)

I am a crocodile.
I am very, very hungry.

I like to eat fish. Mmm . . . good (very sweet)!

I like crabs.
They are yummy (very sweet)!

Another thing I like eating is pig!
I like the flavour (grease) a lot. It is very sweet!

Frogs are excellent! I like eating frogs right now!
They are even sweeter!

Wow! I like eating turtles! They are wonderful. They are even sweeter!

Dogs are good too. I would like to eat a dog today! Mmmm. . . . !

And what else would I like to eat?

YOU!

C8.3

The mountain burns

The following are the lyrics of a song by Panim Wok Band, composed just before a volcanic eruption destroyed the town of Rabaul in Papua New Guinea in 1994.

Mounten ipaiya

Hey yumi no save bai yumi go we
Sapos-mountain paiya bai ipairap
Hey yumi no sawe bai yumi laip yet,
Sapos-maunten paiya bai ipairap

Mi no laik lusim peles bilong mi
Mi no laik stap long narapela hap
Mi laik stap yee et long Rabaul

Mi no laik lusim peles bilong mi
Mi no laik stap long narapela hap
Mi laik stap yee et long Rabaul

(Chorus)

Mi no laik Rabaul taun bai ibagarap
Mi no laik stap long narapela hap
Mi laik stap yee et long Rabaul (2x)

(Chorus)

Mi no laik lusim peles bilong mi
Mi laik stap long narapela hap
Mi laik kam bek long Rabaul

Mi no laik Rabaul taun bai ibagarap
Mi no laik stap long narapela hap
Mi laik kam bek long Rabaul
Mi laik stap yee et long Rabaul
Mi laik stap yee et long Rabaul

C9

NEW ENGLISH

C9.1

Indian English news

The following is a report from the front page of the Calcutta *Telegraph* (Wednesday 8 January 1997):

Sorry, no fish 'n chips for Mr John Major
by Meher Murshed and Shona Bagai

Calcutta, Jan. 7: Mr John Major may have to do without his fish and chips, for chefs at Taj Bengal firmly believe that made-in-India kebabs are better than those grilled in the UK.

And they feel the British Prime Minister's visit will not be complete unless he tastes the roasted delicacy.

Mr Major will be staying at the Taj during his brief visit to the city.

He, however, will not dine at the hotel. He will be lunching with the Prime Minister, Mr H.D. Deve Gowda, at Raj Bhavan, while dinner will be hosted in his honour at Tollygunge Club.

But chefs at the Taj cannot breathe easy. They only have a day to sharpen their skills. For, the hotel will be catering at Raj Bhavan and Tolly.

Mr Major shall have one meal at the hotel – breakfast.

The general manager of Taj Bengal, Ms Shireen Batlivala, said, "We have not decided on a specific menu for him in the morning. He shall be served what he asks for."

Ms Batlivala said the focus at the Raj Bhavan lunch would be on Indian curries. Curry powder, obviously, is a big no-no with the chefs.

But there is bad news for those whose palates do not fancy a spicy meal. There will be no continental dishes, no bland fare for people with delicate alimentary canals.

"The Prime Minister's Office in New Delhi has approved of the menu for lunch. There is no going back now," Ms Batlivala pointed out. [. . .]

Delegates and the British Prime Minister could choose from three kinds of cuisine during dinner at Tollygunge Club. Taj officials said there would be French, Italian and Indian dishes. And, this time, some would be bland too.

The managing member of Tolly Club, Mr Bob Wright, said the meal would be grand, but did not give further details.

"We promise to look after him well," he said. But would there be fish and chips? Mr Wright just guffawed.

Security beefed up for visit

Calcutta, Jan. 7: The state law enforcement machinery slipped into high gear today in the face of sporadic protests against the British Prime Minister, Mr John Major's visit to the city, beginning on Thursday, says our staff reporter.

The city police were on their toes today with Naxalites burning Mr Major's effigy and hawkers demonstrating outside the British Deputy High Commission.

[A photograph of the demonstrators appeared here, holding the burning effigy with the sign 'John Major Go Back' attached.]

In general, written Indian English is characterised by:

❏ particular words that have local reference and specific cultural meaning;
❏ specific idiomatic phrases that are not commonly used in other English varieties;
❏ a choice of register that would seem very formal or conservative in a British or American context;
❏ a form of address that might appear more polite than in the UK/US.

The *Telegraph* is a serious, quality broadsheet, and included this gently humorous report alongside other national and international political news. Perhaps because of the intended tone, the features of Indian English which appear are more prominent than with these other reports. Try to identify all the features of the article that you would not find in a British, American, or Australian press report. Look especially for constructions that would seem to be register-mixing in these other cultures, but which are acceptable in Indian English.

Japanese English news

The following is a collection of headlines and story extracts from the English-language *Asahi Evening News* (Monday 22 May 2000), published in Tokyo:

A former gardener confessed to lacing a soft drink with an agricultural pesticide in a revenge attack for being fired, police said Sunday.

Kunitake Ando, who will become president of Sony Corp., says Nobuyuki Idei will remain the top leader.

Emperor, empress tour Geneva suburb.

9 hurt by schoolyard twister.

Love is in the air for soon-free Keiko [the killer whale].

Sherpa slams Everest record [in the sense of 'breaking' or 'smashing' it].

Chen offers China big door to talks.

Labor and the China vote.

School–police links aim to nip problems in the bud.

Cops and teachers used to rarely cross tracks. Now, though, with children's behavior a mounting concern, that gulf is being bridged in a variety of constructive ways.

Airline cargo hold absolutely no place for an much-loved pet.

TV & Radio/Comics [meaning 'cartoons']

"We expected them to own the ball more. The Marinos have many talented players" [. . .] "It's a good thing (Yoo) Sang Chul wasn't playing. Otherwise they would have figured us out."

Miyabiyama's rise to ozeki in 12 tourneys since first stepping into the dohyo as a professional equals the fastest promotion since the start of the Showa Era in 1926.

> Arden Yamanaka Beauty Salon. US Licensed Beauty Operator. Personalized hair-styling, haircoloring, frosting, permanent waving, manicuring, pedicuring, electrolysis, waxing, etc. Please call Hibiya Park Bldg.
>
> Hiroo: 1 bedroom apartment, ¥220.000, 2 bedroom apartment with washing mod-ern, dryer, refrigerator.
>
> Seijo: Near station, residencile area, 4 bedroom house, 2 bathrooms, power room, living room, dining room, parking, ¥470,000.
>
> Eda (Oimachi Line): 4 bedrooms, German School convenience, few steps to station, large living room, tatami room, greenery area, ¥550,000.

In collecting these, I have excluded items reprinted from international news agencies; nevertheless, even in calling these 'wire reports', the newspaper further illustrates the high level of influence from American English in its usage. Every example above seems to me (a native British English speaker) to be idiomatically non-British English. Many examples (such as narrating an event and adding 'Sunday' rather than 'on Sunday', listing participants in a headline 'Emperor, empress' without adding 'and', and American spelling forms) are common to those used by American reporters and tele-vision news presenters. Other examples simply seem to represent interference from the local indigenous language, Japanese. Try to identify all of these features. Out of your list, can you generalise some of the features of Japanese English, or at least the register of newspapers in this L2 English?

POLITENESS

(Im)politeness

In order to illustrate the reality of very subtle phatic norms, I sent out some of my sociolinguistics students one week with instructions to break the expected conversa-tional norms in specific ways. Some of these follow, with the actual consequences. For each, decide which social expectation of politeness or phatics has been deviated from, and explain the consequence.

(at a bus stop)

Stranger:	beautiful day
Student:	well no – actually. I think you'll find that there is an approaching cold front bringing heavy precipitation from the north-west. followed by high winds tonight.
Stranger:	mmm (*says nothing more, turns to face the oncoming traffic as if searching for the bus*)

(in passing along the corridor)

Friend:	alright?
Student:	no I've just got out of hospital. had a terrible time of it. the old problem playing me up again. still – mustn't grumble I suppose. I'll tell you all about it . . . (*and so on, and on*)

(Friend stands for several minutes listening, nodding and making sympathetic backchannel noise)

(At a supermarket checkout queue a student would pull up with a full basket and ask to go in front of people in the queue. Even though she had more items than them, on 8 of 10 occasions, other people allowed her to push in. The two other occasions went as follows:)

Person A: what? oh. no I'm sorry I'm in a bit of a rush myself and *(shrugs apologetically)*

Person B: ey? you're joking aren't you? you've got a full basket you cheeky sod – piss off

(Students did not make any backchannel noises during any of their telephone calls for a week. Consistently, after around 10 seconds, the other person would stop what they were saying to check whether the student was still there, and would also often ask if there was anything wrong, which the student would repeatedly deny)

(Similarly, students would ask strangers for directions on the street and then listen without nodding or making any utterance or backchannel noise. The person would repeat the information unprompted several times and then ask if the student understood)

(Students were able to categorise their close friends and acquaintances by asking, without any politeness tags: 'Lend me your bike', to see who would simply say, 'OK')

What is non-normative, in terms of Laver's model of phatic tokens, in each of these (invented) situations? What is the effect that is consequently generated?

(Backstage at the Royal Variety Performance 1)
Actor: By God, your Majesty, that's a terrible boil on your neck there!

(Backstage at the Royal Variety Performance 2)
Queen: I'm completely knackered after that!

(Someone rings your doorbell, you open the door, and the person standing there says, 'Yes?')

(Your bank manager begins a meeting with you by saying that his cat has just died.)

(Held at gunpoint by terrorists, you comment to your fellow hostage on how good the weather has been recently.)

C10.2

Face and address

How would you appropriately ask for the following?

- ❏ to borrow a pen from a friend;
- ❏ to borrow a pen from a stranger in the street;
- ❏ to climb onto someone's roof to fetch a football;
- ❏ to get in front of someone in a supermarket queue;
- ❏ to stop someone smoking on a train;
- ❏ to borrow £10,000 from a mafia godfather.

For each, also write out the script of how not to do this.

How are you addressed by the following?

parents	brother/sister	housemate
lover	shopkeepers	waiters
train guards	bus drivers	university lecturer
bank statements	checkout operator	advert for a mail-order firm
personal computer	hospital doctor	priest
television chef	radio DJs	radical newspaper seller

For each, consider the 'face' that each is trying to present, and how this is encoded by naming conventions, politeness strategies and register. Which social factors determine the form? Consider also how you would address each of these in turn.

How would the following conversations begin? Imagine a setting and write short (2–3 line) scripts for each. Try also reversing the order of who initiates the conversation to see if this would make a difference.

❏ teacher – pupil;
❏ teacher – person sitting next to them at a football match;
❏ teacher – referee after a bad decision;
❏ Japanese businessman in Britain – woman on street giving out leaflets for a club;
❏ student – landlord/lady;
❏ beggar – passing office worker in suit;
❏ beggar – passing scruffy student;
❏ drug dealer – drug dependent;
❏ drug dealer – his dog;
❏ driver – broken car;
❏ gardener – tomato plants;
❏ medieval baron – peasant building a wall;
❏ autograph hunter – you, falsely assumed to be someone famous;
❏ armed bank robber – you.

For each, identify the pragmatic rules that are followed (or not).

An intimate conversation

C10.3

For obvious reasons, it is very difficult to obtain naturalistic recordings of intimate style. The following transcript appeared in many non-UK newspapers in the form set out below; it was alleged that the recording had been made by the British security services' electronic monitoring station in 1993. Examine the forms of address, and also track the phatic strategies used to try (and several times fail) to close the conversation.

Charles: What time do they come in?

Camilla: Well usually Tom never wakes up at all, but as it's his birthday tomorrow he might just stagger out of bed. It won't be before half-past eight (pause). Night, night my darling.

Charles: Darling.
Camilla: I do love you.
Charles: (sleepily) before?
Camilla: Before about half-past eight.
Charles: Try and ring?
Camilla: Yeah, if you can. Love you darling.
Charles: Night darling.
Camilla: I love you.
Charles: Love you too. I don't want to say goodbye.
Camilla: Well done for doing that. You're a clever old thing. An awfully good
           brain lurking there, isn't there? Oh darling. I think you ought to give
           the brain a rest now. Night night.
Charles: Night darling. God bless.
Camilla: I do love you and I'm so proud of you.
Charles: Oh, I'm so proud of you.
Camilla: Don't be silly, I've never achieved anything.
Charles: Yes you have.
Camilla: No I haven't.
Charles: Your great achievement is to love me.
Camilla: Oh darling. Easier than falling off a chair.
Charles: You suffer all these indignities and tortures and calumnies.
Camilla: Oh, darling, don't be so silly. I'd suffer anything for you. That's love.
           It's the strength of love. Night night.
Charles: Night, darling. Sounds as though you're dragging an enormous piece
           of string behind you, with hundreds of tin pots and cans attached to
           it. I think it must be your telephone. Night night, before the battery
           goes (blows kiss). Night.
Camilla: Love you.
Charles: Don't want to say goodbye.
Camilla: Neither do I, but you must get some sleep. Bye.
Charles: Bye, darling.
Camilla: Love you.
Charles: Bye.
Camilla: Hopefully talk to you in the morning.
Charles: Please.
Camilla: Bye, I do love you.
Charles: Night.
Camilla: Night.
Charles: Night.
Camilla: Love you for ever.
Charles: Night.
Camilla: G'bye. Bye my darling.
Charles: Night.
Camilla: Night night.
Charles: Night.
Camilla: Bye bye

Charles:	Going
Camilla:	Bye.
Charles:	Going.
Camilla:	Gone.
Charles:	Night.
Camilla:	Bye. Press the button.
Charles:	Going to press the tit.
Camilla:	All right darling, I wish you were pressing mine.
Charles:	God, I wish I was. Harder and harder.
Camilla:	Oh darling.
Charles:	Night.
Camilla:	Night.
Charles:	Love you.
Camilla:	(yawning) Love you. Press the tit.
Charles:	Adore you. Night.
Camilla:	Night.
Charles:	Night.
Camilla:	(blows a kiss).
Charles:	Night.
Camilla:	G'night my darling. Love you.
(Charles hangs up).	

You could also use the framework set out by Schegloff and Sacks in D10 to analyse this passage.

STANDARDISATION

Some non-standard usages

The following are all examples I have recently collected. Every one of these features is regularly denounced in newspaper letters pages for being 'incorrect' English. Can you decide what people see as being 'wrong' in each case?

a   10 items or less (Marks & Spencer).

b   We was just doing us job (Nottingham Council worker on local TV news).

c   We have much to thank the government for (Professor Ron Carter in an article on Standard English).

d   CVs should be included with application forms (university job application rubric).

e   Just along on the left you will pass a dilapidated wooden shed (North Yorkshire Moors walking guide).

f   Just meet with him and talk with him and try to resolve it (agony aunt on 'This Morning' TV magazine programme).

g   To boldly go where no one has gone before ('Star Trek').

h   The data is presented in tabular form (student's sociolinguistics essay, 1999).

i   Hopefully the box office will be open when we get there (overheard on London bus).

j   Look at it's tail! (sign on exhibit, Nottingham Castle museum).

k   The Color Purple (UCI cinema, Preston).

l   Come on down! (Chris Tarrant, 'Who Wants to be a Millionaire?' TV programme).

m   I ain't never done it, Miss (Sheffield schoolchild).

n   If I was rich, I'd still do the lottery (old man in Birmingham newsagent).

o   Donuts (sign at Goose Fair, 2000).

p   The crowd are literally glued to their seats (John Motson, Euro 2000 football commentary).

q   Six cours'es for £5 (Yorkshire pub sign).

r   FRESH HEN EEGS (notice by a farm next door to the pub in q).

Some answers

a   So many people complained to the shop that this should read '10 items or fewer' (since 'items' is a count noun) that Marks & Spencer changed all their signs.

b   This verb agreement and possessive pronoun are non-standard, but are certainly grammatically correct Nottingham dialect, and it would be odd for the man to express himself in Standard English in this context.

c   This is the last line of the article, and it ends a sentence with a preposition, something Bishop Lowth prohibited in the eighteenth century by analogy with Latin. Of course, Professor Carter knows this and is being deliberately mischievous. Winston Churchill lampooned the syntactic knots the rule could cause in declaring, 'This is the sort of pedantry up with which we will not put!'

d   Strictly speaking, CV abbreviates the Latin *curriculum vitae*, and so it should not take the plural '-s' suffix which is part of the English morphological system. Applicants could only hope that the pedant who pointed this out was not on the interview panel.

e   The Latin root of 'dilapidated' comes from *lapis* for 'stone', so, strictly, a 'wooden' shed cannot be dilapidated. Similarly, 'companion' (*cum panis*) should only be someone with whom you share bread. And you should only 'consider' (*cum sideris*) if you are astrologically minded 'with the planets'.

f   The preposition 'with' used twice here is often seen as an 'Americanism'. The speaker is actually a British woman from County Durham. However, the added preposition conveys a greater sense of sharing and participation that is appropriate in this context.

g   This is the most famous 'split infinitive' in history (another of Bishop Lowth's prohibitions, on the grounds that infinitives cannot be split in Latin). However, the alternatives ('Boldly to go . . .', 'To go boldly . . .') sound much more clumsy and destroy the powerful rhythm of the iambic pentameter.

h   The word 'data' is the plural of 'datum' so the verb agreement does not match. However, 'data is . . .' sounds perfectly fine to a lot of people, and it seems likely that this will become the standard 'correct' usage.

i   Within an old-fashioned view of sentence grammar, the adverb 'hopefully' cannot attach to 'the box office' since box offices cannot be hopeful. Of course, what the speaker is doing is using 'hopefully' as a sort of pragmatic adverb to attach to her own hopes. The sentence means 'I am hopeful that . . .'

j   The possessive apostrophe is not used with 'it', since it is a remnant of the Anglo-Saxon genitive (possessive) case ending and 'it' only appeared in English much later. There are more misuses of the possessive apostrophe than any other part of the language, and correct usage is now so confused that we would all be better off if no one used it at all. In fact, possession is usually very clear in context and the feature is largely redundant.

k   This, of course, is the American spelling of the American film from the American novel. Noah Webster was largely responsible for adjusting many American spellings ('plow', 'ax', 'thru', 'nite', 'tire', 'humor', 'defense', and so on) – which are denounced as 'Americanisms' in certain conservative British newspapers.

l   Another American prepositional variant, instead of the more traditional British 'Come down', though appropriate in the context of a glitzy quiz show.

m   The child uses his vernacular non-standard verb 'to be' and employs grammatically correct negative concord. The latter is disparaged as illogical (by ridiculous analogy with maths where 'two negatives make a positive') rather than being emphatic. 'Ain't' (pronounced /ænt/) was the standard negative form of the copula ('to be') and verb 'to have' until it was argued away by ignorant schoolteachers in the 1890s.

n   Since an unrealised speculation is involved, the verb form should be in the subjunctive mood: 'If I were rich'. Nowadays, so few people understand or require the subjunctive in English that it only remains in frozen forms such as 'If I were you . . .'. I confidently predict its unlamented demise in the twenty-first century.

o   This American spelling is fast becoming the standard form instead of 'doughnut'. An examination of national British newspapers suggests similar shifts are happening to 'swap'/'swop', 'gaol'/'jail', 'jewellery'/'jewelry', 'judgement'/'judgment', and recently 'millennium'/'millenium', among others.

p   This non-literal use of the word 'literally' is often lampooned. However, Motson is following common usage in using the adverb as an emphatic marker of a figurative idiom, in order to enliven a dead metaphor. The sentence means roughly the same as, 'The crowd are really glued to their seats here!'

q   Another example of confusion of the historical usage of the possessive apostrophe. The writer obviously knows that it should be used somewhere near an 's', but would be better overall if they just stopped using it altogether.

r   This is the most spectacular example of non-standard spelling I have seen. I know it was not a one-off error, since it was repeated on another hand-drawn notice further down the road. Even so, there is no communicative problem here, though I never called in to see if they really were selling eegs.

EDUCATIONAL   C12

14- to 15-year-old Zoe Taylor undertook a detailed study of writing produced by 50 14–15 year old boys at a state comprehensive school in Stockport near Manchester. Although the school is mixed, English is taught in single-sex groups. She identified those boys from a working-class background using the following criteria for the area in which they lived:

❏ high unemployment;
❏ large numbers of local council-owned houses;
❏ high proportion of lone parents;
❏ large number of households with no car;
❏ large proportion of houses with no central heating.

Replicating the elicitation method of Lawton's (1968) study, Zoe asked the boys to write a short essay on the topic, 'Life ten years from now'. The essays were produced by three classes: Set 1 (the group rated by the teacher as top ability); Set 5 (the least able group); and SEN (a group with 'special educational needs' in terms of behavioural problems and low ability). All essays were thus produced on the same topic by boys from a similar class and family background. She analysed four essays randomly selected from each group using Bernstein's criteria for restricted and elaborated code (see B12).

Here are six of the essays, two from each group; all essays were originally handwritten.

Set 1 essays

1 In 2009 I dont think that life will be much different. There wont be any robots cooking cleaning and doing other household jobs. Cars wont be flying and huge skyrise buildings. Not many inventions will have been made either but one that will be made will be small not very important ones. People still wont be living in space, on the moon or on any other planet and aliens wont be living on earth.

The environment will be better due to cars and other pollutants letting out much less dangerous gases into the air, but the polar ice caps will Probably have melted that would mean the low lying flat countries such as Holland would no longer exist. Weapons will be more advanced and dangerous so more people will be killed in wars. The crime rate will have raised because its always increasing. In home entertainment will be a lot better because of digital TV where you can watch films whenever you want. You can also watch some sporting events on iteractive tv so you can watch the sport anyway you like.

2 I think life in 10 years will not be that different from now. I think small things will have changed but on the larger scale things will be very similar e.g. Homes, food and Pubs will stay the same, but music, clothes and appearances will have changed.

10 years ago in 1990 people would have thought that it will have been different by now but again only small things have (music, cars, clothes). Some people think that everything will change, like flying cars and learning off computers but I disagree, and think that things will stay similar.

C

Set 5 essays

1 In the year 2009 everybody will start thinking about things like kids drinking on the street and they will put an end to it, the same with violence they will try to stop it but I don't think alot of the violence will stop some of it will but not a lot things like (etc) kid fighting in the street older men when there drunk in a pub will fight over something stupid. I don't think there will be many drugs in the year 2009 than there is know. I think fags will be band because there is to many kids smoking and its there parent fault because they see them smoke so they think that it is alright for them to smoke.

In britain I think they will make new money like bringing new coins and notes out. There won't be as many cars with fumes coming out of them they will run of bactery or the sun.

2 I think that life would be very different because every thing would of changed, new people around you, go to better places with other friends. I think transport would be different. I wish Stockport County will go in the premiership. There will be lots of new buildings.

SEN essays

1 In the future I recon We are going to live in space and the moon and hovering car's. I said that because most of the planet might be mostly covered in water and we would be friends with alien beings.

Dinosaurs may rule the earth like tyrannosaurus rex and smilodons (this is a big cat) and new animals may be created or transported to earth. I thingk the earth it self would be hoter because of Global warming.

I recon there we be able to have a teleporter on the internet shopping.

2
1   fossile fules bured out.
2   space ships hovering everywhere in the shape of cars.
3   ground which was groud would be under water.
4   all cars eletrik.
5   live on the moon in ecow buble.
6   could all die of world war 3.
7   more space like clothes.
8   more cloning.
9   all paper would run out.
10 so that leads to computer work.
11 By your owr engergy electicity boxes.

Can you identify any features characteristic of elaborated or restricted code here (see B12)? Alternatively, can you set up a systematic linguistic account of the differences between these essays? Are the variations necessarily evidence of cognitive differences, indexes of social class background or supportive families?

E-DISCOURSE

Both Miranda Chadwick and Naomi Holdstock produced detailed analyses of electronic chatroom discourse on the internet. Neither the normal patterns of writing nor the characteristic features of speech apply perfectly to this mode of discourse, leading them to the conclusion that e-mail, electronic chat and telephone texting all represent not a 'mid-point' between speech and writing but a new, third mode of discourse.

The samples from Internet discourse come from Miranda and Naomi's data, and some of my own. I now communicate with colleagues around the world far more by e-mail than by any other form, and it is clear that we have started using a sort of 'World Standard Electronic English'. This is mainly a code of avoidance of idiomatic or culturally specific British features that I know colleagues in Japan or America would not understand. Electronic discourse, however, operates within well-defined domains (academic discussion, teenage chat, student bulletin board, and so on); the fact that the participants share common assumptions means that it is often characterised by restricted code features (see B12, C12).

Chatroom discourse

This is a 'webcast' discussion with founder of the Cyber Angels Internet Safety Organisation, Colin Gabriel Hatcher:

Colin Gabriel Hatcher:	hi folks :)
Petal262:	err gabrielca
Colin Gabriel Hatcher:	lol
Petal262:	dang . . . can't type today . . . sorry
Colin Gabriel Hatcher:	I am loggin by telnet . . . ugh : /
Petal262:	oh. . . .
Colin Gabriel Hatcher:	my new puter just broke down . . . power supply . . .
Petal262:	I hope you don't mind that I forwarded my invitation to Cheron. . . . she is trying to connect up now . . .
Colin Gabriel Hatcher:	telnet was not made for fast chat!!
Colin Gabriel Hatcher:	she should have got one too
Petal262:	she said no . . . so I forwarded mine to her
Colin Gabriel Hatcher:	hmmm well she is on the list
Petal262:	maybe something she overlooked. . . .
Jady:	gabriel :)
Colin Gabriel Hatcher:	jave/telnet reminds me why I like irc ;)
Petal262:	:)))
Petal262:	Hello Commander Morg
Commander Morg:	hey, just checking out what "electronic Fronties" is . . .
Colin Gabriel Hatcher:	hi morg

Commander Morg:	oops, just realized I put another space in my name, must remember to stop doing that . . .
Colin Gabriel Hatcher:	its a discussion forum morg
Jady:	hi morg :)
Commander Morg:	oh, ok
Colin Gabriel Hatcher:	starting I believe in 10 mins
Commander Morg:	sorry to interrupt, were you discussing something?
Jady:	just waiting for it to start : 0
Colin Gabriel Hatcher:	nope morg :) I was just whining about telnet
Petal262:	there were a couple here earlier that said they missed it by about 2 hours . . .
Commander Morg:	oh
Jady:	I saw that . . . had to figure my time stuff again
Commander Morg:	I'm in the Java client, works pretty well
Colin Gabriel Hatcher:	2 hours??
Petal262:	Hi BypsyRogue
Petal262:	GypsyRogue
Jady:	hi Gypsy :)
GypsyRogue:	thanx for the correction
Colin Gabriel Hatcher:	lol petal. . . . i c you r having a b-g prob today :)
GypsyRogue:	sound like some teeny bop w/ a b
Jady:	hehehe
Colin Gabriel Hatcher:	morg my netscape 3 is down so I am stuck with telnet :)
Colin Gabriel Hatcher:	lol jady
Commander Morg:	oh, bummer
Colin Gabriel Hatcher:	: D
Commander Morg:	try to the new Netscape PR3
Commander Morg:	Netscape 3 Java was really bad, I think the programmers were on crack
Commander Morg:	:)
Colin Gabriel Hatcher:	lol . . .
GypsyRogue:	comp talk – how dull

Notice how the usual turn-taking mechanisms from speech do not apply here. Other 'voices' appear while a user is typing, so it seems as though there is a lot of 'skip-connecting' back to previous topics. This means that participants have to keep track of several threads of chat, only one or two of which will be developed. You will see by comparing this with other chatrooms that there is a great deal of variation in linguistic usage, with different registers and dialects in the process of emerging. It seems that the main determinant of sociolinguistic stratification and variation in e-discourse is the level of technical expertise of the user.

Glossary of emoticons and net acronyms   C13.2

There are very many internet catalogues of 'emoticons' (graphic keyboard tricks to encode tone of voice, irony, sarcasm, gesture, and so on) for the novice 'newbie' user. However, many of these are simply clever jokes and are almost never used:

:^)   user has a broken nose
:-#   user wears braces
:-Q   smoking cigarette

However, Miranda discovered a chatroom for experienced netizens with the following:

room: #weed
Thunder: :-Q :| :| :/sssss :-)

Here, 'Thunder' has renamed the room and smokes a virtual joint with the other chatters.
    More common emoticons include:

:-)   the basic smiley
;-)   wink, used to mark a joke
:-(unhappy or frowning
:-I   indifferent
{{{you}}}   hugging 'you'
:-@   screams
:-D   laughing
:-s   confused or unsure
: 0   yawn, tired
:-x   user's lips are sealed, confidential

and the acronyms

BTW   by the way
HH   holding hands
r   are
u   you
c   see
lol   laughing out loud
a/s/l   age, sex, location

For example:

Kt1_red: a/s/l???
Spunky2000_uk: gloucester, and u
Juicyjess: scotland, 19
Dr_rich3:   call me stoopid, but i dunno what a/s/l means
Kt1_red: stoopid
Jamieton99:   stupid
Dr_rich3:   24, bloke manchester :-s ??
Kt1_red: cool thats ur a/s/l ☹☺☺
Dr_rich3:   I've learnt somethin. What's your a/s/l?

It is an easy matter to 'lurk' in a chatroom and print out some discourse data. What are the naming and address conventions in e-mail and electronic discourse? What other means are used to maintain 'netiquette'? Is e-discourse a third mode of communication, or is it mainly a blend of speech and writing? Is there such a thing as an emergent World Standard Electronic English? What do you think will be the impact of improved voice-recognition software on world accents, when the computer keyboard finally becomes a quaint relic of the past?

IDEOLOGY

Here are two texts which come from roughly the same source. The first is a letter confirming an offer of a job at a British university. It is a standard letter that was sent in this form to all newly contracted staff. The second text is from the same office, sent to all staff in post at the university, to warn them of procedures in the event of a planned demonstration by students. In both cases, names and locations have been changed or obviously disguised.

Contract

Our ref	P/JDM/MSC/MPA	Personnel Department
Your ref		Bigcity University
Date	22 April 1992	[Address details]

John D Bossman
BA(hons)
Personnel Manager

Dear Mr Newboy

I am delighted to be able to offer you the post of Lecturer in English at Bigcity University. The post is offered with effect from 1 September 1992 subject to medical clearance.

I enclose with this letter two copies of the university's contract of employment. I should be grateful if you would indicate your acceptance of this offer by signing and returning the top copy. The second copy is for you to retain.

As a result of recent changes under the Education Reform Act 1988, the university is revising its procedures. Therefore new arrangements covering such matters as grievance procedures, disciplinary procedures and other provisions are included in the staff handbook which will be issued to you in due course.

I should be grateful if you could come to the Personnel Office on the fourth floor of Labov Building at the Nice View site at 9.00 am on your first day of employment. You should bring your P45, birth certificate and qualifications.

I look forward to meeting you.

Yours sincerely

J D Minion
Director of Resources

Memo

To	All Staff	Bigcity University
Our ref	KCB/SJK	Memorandum
Your ref		
From	Dr K.C. Bigcheese	
Centre	Labov Building	
Telephone	5555	
Date	16 January 1992	

Demonstration

To minimise any consequences of the demonstration, the following action will be taken:

1. Between 12.30 p.m. and 2.30 p.m. all lights will be extinguished in offices on the fourth floor of Labov Building facing the quadrangle.

2. When unoccupied, all offices are to be kept locked and all papers to be kept locked in drawers if possible.

3. People are not to look out of the window; it will only encourage the rabble.

4. The entrance doors to the Directorate are to be shut and not held open on the magnetic locks.

5. Someone is to test the button.

6. Finance, Personnel and Payroll are also to keep their offices locked when unoccupied.

7. Occasionally in these events, idiots press fire alarms. If the fire alarm sounds, the building is to be evacuated in an orderly manner and if time allows offices are to be locked.

8. If staff are nervous about the effects of a demonstration, they are to take a long lunch hour.

9. I will not be on site, I will be at the Cityview site. In the event of a crisis, I am available on the mobile phone.

Sylvia
pp. Dr Keith C. Bigcheese
     Director

Both texts encode an ideological view of the event and the participants in particular ways. Try to draw up a systematic linguistic analysis to uncover the ideological viewpoints realised by these two texts. Categories you might focus on could include, for example:

❑ how layout signals the text type;
❑ naming strategies including titles, job titles, forms of address and nouns used for reference to people;
❑ formality expressed through lexical choice and syntactic pattern;
❑ assignment of blame, or delineation of inclusive and exclusive participants ('us' and 'them') by naming, lexical choice, or verb form.

Both texts are, at a fundamental level, instructional, but how do they each go about encoding their viewpoints of different participants and groups?

You probably work or study within an institutional setting. How is your behaviour regulated linguistically by your institution? How is your identity and 'face' delineated by the institution, and how far do you conform to this when you are in the institutional setting? Do you code-switch into a different register when you leave for other parts of your life?

EXTENSION

SOCIOLINGUISTIC READINGS

HOW TO USE THE READINGS

Throughout this book I have been at pains to emphasise the importance of reading in the area of sociolinguistics. Extensive reading of books and articles has several benefits:

- ❏ it provides you with the necessary background of the history of the discipline;
- ❏ it familiarises you with the main current research areas;
- ❏ it allows you to see the sorts of methods and approaches that are used by different sociolinguists;
- ❏ it gives you a model for how to express yourself in appropriate academic and scholarly language.

Reading with a critical awareness (that is, reading and thinking rather than simply being a passive reader) allows you to see that different writers come to different conclusions and interpretations. This sort of critical engagement will spark your own ideas and allow you to see areas that need further investigation. The journey from being introduced to sociolinguistics to being a serious researcher doing valuable and innovative work is a short one, and by this point in the book you are already well on the way.

The ten readings in this section have been selected to give you a useful resource across the field of sociolinguistics. They range from surveys to specific details of research studies; they include classic articles as well as extracts that are more difficult to find; and they cover material which is accessible as well as writing that can give you a taste of complex analysis and argument. After each reading, some suggestions for thinking and critical engagement are offered. It is often useful if you make brief notes and ideas either in the margins (if this book is yours) or in a notebook. If you get into the habit of 'reading with a pencil' you will find you are never short of ideas.

The numbered sections roughly correspond with the corresponding sections earlier in this book, though sometimes the readings combine several areas of interest.

The first reading, below, uses many of the terms introduced in A1, though Hamer also discusses issues of standardisation (A6, B6, C6) in relation to language change (B11, C11), and refers to Labov's work (A5) in order to make a point about language and education (B12, C12).

Andrew
Hamer

Sociolinguistics and language change

Early Standard English: linguistic confidence and insecurity

Andrew Hamer (reprinted from *Proceedings of the English Association North* Vol.VII (1993), Liverpool: Liverpool University English Department, pp. 31–42)

The advantage claimed for studying developments in the history of English has traditionally been the insight these provide into trends in the modern language. This is a view which may be attractive to teachers faced with presenting unfamiliar material to students they fear may find it irrelevant, but which relegates language history to the status of a discipline not worth studying for itself. Less commonly appreciated is the fact that diachronic developments in English can be studied using linguistic insights gained from examining the modern speech community. In this way, the past ceases to be relevant only as an aid to understanding what is *really* important, the modern period, and becomes an exciting challenge, a laboratory where students can apply the analytic techniques they have learnt elsewhere in their course.

In what follows, I intend to look at the consequences for the speech community of the establishment of a written standard form of English during the late fifteenth and sixteenth centuries. One might reasonably expect to be able to apply sociolinguistic insights here. After all, defining the sociolinguistic situation in modern Britain is made possible largely by the existence of a prestigious dialect (Standard English) and accent (Received Pronunciation – RP). The speech patterns of groups of individuals, whether these be social classes, or regional or gender groupings, can be shown to vary systematically in terms of the percentage of occurrence within them of prestigious forms.

One should probably *a priori* expect the linguistic situation during the century after *c.*1470 to have differed from that of our own time in one important respect, however: there might well exist a great variety of competing forms in texts written in a transitional period, during which a standard dialect was becoming established. Since this has been shown indeed to be the case (see Dobson 1968), it follows that there must at that time have been some confusion about the relative status of linguistic variants, confusion that can only have aggravated any linguistic insecurity a vulnerable social group might have felt. It is the evidence for this nervousness about language which interests me here.

Texts from this period show evidence of two sorts of linguistic anxiety: a speaker's insecurity about his own dialect; and a nervousness about the ability of English to serve as a vehicle for all kinds of written communication. The view normally taken is that the second type of insecurity disappeared 'quite suddenly between 1575 and 1580. Before 1575, nearly everybody agrees that English is barbarous; after 1580 there is a whole chorus of voices proclaiming that English is eloquent' (Barber 1976: 76–7). Such a sudden change may well strike the reader as unusual, to say the least. In this essay, I hope to show that scholars have taken too uncritically expressions of the second type of insecurity, and that in fact from *c.*1500, members of elite groups had considerable confidence in their own articulatory powers in English.

Andrew
Hamer

Between the time of the Norman Conquest and the first half of the fourteenth century, the sociolinguistic situation in England could roughly be characterised as follows: there existed a set of English dialects, none of which enjoyed any more prestige than the others; the functions which are now the domain of Standard English were then largely carried out by dialects of Latin and French. This situation changed from the late fourteenth century, when a number of standardised forms of English started to appear in texts, a trend which culminated in the widespread appearance, by 1470, of 'Chancery Standard,' which provided the ancestor of the later standard dialect.

The use of Chancery Standard, though widespread by 1470, was by no means universal. Caxton, in the famous Preface to his *Eneydos* (published in 1490), complains that the lack of an agreed standard causes particular problems for the printer. Baugh and Cable (1978: 195) quote the complaint with no more comment than: 'it was not easy for a writer at the end of the fifteenth century to choose his words so that his language would find favor with all people.' Attempts to assess Caxton's motives in more recent histories than theirs are clearly influenced by Sociolinguistics: Dick Leith (1983: 40) notes that Caxton's complaint that English has changed much since he was young has been followed by 'a good many people since'; more interestingly, Barbara Strang (1970: 157, 197) urges Caxton's modern readers not 'to take too much at face-value his observations on variation', since 'he does seem to be picking an example to labour a point.' In the light of these comments, it is worth looking again at this Preface to see whether anything more can be gleaned from it that might add to our knowledge of the sociolinguistic situation in the late ME period.

> And that comyn englysshe that is spoken
> in one shyre varyeth from a nother. In so
> moche that in my dayes happened that certayn
> marchauntes were in a shippe in tamyse, for
> to have sayled over the see into zelande, and
> for lacke of wynde, thei taryed atte forlond,
> and wente to lande for to refreshe them. And
> one of theym named Sheffelde, a mercer, cam
> in-to an hows and axed for mete; and specyally
> he axyd after eggys. And the goode wyf answerde,
> that she coude speke no frenshe. And the
> marchaunt was angry, for he also coude speke
> no frenshe, but wolde have hadde egges, and
> she understode hym not. And thenne at laste
> a nother sayd that he wolde have eyren. Then
> the good wyf sayd that she understod hym wel.
> Loo, what sholde a man in thyse dayes now wryte,
> egges or eyren? Certaynly it is harde to playse
> every man by cause of dyversite & chaunge of
> langage.

D

Andrew
Hamer

We must ask ourselves at the outset, who were the likely readers of Caxton's *Eneydos*? This text is an English translation of a French prose version of Virgil's *Æneid*, and must therefore have been aimed at literate, monolingual English speakers. In other words, Caxton's intended audience did not include either of the two elite groups: those who were educated to the level where they could read Latin with any fluency would not be interested in this text, as they would certainly have read Virgil's epic in the original, while the French-favouring social elite would naturally read the French version.

It is also clear that during the early printing period the very wealthy were not interested in buying printed books. They continued to be attracted by manuscripts, in part because these represented sound investments, being individual and exclusive. It is more likely, therefore, that Caxton would have to find his readers among sections of the community which traditionally had wielded little power, but which now, for the first time, had a little spare money and some leisure. Significant numbers of this group were by now literate also, and this combination of factors meant that conditions were ripe for some of these people to want to improve themselves, through an acquaintance, however indirect, with the classics. A shrewd entrepreneur, Caxton catered for the emerging lower middle class, those beneficiaries of the collapse of the old economic system.

What evidence is there in the text to support this view? It seems to me that a lower middle class audience is precisely the group that will identify with the predicament of Sheffelde the mercer. By the time that Caxton wrote this Preface, southerners had for more than a century been poking fun at Norse-influenced Northern dialects. Writing in 1385, John of Trevisa (in Cornwall) claims that:

> *Al þe longage of þe Norþhumbres, and*
> *specialyche at ʒork, ys so scharp,*
> *slyttyng, and unschape, þat we*
> *Souþeron men may þat longage unneþe ('scarcely')*
> *undurstonde.*

Little wonder if Sheffelde (note the name) felt sensitive about his dialect when in the South-east. (His word comes from the Norse 'egg' /ɛg/ while the good wyf's is from Old English 'æg' /æj/.) His anger at the woman's response, that she couldn't understand him because she couldn't speak French, is understandable when seen against the background of this long tradition of southern superiority. Of little education himself ('for he also coude speke no frenshe'), he assumes that the woman is pretending he is French in order to mock his uncouth dialect. To the monolinguals to whom Caxton addressed his translations, Sheffelde's predicament may well have been embarrassingly familiar.

To suggest in this way that Caxton's intended readership was a lower middle class one which would empathise with Sheffelde fits well with what is known about the sensitivity to linguistic variation of today's lower middle class. In a famous study, William Labov (1972b) examined a series of phonological variables in the speech of a random sample of New Yorkers. Among the variables studied was /r/ in such words as *guard, floors, certain* (i.e. when not before a vowel). The results of his findings were summarised in the following diagram.

Andrew
Hamer

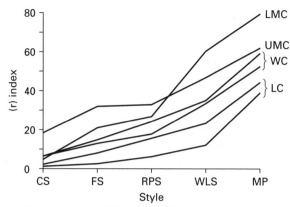

Figure D1.1 Social stratification of a linguistic variable undergoing
change – post-vocalic (r) in New York City (Labov 1972b: 114)

In New York city, the presence of /r/ in words such as these can be shown to
be prestigious by the fact that for all social groups, there is a correlation between
increasing frequency of pronunciation of /r/ and increasing formality of speech
styles. As Labov (1972b: 115) says: 'at the level of casual, everyday speech, only
the upper middle class shows a significant degree of r-pronunciation. But in more
formal styles, the amount of r-pronunciation for other groups rises rapidly. The
lower middle class, in particular, shows an extremely rapid increase, surpassing
the upper-middle-class level in the two most formal styles.' This 'crossover pattern' for the lower middle class is found 'for all those linguistic variables which
are involved in a process of linguistic change under social pressure,' and may therefore be taken as an 'indicator of linguistic change in progress.'

The only explanation possible for this regular hypercorrecting among the lower
middle class appears to be this group's linguistic insecurity, which 'is shown by
the very wide range of stylistic variation used by lower-middle-class speakers; by
their great fluctuation within a given stylistic context; by their conscious striving
for correctness; and by their strongly negative attitudes towards their native speech
pattern' (Labov 1972b: 117). If the interpretation given above of Caxton's account
of Sheffelde the mercer is correct, the linguistic insecurity of the lower middle
class has a history in this country of five hundred years.

The linguistic insecurity typical of the modern lower middle class is a largely
unconscious response to social pressures on the part of a group that is peculiarly
susceptible to social change. We do not find indicators of this insecurity in the
speech patterns of today's upper middle class, and would certainly not expect to
find them in the writings of those among Caxton's contemporaries who enjoyed
a privileged social status. Oddly enough, at least at first glance, this is exactly
what we do appear to find, in a number of statements about English from the
first half of the sixteenth century.

[. . .]

It would appear, [. . .] that the speech community of Tudor England shared
some sociolinguistic characteristics with that of the modern period: a linguistically

Andrew Hamer

insecure lower middle class; and a social-cultural elite, confident about their own articulacy. Any tendency among the latter group to feel linguistically, as well as socially, financially and educationally, superior to others could only be reinforced by the former group's attempts to imitate the speech patterns, as well as the lifestyles, of those who they believed enjoyed social prestige.

Whether the complementary attitudes to language of these two social groups were the reflection or cause of the belief that some forms of English were 'better' than others is not clear, but certainly, two significant attitudes to language variation developed during this period. These attitudes, which were both destined to have a long, and some would say still unfinished history, can be summarised as follows: (i) some speakers, through their own fault, lack the ability to express themselves as well, eloquently, elegantly as they ought; and (ii) things were better in the past.

Caxton prefaces his simple observation that 'that comyn englysshe that is spoken in one shyre varyeth from a nother' with a hint that he sees language change through time as the result of a fault in the speakers: And certainly our 'langage now used varyeth ferre from that whiche was used and spoken whan I was borne. For we englysshe men ben borne under the domynacyon of the mone, whiche is never stedfaste, but ever waverynge, wexynge one season, and waneth & dyscreaseth another season.' Such blame as Caxton does apportion here, he does so indiscriminately to the whole nation.

Sixty years later, Richard Sherry's writing shares Caxton's nostalgia for a better past, but coupled with it is a confidence that certain of the author's (socially prestigious) contemporaries are fully the equals in articulacy of even their most famous predecessors. Any failure of articulacy in an Englishman, moreover, can only be the result of his not availing himself of the opportunities that the language offers him. For Sherry, this involves actively seeking out eloquence, something which the lazy will not do:

> It is not vnknowen that oure language for the barbarousnes and lacke of eloquence hathe bene complayned of, and yet not trewely, for anye defaut in the toungue it selfe, but rather for slackenes of our countrimen, which haue alwayes set lyght by searchyng out the elegance and proper speaches that be ful many in it: as plainly doth appere not only by the most excellent monumentes of our auncient forewriters, Gower, Chawcer and Lydgate, but also by the famous workes of many other later: inespeciall of the ryght worshipful knyght syr Thomas Eliot.
>
> (Sherry, reproduced in Hildebrandt 1977: 4–5)

Linguistic performance is now plainly considered the reflection of moral worth. Coincidentally, this period sees the emergence of an educational attitude which will be familiar to many modern readers: those concerned with the education of the young must teach the standard dialect, and those determined to improve themselves must learn it. Peter Levins's English rhyming dictionary (*Manipulus Vocabulorum*, 1570) offers an opportunity to learn something of 'the chiefe grace and facilitie of our Englishe tong', whereby 'children and ruder schoolers, as also

Andrew
Hamer

the Barbarous countries and ruder writers, may not a little (if they wil enioy the offered occasion) well and easely correct and amend, both their pen and speache' (in Dobson 1968: 20).

Levins's own dialect, though 'plentifully sprinkled with Northernisms, . . . was certainly accommodated in many ways to the language of the South' (Dobson 1968: 20). This was probably the safest course for an educator at that time: the inspectors who made the first visitation of Merchant Taylors' School (16th August, 1562) under the headmastership of Richard Mulcaster, reported only one fault in the teachers: 'that being northern men born, they had not taught the children to speak distinctly, or to pronounce their words as well as they aught' (quoted in Dobson 1968: 125).

Mulcaster's *Elementarie* was planned as a text book on the whole range of elementary education, including, as far as English is concerned, reading, writing and grammar. Indeed, the study of orthography which forms most of the work as published was intended as a background to the teaching of reading and writing, and not as a guide to 'better' pronunciation. Four hundred years ago, Mulcaster's concern to improve the literacy skills of his pupils contrasted with the inspectors' concerns that those pupils were not being taught 'to pronounce their words as well as they aught'. The comments of these inspectors, whether they were reacting to their own prejudices or to real or perceived pressure on the part of parents or governors, show that linguistic insecurity was a real force at this time. Indicative of this insecurity is the refuge sought in rules: 'as well as they aught'.

The English-teaching aims, no doubt only slightly different, of Mulcaster and the inspectors may be compared with a shift in emphasis between the Kingman Report (1988) and the National Curriculum Council's (1993) revision of the English Order. Both reports recognise the need to teach written and spoken Standard English, and both also accept that the standard dialect can be spoken 'in a variety of regional and social accents'. But whereas in the Kingman Report the Standard is an indispensable, though not intrinsically superior, variety, those who have revised the English Order are certain (p. 9 para. 6) that 'Standard English is characterised by the correct *(sic)* use of vocabulary and grammar'. The concept of correctness in language does not tolerate the existence of variation, since a form is either 'correct' or not. It would appear therefore that, if implemented, the revised English Order may well prove a fertile breeding ground for future linguistic insecurity.

Issues to consider

D1.2

Activity

The 'English Order' referred to at the end was the UK government's curriculum for English teaching in England and Wales. The 1993 proposed revision to the curriculum for English met with a great deal of criticism from teachers and academics, centring round the question of standardisation. The proposal in its 1993 form was quietly dropped. Shortly afterwards the National Curriculum Council was replaced by a body with a wider authority for maintaining standards in the curriculum and assessment.

The intersection of sociolinguistics and politics is an interesting area of investigation, touching upon issues of language planning, and notions of standardisation,

D

codification, prescriptivism and linguistic authority. Any government around the world has to decide how language skills and literacy are to be taught in their education systems, and decisions are often made on the basis of politics, ideology, history and economics, as well as on the state of linguistic understanding. The places to begin to explore these matters are newspapers (especially educational supplements), political manifestos and the documents that schools in your area will have received from their authorities. You could compare the view of language practice embodied in these official documents with the reality around you. Alternatively, you could use your sociolinguistic knowledge to explore issues of historical language change in the past, and see connections and continuities with the present, as Hamer has done. Practical investigations might include:

❏ analysing official documents to discover which dialect(s) of your national language is/are privileged, and then investigating the consequences for students who do not use that dialect;

❏ using your reading and skills as a sociolinguist to evaluate the pronouncements of politicians, journalists and other commentators when they discuss issues of language policy, linking the issues to published work in the field;

❏ using data such as schoolchildren's written work to explore differences in class or other social background, or to see whether important local dialects affect their writing, and what attitude teachers take to these effects in assessing the work;

❏ focusing on a specific feature of a change in language in the past, and using your knowledge of sociolinguistics to re-evaluate it;

❏ speculating on one main historical difference in the past (e.g. the Norman Conquest of England did not happen in 1066; a Spanish empire was maintained in North America; steam computers and the internet were perfected in the early nineteenth century; Germany and Japan won the Second World War, and so on) and using your sociolinguistic knowledge to discuss what the differences in language use might be, based on real principles from your reading;

❏ imagining how language might change in the near future, based on what you observe around you and what you know about the sociolinguistic principles of language change.

D2

FOREIGN ACCENTS IN AMERICA

In those countries of the world in which English is the official language (see A9), monolingualism can often seem to be the global norm. Not only is this a delusion across the world, it is also often a distortion of the multilingual and multi-ethnic composition even within those countries. In the following chapter from her book, Rosina Lippi-Green provides a well-argued antidote to such views. She takes a macro-sociolinguistic approach, using historical and census data to discuss the importance of recognising all of the accents of American speech. She emphasises in the rest of the book the importance of attitudes to accent differences in relation to educational performance and ethnic discrimination.

D

You will recognise connections here with the terms we covered in A2, B2 and C2. Notions of prestige (A6, B6, C6) are central to Lippi-Green's approach, as well as the linguistic effects and markers of ethnicity (A4, B4, C4). Her book is concerned with exposing the educational consequences of prescriptive linguistic attitudes (B12, C12).

The stranger within the gates

D2.1

Rosina Lippi-Green (reprinted from *English with an Accent: Language, Ideology and Discrimination in the United States*, London: Routledge, 1997: 217–39)

The 1990 census established that the United States is a nation of some 248 million persons, of whom 2,015,143 are Native American and 205,501 Hawai'ian. Thus it is an obvious and inescapable truth that the majority of people residing in the US are immigrants, or the descendents of immigrants, the greatest portion of whom came of their own will, while others came in chains. We are a nation of immigrants, but having made the transition and established ourselves, we have a strong urge to be protective of what is here; we talk at great length about closing the door behind us. At times, we have acted on this impulse:

❑ In the 1840s during a depression, mobs hostile to immigrant Irish Catholics burned down a convent in Boston.
❑ Congress passed the Chinese Exclusion Act in 1882, one of our first immigration laws, to exclude all people of Chinese origin.
❑ In 1942, 120,000 Americans of Japanese descent had their homes and other property confiscated, and were interned in camps until the end of the Second World War. At the same time, many Jews fleeing Nazi Germany during that war were excluded under regulations enacted in the 1920s.

(American Civil Liberties Union 1996)

Language often becomes the focus of debate when these complex issues of nationality, responsibility, and privilege are raised. English, held up as the symbol of the successfully assimilated immigrant, is promoted as the one and only possible language of a unified and healthy nation. Using rhetoric which is uncomfortably reminiscent of discussions of race in fascist regimes, a California Assemblyman notes the multilingual commerce in his home town with considerable trepidation: 'you can go down and apply for a driver's license test entirely in Chinese. You can apply for welfare today entirely in Spanish. The supremacy of the English language is under attack' (report on pending English Only legislation in California, CBS Evening News, October 1986).

In considering the history of multilingualism and public fears around it, Ferguson and Heath noted that 'whenever speakers [of other languages] have been viewed as politically, socially, or economically threatening, their language has become a focus for arguments in favor of both restrictions of their use and imposition of Standard English' (1981: 10). This is illustrated by the history of German use in the US, a language (and people) which particularly irritated Benjamin Franklin.

[. . .]

D

Rosina
Lippi-Green

WHO HAS A FOREIGN ACCENT?

The census bureau estimates that 22,568,000 persons or 8.7 percent of the population of the United States was foreign-born in 1994, a figure which is nearly double the number of foreign-born in 1970 (4.8 percent). A total of 31,844,979 persons – many of these not foreign-born – reported that they spoke a language other than English in the home, as is seen in Table D2.1. We note that this list does not specify a single language from the continent of Africa beyond the Arabic languages of the north. It must be assumed that as immigration from the mid- and southern African nations is limited, speakers of languages such as Swahili and Zulu are subsumed under the category 'Other and unspecified languages.'

Table D2.1   Language spoken at home by persons 5 years and older

Language	*No. of people*
English only	198,600,798
Spanish or Spanish Creole	17,345,064
French or French Creole	1,930,404
German	1,547,987
Chinese	1,319,462
Italian	1,308,648
Other and unspecified languages	1,023,614
Tagalog	843,251
Polish	723,483
Korean	626,478
Other Indo-European language	578,076
Indic	555,126
Vietnamese	507,069
Portuguese or Portuguese Creole	430,610
Japanese	427,657
Greek	388,260
Arabic	355,150
Native North American languages	331,758
Other Slavic language	270,863
Russian	241,798
Other West Germanic language	232,461
Yiddish	213,064
Scandinavian	198,904
South Slavic	170,449
Hungarian	147,902
Mon-Khmer	127,441

Source: 1990 US census data. Database: C90STF3C1

Rosina
Lippi-Green

If the purpose is to come to an approximation of who speaks English with a foreign accent, it is useful to have some accounting of proficiency in English. The census bureau attempts to access this information by simply asking the question. The published results are conflated into four groups: native English speakers who have no other language in the home (this would include, for example, people who have limited second-language ability through schooling) and then three universes, as seen in Table D2.2: speakers of Spanish, speakers of Asian and Pacific Rim languages, and speakers of other languages which do not fall into any of the previous groups. This last group must include a great variety of languages, from those spoken in Africa to Scandinavia and middle and eastern European.

A graphic representation of the 18–65-year-old group from this table is given in Figure D2.1. Here we see that there is in fact a differential in the individual's assessment of ability to speak English according to national-origin subgrouping. In all three groups, the majority of non-native English speakers claim a very good command of their second language. The differential between 'very good' and 'not well at all' is smallest for the Asian-languages group, which is in turn the smallest of the three groups overall.

We note especially that there are four million people in the 'Other language' category who call their own English 'very good' and another million or so of this same group who find their English not very good at all. This mysterious 'Other language' group is in fact larger than the Asian-languages group. While this profusion of numbers still does not provide an exact count of how many people speak English with a foreign accent, it does raise two crucial points.

Table D2.2 (Non-English) language spoken at home and ability to speak English, by age

Age	Language spoken	Evaluation of English-language skills: census count		
		'Very well'	*'Well'*	*'Not well'* or *'Not well at all'*
5–17	Spanish	2,530,779	993,417	643,457
	Asian or Pacific Island	455,339	224,821	135,430
	Other	948,573	262,442	128,676
18–64	Spanish	6,105,722	2,589,195	3,425,937
	Asian or Pacific Island	1,496,466	1,048,835	755,324
	Other	4,312,500	1,315,685	658,210
65+	Spanish	398,568	223,350	434,639
	Asian or Pacific Island	99,461	82,351	173,594
	Other	1,515,069	570,205	316,934

Source: 1990 US census data. Database: C90STF3C1

Rosina Lippi-Green

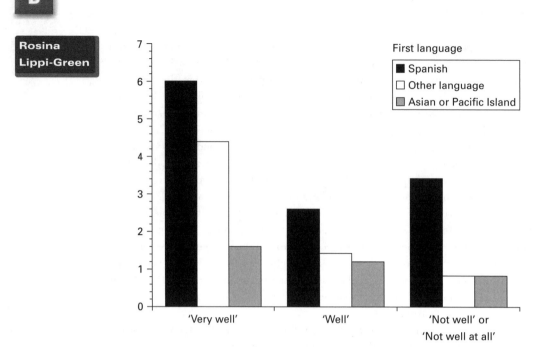

First language
- ■ Spanish
- □ Other language
- ▨ Asian or Pacific Island

Figure D2.1 Persons between 18 and 65 years who claim a first language other than English, and their evaluation of their English-language skills
Source: 1990 census

First, millions of people resident in the US are not native speakers of English, and use a language other than English in their homes and personal lives. Any individual who takes on the task of learning a second or third language in adulthood will have some degree of L2 accent, a degree which is not readily predictable and will not correlate, overall, to education, intelligence, or motivation. Thus there is a large population of US residents who speak with an L2 accent.

Second, there are preconceived notions about non-native speakers of English which have repercussions even in the way we count their numbers and talk about them. The US Census Bureau distinguishes between Spanish, Asian, and other languages. It is from this departure point that we look at the way foreign-language groups and the language stereotypes associated with those groups are used to classify – and often to dismiss – individual needs and rights.

FROM BALI HAI TO NEW DELHI: WHAT IT MEANS TO BE ASIAN
[. . .]

The Census Bureau lists a figure of almost 7.3 million Asians in the US population. Figure D2.2 breaks down this figure, according to census data, into more specific national origins. In examining this chart, it immediately becomes apparent that even in its more specific form, the subgrouping 'Asian' is internally immensely complex and diverse. It might be argued that generalizations are necessary when dealing with this kind of data, for the nations of Asia and the Pacific are numerous. In linguistic terms, even this breakdown is deceiving.

Rosina
Lippi-Green

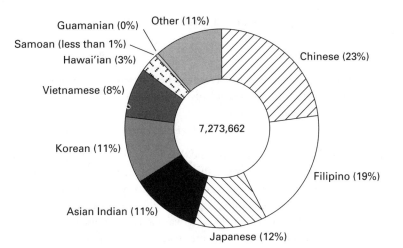

Figure D2.2 Breakdown of 'Asian or Pacific Islander' category in the 1990 US census, by national origin

We take for example India, a nation of 844 million persons which recognizes fifteen official national languages each with a large number of dialects. India is linguistically complex, especially when viewed in comparison to the US, but it is not the exception to the rule. It is not even extreme in the larger global view. We consider China (population 1.1 billion), with fifty-five official minority nationalities and eight major languages in addition to literally hundreds of other languages from Mongolian to Hmong; or Fiji with a mere 740,000 residents spread out over 7,000 square miles of islands on which fifteen languages (in addition to Fijian) are spoken.

While it would be an unreasonable burden on the Census Bureau to make note of each and every world language spoken in the US, the great disparity between *how* we make official note – what we see when we look outward at the majority of the world's population – and the *reality* of those nations, bears some consideration. What are the repercussions of the fact that we group together persons as different as the native people of Hawai'i – US citizens with a history which should be very familiar to us – with Cambodians who sought political asylum in the US and middle-class exchange students from New Delhi? How can policies which do not distinguish between the immigration patterns and educational and language backgrounds of such disparate peoples be functional?

And why do we do this? Is expediency the single most viable answer? Or is it simply that when it comes to language, we hear a single 'Asian' accent?

An obvious but disturbing answer is that we feel justified to group so many distinct nations and peoples and languages together because they all look alike to 'real' Americans, to European Americans. *Asian* evokes an association not to national origin, but to race.

[. . .]

The issue is not so much accent as 'otherness,' as illustrated in a series of court cases involving Asian American English:

**Rosina
Lippi-Green**

Managerial level employee [LS] told Xieng he was not being promoted because he could not speak 'American.'

(*Xieng* 1991: Appeal Court Opinion: 5)

the complainant's supervisor had removed her because of concern about the effect of her accent on the 'image' of the IRS, not any lack in either communication or technical abilities.

(*Park*: EEOC press release, June 8, 1988)

Our relationship to the Far East and Pacific is shaped to a great degree by the facts of nineteenth-century colonialism, in which the US, young in comparative terms, followed the European model in the way that smaller nations were overcome and dominated politically, economically, and socially. We have a history of dealing with the Asian world as a warehouse of persons and goods available to suit our own purpose and fill our own needs, a practice justified by the supposition that those people are inherently weaker. Because they are also cast as manipulative and wont to use natural wiles and treacherous means to achieve their own ends, we are able to rationalize aggressions toward them. Thus the primary male Asian stereotype is of an intelligent, clever, but crafty and unreliable person. A secondary stereotype grows out of the mystification of Asia, the mysterious 'Orient' where hardworking but simple people ply their crafts and study arcane philosophies, attaining wisdom and a spirituality specific to their race. We are uncomfortable with Asians unless they correspond to the stereotypes we have created for them.

[. . .]

Like African Americans, Asian Americans have more and more difficult hurdles to leap before they can transcend stereotype and be accepted as individuals. Accent, when it acts in part as a marker of race, takes on special power and significance. For many in the African American community there is little resistance to the language subordination process, in part because the implied promises of linguistic assimilation – while obviously overstated – are nevertheless seductive, *precisely because the threats are very real*. The seduction of perfect English, of belonging absolutely to the mainstream culture of choice, is one that is hard to resist for Asian Americans as well.

It is easy to establish that language variation is linked to race, and more specifically that foreign-language accent is linked to national origin. But once accomplished, what is to be done with such a collection of facts? Perhaps the only realistic thing is to ask harder questions of ourselves. Discrimination against Asian Americans which centers on language, but which has more in actual terms to do with race, is an established practice. How is it that in a nation so proud of its civil rights legislation and democratic ideals, people can so easily use *accent* to exclude, to limit discourse, and to discredit other – very specific – voices, because they simply do not sound white enough?

It is necessary and important at this point to look at another large group, composed in large part of non-native speakers of English. The Spanish-speaking people of this country comprise nations within the nation. As speakers of lan-

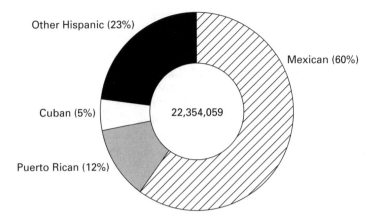

Figure D2.3 Hispanics counted in the 1990 US census

Table D2.3 Hispanic origin by race

Race	Non-Hispanic	%	Hispanic	%
White	188,424,773	83.1	11,402,291	52.1
Black	29,284,596	12.9	645,928	2.9
American Indian, Eskimo, or Aleut	1,866,807	0.8	148,336	0.7
Asian or Pacific Islander	6,994,302	3.1	232,684	1.1
Other race	239,306	0.1	9,470,850	43.2
Total	226,809,784	100	21,900,089	100

Source: 1990 US census data. Database: C90STF3C1

guages other than English, they are also subject to the process of homogenization which has been seen for other groups.

CHIQUITAFICATION

The group of peoples which the Census Bureau calls 'Hispanic' included some 22 million US residents in the 1990 census. As was the case for the Asian population, this overarching term hides a great deal of ethnic variety, in this case compounding the racial diversity, as seen in Figure D2.3 and Table D2.3.

As might be predicted, Mexican Americans account for most of the Latino population, with a much smaller Puerto Rican population and a Cuban population of just over one million, or about 5 percent of the whole. Almost a quarter of *Latino* is made up of 'Other,' in this case comprising primarily Central and South Americans (just over a million residents each) and half a million Spaniards. About half a million persons could or would not be specific in identifying their national origins.

It is important to note that the racial classifications do not include *mestizo*, and thus persons of mixed European and Native American ancestry – a large portion of the population of Mexico and Central America – must choose between allegiances (a fact which probably accounts for the large number of persons who identified themselves as 'other race'). This oversight is compounded by the assumption of an overarching Spanish monolingualism which spans more than ten countries in three continents. The Mexican population of more than 88 million includes more than 5 million speakers of indigenous Indian languages (about 8 percent of Mexico's total population), of whom almost half a million are monolingual and speak no Spanish at all (Grimes 1992). Guatemala's population of 9.3 million is approximately 55 percent Indian and 44 percent mestizo. The Indian population includes some 20,000 speakers of Kanjobal, 5,000 of whom are reported to be in Los Angeles (ibid.).

In addition to racial and ethnic diversity, 'Latino' subsumes persons from all economic groups, political and religious backgrounds, and does not recognize a residency status differential. It overlooks the fact that many ethnically Spanish-speaking persons live here on land their families have owned for many generations, and predate European settlement. In addition to this group, which cannot logically be called 'immigrant,' there are populations of more recent arrivals, short-term residents, cyclical immigrants made up primarily of farmworkers, and individuals who seek asylum in the US to escape political persecution, in addition to undocumented workers.

The use of language as a preliminary qualifier in the construction of ethnicity is an established custom, but it is nevertheless a troublesome one, as the scope and depth of 'Hispanic' has made clear. Zentella (1996) speaks and writes of what it was like for her as a child to have had a singing and dancing Chiquita Banana as a solitary Latina figure in the public eye. Thus she uses the term *chiquitafication* to speak of public policies and practices which homogenize Latino cultures and languages into a tidy and digestible package for the rest of the nation. Three areas which concern her greatly are

❑ the construction of a homogenous 'Hispanic community' that refuses to learn English;
❑ the belittling of non-Castilian varieties of Spanish;
❑ and the labeling of second-generation bilinguals as semi- or a-linguals.

(1996: 1)

The second of these concerns points to an issue which has not been raised much in this discussion, and that is that language ideologies are not restricted to the English-speaking world. Discourse around 'good' and 'lesser' language, 'appropriate' and 'inappropriate' varieties can be found wherever people care to look. For each nation, there is a supra-cultural awareness of which are the 'right' varieties, although there will also be competing constructions of social acceptability – for without those who find the 'right' language unacceptable in social terms, stigmatized language would not flourish as it does. Table D2.4 presents the simplest answers one would be likely to get in asking an average person on the street 'Where is the best [language] spoken?' and 'Where is the worst [language] spoken?'

Table D2.4 Popular constructions of 'good' and 'bad' language for other countries

Country	'Good' 'Proper' 'Cultured' 'High'	'Low' 'Bad' 'Inappropriate'
Italy	Florence	Sicily
		Calabria
Spain	Burgos	Huelva
	Valladolid	
England	Oxford	Liverpool
	Cambridge	Birmingham
Turkey	Istanbul	Black Sea
		Southeast Anatolia
Northern India (Hindi)	Delhi	Bombay
		Calcutta
Pakistan (Urdu)	Lucknow	Hyderabad

For Spanish, with a much greater geographic coverage than any of the other European languages with the exception of English, standard language ideology has established Castilian Spanish and, following therefrom, Castilian literature and culture as inherently superior and more worthy of study than New World language or language artifacts, as Zentella notes. Within Central and South American nations, there are similarly constructed ideologies, so that in Mexico there is a conception of three *normas* or levels of speaking: *la norma culta*, which Valdés (1988: 119) calls 'educated standard,' *la norma popular* ('a less elaborate and cultivated style'), and *la norma rural* ('This style of speaking generally sounds rustic to city people and is normally associated with rural lifestyles and backgrounds') (ibid.), as well as a conception of good and bad varieties over space, so that the Spanish spoken in the Yucatan is stigmatized. Overarching the national constructions of 'good' and 'bad' language, however, is a very persistent idea that *Castilian* is the only real, original language. This functions much in the same way as it does in the US, when popular belief may point to Ohio as 'Standard US English' but then defer to that mythical beast 'the King's English,' or a British norm.

As interesting as it would be to compare the way language subordination tactics function across language and cultural boundaries, here I would like to concentrate instead on the first and third of Zentella's concerns. Together they summarize some conflicts about the process of language subordination which are instructive and important.

Zentella states that there is a troublesome, contrary-to-fact 'construction of a homogeneous "Hispanic community" that refuses to learn English' in the US, and she goes on to demonstrate how dangerous such homogenization can be. This is a willful policy which encourages wholesale demonizing of the type reflected in a memo written by John Tanton when he was Chair of US English, the group that has been lobbying to make English the official language of the United States since 1981. Tanton portrayed Hispanic Catholicism as a national threat to the separation of church and state, and declared that a Latin American tradition of bribery imperiled US democracy. His most outrageous insult was a vulgar reference to 'the Hispanic birthrate,' charging that 'perhaps this is the first instance in which those with their pants up are going to get caught with their pants down.'

(Zentella 1996: 9)

Zentella's analysis of US English and other English Only movements as xenophobic, hostile, and threatening to more than just language rights is clear and convincing (see also Crawford, ed., 1992 for a lengthy discussion). When she sets out to counter their arguments with hard data, she does so carefully:

Despite the continued influx of monolingual immigrants, Veltman (1983) found that Hispanics are undergoing language loss similar to, and even exceeding that of other groups in US history. Language shift is most advanced among the US born, who constituted the majority (64%) of the US Latino population in 1990; immigrants shift to English within 15 years . . .

(1996: 10)

But somewhere an issue has gone missing.

Tanton and his colleagues construct not only a *homogenous* 'Hispanic' community, but a *resistant* one. Zentella attacks both premises: it is not true, she asserts, that Hispanic immigrants are resistant to, and reject, the importance of English or the necessity of learning it. She claims that this is not true because the numbers show us that they do indeed learn it. But does the result preclude resistance to the process, or resentment of the necessity? Further, if this kind of resistance does exist, is it necessarily bad? Would the existence of a Spanish-speaking community in Florida or Texas or New Mexico which does not use and manages to function without English render Tanton's claims credible? Would asserting the right not to be bilingual (a right which would bring along with it many great difficulties) be tantamount to an attack on American democracy? It is clear that Zentella does not mean to make this claim, and that she is constructing 'resistance' in a purposefully narrow way.

However, the third concern (*the labeling of second-generation bilinguals as semi- or a-linguals*) does demand a wider conception of resistance. This question moves beyond the issue of whether or not bilingualism is necessary and reasonable (something she, and most others, take for granted) to the issue of *Which English?*

Some immigrants live in communities of monolingual English speakers, where a Spanish accent stands out. Others live in communities where multiple varieties of English coexist in relative harmony, in which Spanish, English, and Chicano or another variety of Latino English each have a sphere. Chicano English, Puerto Rican English and Cuban English in Los Angeles, New York, and Miami are individual varieties of English, distinct in certain syntactical, morphological, and discourse

Rosina
Lippi-Green

markers from one another and from other varieties of English (Penfield and Ornstein-Galicia 1985; Zentella 1988; Valdés 1988; García and Otheguy 1988). There is a recognized Chicano American and Latino American literature which is taken as a serious object of study.

When Zentella protests the labeling of second-generation Spanish-language immigrants as semilingual or a-lingual, she is discussing a related phenomenon, that of code switching. Code switching is the orderly (rule-based) alternation between two or more languages, a subject of great interest to linguists and one which is widely studied. This complicates the picture of the Spanish-speaking universe considerably. We have distinct languages, each with its own stylistic repertoires: Spanish and English. To these we add more recently developed but distinct varieties of English, for example Chicano English as it is spoken in Texas. Now we have also the phenomenon of living and working with three languages, and switching among them as determined by language-internal (syntactical and morphological) rules as well as social and stylistic ones. The criticism Zentella discusses is aimed at switching, which may seem to an unsympathetic outsider nothing more than a language hodge-podge, and is often labeled *Spanglish*.

In fact, I would argue that whether the object of subordination is the act of style switching, or pressure to use a specific language, the ultimate goal of language subordination remains the same: to devalue and suppress *everything Spanish*.

To call code-switching *Spanglish* in a dismissive way is just another subordination method with a long history: to deny a language and its people a distinct name is to refuse to acknowledge them. There is a shorthand at work here, and that is, there is only one acceptable choice: it is not enough for Spanish speakers to become bilingual; they must learn the *right* English – and following from that, the right US culture, into which they must assimilate completely.

[. . .]

Stereotypes around Chicano and Latino Americans are almost exclusively negative, in all forms of popular culture. Penfield and Ornstein-Galicia identify the exception to this, the Californian *Don* or the New Mexican *Rico* who as 'symbols of the aristocratic class . . . were both linked more to Spain than Mexico' (1985: 78). These characters in film (*The Mark of Zorro*) or popular fiction speak an English which is accented, but elegant and archaic. Both men and women speak this kind of 'noble Spaniard' English:

> 'Come out,' she said.
> 'Ay! They have me fast. But when they do let me out, *niña*, I will take thee in my arms; and whosoever tries to tear thee away again will have a dagger in his heart. *Dios de mi vida!* ' . . .
> 'But thou lovest me, Carlos?'
>> (Gertrude Atherton (1901) *The Doomswoman: An historical romance of old California*, as cited in Simmen 1971: 40)

More usually the stereotypes for Mexican Americans depart from the *greaser*, a classification subdivided into three types: 'a Mexican *paisano* – poor rural inhabitant; as a *mojado* – "wetback" or illegal alien; and as a *bandido* – a robber wearing "huge

sombreros . . . tobacco-stained fingers and teeth, and grotesque dialect and curses"'
(Penfield and Ornstein-Galicia 1985: 78). These characters are portrayed as speaking
English with extreme dialect features; the more stereotypical the role, the more
extreme the features:

> Billee the Keed. Ah, you have heard of heem? He was one gran' boy, senor.
> All Mexican pepul his friend. You nevair hear a Mexican say one word against
> Billee the Keed . . . so kind-hearted, so generaous, so brave. And so 'andsome.
> Nombre de Dios! Every leetle senorita was crazy about heem . . .
>
> (Walter Noble Burns, The Saga of Billy the Kid,
> as cited in Pettit 1980: 162)

Recent stereotypes in film and television, note Penfield and Ornstein-Galicia,
have one thing in common: Mexican Americans are almost always portrayed as
violent; they are drug-pushers, gang-members, pimps. A particularly extreme example of a trivialized character was Frito Bandito, a 1980s counterpart and mirror
image of the wholesome Chiquita Banana. In the 1980s, however, the Latino community was vocal and persuasive enough to convince the Frito-Lay company to
drop that negative character (1985: 84).

The Spanish-speaking population of the US is very large, and has more resources
and expertise with US law and the legal system than other groups. Latino resistance to all kinds of discriminatory practices is well organized, and extends to language matters, especially when education is at issue. Unlike a smaller and more
fragmented Asian population, many Spanish speakers are ready and willing to speak
out on these issues. Unfortunately, they continue to have to battle, because as the
San Diego businessman makes clear, equal opportunity and equal standing are not
always forthcoming.

SUMMARY

[. . .]

It is crucial to remember that it is not *all* foreign accents, but only accent
linked to skin that isn't white, or which signals a third-world homeland, that evokes
such negative reactions. There are no documented cases of native speakers of Swedish
or Dutch or Gaelic being turned away from jobs because of communicative difficulties, although these adult speakers face the same challenge as native speakers of
Spanish, Rumanian, and Urdu.

Immigrants from the British Isles who speak varieties of English which cause
significant communication problems are not stigmatized: the differences are noted
with great interest, and sometimes with laughter.

[. . .]

But most do not have these resources. People have always come to the United
States because in the mind of the world it is a place of real opportunity. The hid-
den costs of democracy, of assimilation, are not spelled out in the papers they
must file to live here, but in the stories of people like Henry Park. The narrator
of *Native Speaker* draws a vivid picture of himself and all immigrants: 'They speak

... not simply in new accents or notes but in the ancient untold music of a new-comer's heart, sonorous with longing and hope' (Lee 1995).

What the newcomer must learn for him or herself is the grim reality of limitations imposed by a standard language ideology.

Issues to consider

D2.2

⊛ Activity

The approach demonstrated in this reading shows that sociolinguistic data is not necessarily 'raw' data: processed data such as census information, and interpreted data such as film and television representations can be used in sociolinguistic explorations. This latter sort of mediated information can be used to investigate attitudes to different forms of language. Cartoons, film, television, literature, newspapers and magazines have all been used to gather sociolinguistic data in recent years. As long as you remember that mediated data must be treated differently from 'raw' data, there is a lot of useful material that can come to you in this way.

Some practical investigations might include the following.

❑ Make a list of all the different linguistic codes available within a particular boundary: accents, dialects, registers, languages. You could define the boundary in different ways: the people in your classroom, the people in your extended family, the people near where you live, your town or city, your region, your nation, and so on. You could also make decisions on the level of competence of each code for each person. Who has a large repertoire of codes available to them, and what difference does this make to their lives? Are some codes more socially valued than others?

❑ You could investigate the history of what dictionary compiler Noah Webster called 'the American language'. What were the language-planning motivations of American politicians and thinkers in promoting an American style of English? How did they go about codifying this and encouraging its use in the US?

❑ The influence of American forms of English on the other Englishes around the world has been immense. Take one local area (in the UK, Australia, Singapore, or non-English places like Japan, Thailand, France, Germany, and so on) and explore the influence of American English. This could have effects at the level of accent, or particular word usage and spelling, or at a dialectal level. See if you can find examples of local resistance to 'Americanisms', such as in the letters pages of conservative newspapers.

❑ How does the English spoken by ethnic minorities in general English-speaking environments show interference patterns? You will need to compare real examples of the community speech in English with what you know or can discover about the grammar of the influencing language.

❑ How are attitudes to particular linguistic codes represented by the media? You should focus on one aspect of the media (such as television news, newspaper cartoons, magazine advertisements, the representation of African-Americans by Hollywood, and so on) and draw out the attitude to the language involved. Is the representation consistent across your data, or are there shifts in attitude over time or between different texts?

D

**Norman
Fairclough**

STYLE AND IDEOLOGY

In the article by Norman Fairclough below, the notion of metaphor is used as a means of describing two different sorts of ideological representation in newspaper reporting. Elsewhere in the book from which this extract is taken, Fairclough uses a linguistic analysis to draw out many different aspects of media representation, linking the form of expression with the ideological motivations underlying the discourses.

In discussing forms of register, metaphor and euphemism, this reading complements issues discussed in A3, B3 and C3. Language and ideology were also treated in B14 and C14.

D3.1

Analysis of discourses in newspaper texts

Norman Fairclough (reprinted from *Media Discourse,* London: Edward Arnold, 1995: 94–102)

Discourses are [. . .] constructions or significations of some domain of social practice from a particular perspective. It is useful to identify discourses with names which specify both domain and perspective – for instance, one might contrast a Marxist political discourse with a liberal political discourse, or a progressive educational discourse with a conservative educational discourse. I shall illustrate the analysis of texts in terms of discourses using press coverage of an air attack on Iraq by the USA, Britain and France on 13 January 1993 (two years after the Gulf War), referring to 14 January editions of five British newspapers: the *Daily Mirror,* the *Sun,* the *Daily Mail,* the *Daily Telegraph* and the *Guardian,* and the *Guardian Weekly* for the week ending 24 January 1993. I focus upon two issues: the 'congruent' as opposed to 'metaphorical' selection of discourses for formulating who did what to whom and why within the attack; and the role of *configurations* of discourses in the construction of these events.

The distinction between congruent and metaphorical discourses is the extension of a terminology used by Halliday (1985). A congruent application is the use of a discourse to signify those sorts of experience it most usually signifies; a metaphorical application is the extension of a discourse to signify a sort of experience other than that which it most usually signifies. The distinction is a rough one, but a useful one. Metaphorical applications of discourses are socially motivated, different metaphors may correspond to different interests and perspectives, and may have different ideological loadings. The following examples (headlines and lead paragraphs) illustrate how congruent and metaphorical discourses combine in the coverage of the attack.

Spank You And Goodnight
Bombers Humble Saddam in 30 Minutes
More than 100 Allied jets yesterday gave tyrant Saddam Hussein a spanking – blasting missile sites in a raid that took just 30 minutes.
(*Sun*)

Saddam's UN Envoy Promises Good Behaviour After Raid by US, British and
French Aircraft

> *Gulf Allies Attack Iraqi Missiles*
> More than 100 aircraft blasted Iraqi missile sites last night after the allies' patience with Saddam Hussein's defiance finally snapped.
> (*Daily Telegraph*)

In the examples I looked at, it is a discourse of military attack that is congruently applied (e.g. *jets* or *aircraft blasting missile sites* and *Gulf Allies Attack Iraqi Missiles* in the examples above). Not surprisingly, we find such formulations in all the reports, along with expressions like 'retaliate' and 'hit back' (e.g. *Iraq To Hit Back*, in the *Sun*) which represent these events as a contest between two military powers. But there are distinctions to be drawn. Whereas the *Guardian*, the *Daily Mail* and the *Daily Telegraph* use what one might call an 'official' discourse of military attack – that is, they use the sort of language that might be used in official and military accounts – the *Sun* and the *Daily Mirror* (and exceptionally the *Daily Telegraph* in the example above: *more than 100 aircraft blasted Iraqi missile sites*) use a fictional discourse of military attack, the discourse of stories about war (whether purely fictional, or fictionalized versions of fact), which highlights physical violence. The *Daily Mirror* is particularly rich in expressions for processes of attack which link to this discourse: *blitz, blast, hammer, pound, blaze into action*, (warplanes) *scream in*. While the attacks are mainly formulated as action by aircraft or 'the allies' against 'Iraq' or specific targets (e.g. 'missile sites' or 'control centres'), both the *Daily Mirror* and the *Sun* also formulate them in a personalized way as directed at Saddam Hussein (*The Gulf allies struck hard at Saddam Hussein*, '*Spot Raids Give Saddam Pasting*', *allied warplanes have bombed the hell out of Saddam Hussein*).

The main headline and lead paragraph from the *Sun* above show that formulations of the attack do not by any means draw only upon military discourse: *Spank You And Goodnight* (notice the play on 'Thank you and goodnight' which makes a joke even of this serious event) and *More than 100 Allied jets . . . gave tyrant Saddam Hussein a spanking*. This is a metaphorical application of an authoritarian discourse of family discipline which is a prominent element in representations of the attack – Saddam as the naughty child punished by his exasperated parents. The *Guardian* editorial sums it up as *an act of punishment against a very bad boy who thumbed his nose several times too often* – also notice *the allies' patience . . . finally snapped* and *good behaviour* in the *Daily Telegraph* example, both consistent with this disciplinary discourse. (One might also be tempted to read 'spanking' in terms of a discourse of sexual 'correction'.) The attack is formulated several times in the reports as 'teaching Saddam a lesson' (for instance, *The allies launched 114 war planes to teach defiant Saddam a lesson* in the *Daily Mirror*, and *Let's hope he's learnt his lesson*, attributed to a US official in the *Sun*). This is again consistent with the discourse of family discipline, or disciplinary discourses more generally. So too with *Toe The Line Or . . . We'll Be Back!*, the main page-one headline in the *Daily Mirror*. Such conditional threats ('do x or we'll do y', 'if you do x – or don't do x – we'll do y') occur several times in the report.

A related but rather more specific metaphorical discourse that is evoked is that of the disciplining of young offenders, juveniles found guilty of crimes (with

Norman
Fairclough

the focus on crimes of particular sorts, such as 'joy-riding'). A British government official is quoted in most reports as saying that the attack was *a short, sharp and telling lesson* for Saddam. This evokes the expression used by the British Conservative government in the 1980s, when it tried to develop the policy of delivering a 'short, sharp shock' (in the form of incarceration in highly disciplined quasi-military institutions) to juvenile offenders. The same group of discourses is indicated in reasons given for the attack. The headline for a report on pages 2–3 of the *Sun* is *He Had It Coming*, and the lead paragraph refers to the *pasting* that Saddam Hussein *has been asking for*. According to the *Daily Mirror*, Saddam had *pushed his luck too far*. These formulations evoke a conversational or 'lifeworld' version of an authority-based discourse of discipline, referring to what is elsewhere frequently formulated in the reports as the 'provocations' of the subordinate party in this disciplinary relationship, i.e. Saddam (note also formulations such as Saddam 'goading' or 'taunting the West'). Disciplinary formulations such as 'provocations' alternate with legalistic formulations such as 'breaches' and 'infringements' (of the UN ceasefire conditions).

The metaphorical application of such discourses is a very prominent feature of these reports, and in assessing that application one might wonder whether such a disciplinary relationship applies or ought to apply in relations between nations, or indeed whether the relations between nations ought to be personalized as they consistently are here: the target of discipline is Saddam, not Iraq or the Iraqi government – whereas its source is mainly 'the (Gulf) allies' or 'the West', and rarely George Bush (the American president at the time).

Other discourses are metaphorically applied, though they are less prominent in the reports. One is evident in the *Sun* headline *Bombers Humble Saddam in 30 Minutes* as well as the *Daily Mail* headlines *Allies Humble Saddam* and *Retribution in the Gulf*. I think these can be read in terms of a (Christian) religious discourse, though 'retribution' also evokes a legal discourse. Another discourse which features only once here – attributed to a Whitehall official by the *Daily Mirror* – but was quite common in coverage of hostilities in the Gulf at the time, is a discourse of communication exchange, of 'signals' sent through military actions. (In the words of the Whitehall official, *If Saddam does not get this message . . . he knows there will be more to come*.) Again, both the *Sun* and the *Daily Mirror* draw upon a discourse of dangerous-animal control in their editorials: the air strikes are intended to 'curb' Saddam, and if *he doesn't learn this time, he will have to be put down for good like the mad dog he is* (*Daily Mirror*), *the tragedy is that we did not finish him off last time* (the *Sun*).

An important distinction within a report, which takes us back to the discussion of discourse representation earlier in this chapter, is between discourses which occur in represented discourse attributed to the 'voices' of others in quotations or summaries, as opposed to discourses which are unattributed and are drawn upon by the 'voice' of the report itself. However, a key question (which requires historical research and research on production processes) is where the discourses of reporters come from. By comparing attributed and unattributed formulations within and across reports, one can often see the same discourses being drawn upon by reporters and official sources. For example, the discourse of correction (in *Spank You And Goodnight*, also in the *Daily Mirror* inside-page headline *A Spanking Not A Beating* and in the headline of the *Guardian* editorial *More A Smack Than A Strike*) may have originated in a statement by a US official: *It's just a spanking for Saddam, not a real beating*. Similarly the *Sun* headline *He Had It Coming* and more generally 'teach-Saddam-a-lesson' formulations apparently echo official sources – the *Sun* quotes a White House statement: *Saddam had this coming. Let's hope he has learnt his lesson*.

Official influence upon media formulations is built up over the longer term rather than just on a day-by-day basis; 'teach-Saddam-a-lesson' formulations had been widely used officially and by the press for a period before the attack, and similarly official sources including President Bush had spoken of 'patience running out' in the weeks before the attack. (Also, this relatively minor Iraq crisis was intertextually linked to earlier ones including the Gulf War, and fed discoursally from them. See the discussion of 'discourse-historical' method of analysis in Wodak 1990.) The *Guardian*, the *Daily Telegraph* and the *Daily Mail* are more likely generally to use such formulations only as attributions. There is a constant flow between official sources and the media: the latter may take up the discourses of the former, but the former also design their statements and press releases to harmonize with discourses favoured by the media. Bruck (1989) points out that the influence of official discourses on media discourse depends upon the discourse type – it is, for instance, likely to be greater in news reports than in editorials or features.

While the discourses and specific formulations of certain favoured sources are massively present and foregrounded, those of other – and especially oppositional – sources are either omitted altogether from some reports, or backgrounded. For example, the Labour Party leftwinger Tony Benn described the attack as the *last piece of gunboat diplomacy* of a *lame-duck US president* according to the *Guardian*, but that was the only report of Benn's comment, and it was backgrounded (positioned in a single paragraph in the middle of a report in the bottom left-hand corner of a centre page). Formulations of the attack attributed to the Kuwaiti government, which draw upon a discourse of disease and surgical intervention (*bursting the abscess of the Baghdad government* according to the *Sun*, *removing the Iraqi cancer* according to the *Daily Telegraph*), were quite widely reported though backgrounded. By contrast, only the *Guardian* reports formulations of Saddam's actions prior to the attack as 'acrobatics' and 'mere fireworks' (from the newspaper *al-Ahram*, Cairo), and 'clownish' behaviour (*al-Thaurah*, Damascus), constructing Saddam in the less threatening role of a clown/performer (clowns don't generally merit bombing). Significantly, the same reports highlight the 'double standards' applied by the West, in not reacting as vigorously to the plight of Muslims under attack by Serbians in Bosnia, or of the 400 Palestinians extradited by Israel and isolated in No Man's Land between Israel and Lebanon at that time, in defiance of a United Nations resolution. Why no air attacks on Israel?

If selection between alternative congruent and metaphorical discourses is one issue, another is configurations of discourses, how discourses are articulated together within discourse types. Bruck (1989), for instance, suggests that five main discourses were drawn upon by the Canadian media in the mid-1980s in their coverage of

disarmament, peace and security issues, which he calls: the discourse of state
leaders, bureaucratic-technical discourse, scientific-technical discourse, the discourse
of victims, and the discourse of survival. The first three are dominant discourses,
the last two oppositional discourses. The analysis of news output is concerned with
both the selections made between these discourses, and the ways in which they
are articulated together, which between them allow the analyst to describe the
range of discursive practice in the coverage of these issues.

The following report was inset in a double-page spread in the *Daily Mirror* of
14 January, dealing with the attack in Iraq. (Major reports are often made up in
this way of combinations of smaller reports, and the relationship between articles
on a page in such cases is worth attending to.)

The Mother Of All Rantings

Evil dictator Saddam Hussein promised Iraq last night they were winning
a new great victory – just like they had in the 'Mother of All Battles' in
Kuwait. His pledge came three hours after allied aircraft pounded his missile sites.

In a ranting, confused speech, he told his nation on television that a
new jihad – holy war – had begun. He urged the Iraqis to fight 'in the
name of God' . . . and he promised them they would humiliate the allies.

Saddam called the allies 'the infidels' and said they were 'under the
influence of Satan'. And he raged: 'Every aeroplane of the aggressors in
the Iraq sky shall be a target for us and we shall fight in the name of
God and down their aircraft. The aggressors will be defeated.'

Reading stiffly from hand-held notes, he said: 'The criminals have come
back. But tonight they came back without any cover, not even a transparent one.

'They came back for the purpose they never spoke about the first
time in their evil aggression, namely to impose colonialism.'

This report includes a new and clearly oppositional configuration of discourses for
formulating the attack, attributed to Saddam himself: an Islamic religious discourse
(*infidels, under the influence of Satan*), and political discourses of aggression and colonialism. The reference to the absence of any 'cover' obliquely cues also a legal discourse – the attacks were condemned as 'illegal' by those who opposed them. Notice
also that the allies are referred to here as *criminals*.

However, this oppositional configuration of discourses is framed within a larger
configuration by the dominant discourses I have discussed above. Saddam's speech
is firstly formulated and summed up in the headline in an ironic play upon his
own (in)famous description of the Gulf War as 'the mother of all battles', with
rantings evoking discourses of madness and political fanaticism. In the lead paragraph, Saddam is referred to as an *evil dictator*, deploying the religious and political discourses I referred to earlier as part of the anti-Saddam armoury. The summary
of Saddam's speech in the second paragraph is framed by the initial thematized
phrase in a ranting, *confused speech*, and similar framing devices are used where
Saddam is directly quoted – notice the choice of *raged* as a reporting verb, and

reading stiffly. In the first two of these cases there is again an evocation of the discourse of madness. The net effect of the framing of Saddam's oppositional discourses with the dominant ones is to undermine and ridicule the former.

Diverse discourses are articulated together in the naming and identification of both the protagonists and the antagonists, though to quite different effects. The identification of the protagonists caused some difficulty in that the USA, Britain and France were claiming to act to enforce a United Nations resolution, but neither the 'no-fly' zone they had imposed on southern Iraq nor the attack had been endorsed by the UN. The attackers are referred to in the reports as 'the Gulf allies', 'the West', and most frequently 'the allies'. 'The Gulf allies' is problematic in that the alliance which fought Iraq in the Gulf War was actually divided on this later attack, and none of the Arab members of the alliance was involved. 'The West' is problematic because a number of members of 'the West' were also critical. 'The allies', with its reassuring evocation of the Second World War, seems to have been the least problematic label. The *Guardian* also refers 'correctly' to 'the United States, Britain and France'. A number of other identifications were used elsewhere: in the *Guardian Weekly* 'the coalition' and 'the US and its allies' were used, and President Clinton was quoted as supporting *the international community's actions*. The variety of these formulations, the range of discourses they draw upon, and the instability of naming practices here, are indicative of the difficulty in constructing an identity for the protagonists.

By contrast, the considerable range of expressions used to refer to Saddam Hussein shows a number of discourses working together to discredit him, as in the following editorial from the *Sun* on 14 January:

Wipe Out The Mad Menace
At long last, Allied warplanes have bombed the hell out of Saddam Hussein.
    The Iraqi madman has pushed the West too far.
    He has played a dangerous game and now he must pay the price.
    Four times Saddam has sent raiding parties over the border into
Kuwait.

Menace
His boast that Iraq planned to 'recover' Kuwait was the last straw.
    The tinpot tyrant could not be allowed to cling onto power a moment
longer.
    He is an international terrorist, a constant menace to peace.
    The tragedy is that we did not finish him off last time.
    Go get him, boys!

This is discoursal overkill: a remarkable range of discourses are articulated together in the verbal annihilation of Saddam Hussein. The density of the assembled discourses is no doubt attributable to the fact that the genre is editorial rather than news report: this is an apologia for the attack, based upon a thorough discrediting of Saddam Hussein. He is referred to as a *madman*, a *menace to peace*, a *tyrant*, a *terrorist*, a *blusterer* (cf. *his boast*), and a figure of ridicule (the implication of

Norman
Fairclough

tinpot), yet at the same time a calculating politician (who has *pushed the West too far*, and *played a dangerous game*), and actions against him are formulated in terms of discourses of legal retribution (*he must pay the price*), war fiction (*bombed the hell out of*) and even westerns (*wipe out, finish off, go get him, boys*). We find the range of discourses extending further elsewhere – he is referred to, for instance, in the terms of religious and ethical discourses as 'evil' and a 'coward'.

A configuration of discourses is put to different effect in the editorial in the *Guardian Weekly*, where evaluation of competing discourses is itself a topic. The editorial is a critique of the attack, under the headline *What Signal Will He Read?* The editorial is a dialogue with opposing positions represented by different discourses. Thus it refers to – and distances itself from – *headmasterly talk of Teaching Saddam a Lesson*, and attributes the discourse of *delivering a signal* to Saddam to what it calls *the tough-minded* (this discourse generates the expression 'coercive bombing' in another report in the same edition). It does, however, in its own voice draw upon some of the dominant discourses for formulating Saddam and his actions (he is *evilly brutal Saddam*, with a *record of provocation* – though perhaps *deliberate*). The editorial also formulates the attack, tentatively, in a different discourse: *Mr Bush's likely desire to settle accounts before leaving office*.

Other terms which are roughly equivalent to 'discourses', but derive from different theoretical frameworks and traditions, are quite widely used, including schemata, frames, and scripts (from cognitive psychology), metaphors, and vocabularies. I have discussed metaphorical applications of discourses, and for the most part the discourses I have referred to are realized in the vocabulary of texts. Aspects of grammar may also be involved in the realization of discourses. For instance, I noted earlier that conditional threats (e.g. *Toe The Line . . . Or We'll Be Back*) are a feature of disciplinary discourse, and these are realized in particular syntactic constructions (in this example, imperative clause + *or* + declarative clause).

Analysis of *collocations* in texts (patterns of co-occurrence between words) is a way of linking analysis of discourses to the linguistic analysis of texts (Sinclair 1992). Configurations of discourses identified in the analysis of discourses may be realized in – condensed into – collocational relations in phrases or clauses (Fairclough 1991). Collocations are often a good place to look for contradictions in texts. For example, in the editorial from the *Sun* above, the following collocations occur: *mad menace, tinpot tyrant, the Iraqi madman has pushed the West too far. Mad* evokes the discourse of madness whereas *menace* evokes the discourse of political extremism, and the collocation bonds the two discourses together in a detail of the text. Similarly, *the Iraqi madman has pushed the West too far* compacts together the discourse of madness and the discourse of political calculation.

Both selections amongst available discourses and selection of particular ways of articulating them together are likely to be ideologically significant choices. There may, for instance, be various ways of rationalizing the decision to construct relations between 'the West' and a 'Third World' country like Iraq as relations between a teacher and a recalcitrant child, but such a construction implicitly evokes an imperialist and indeed racist ideology of relations between nations, which contributes to the continuity of imperialist and neo-colonialist relations in practice. Of course,

[. . .] one cannot assume ideological effects consequent upon selections of discourses, merely that the question of potential ideological effects is always worth raising.

Issues to consider

D3.2

✪ Activity

Norman Fairclough

Exploring ideology or metaphor or euphemism are fruitful dimensions of study. Sociolinguistics students, however, must be careful that work in these areas has a social dimension as well as a purely grammatical analysis. The key is to engage in both social theory and linguistics, and relate the two. Many students' essays in ideology remain general and simply opinionated; the way of avoiding this is to ensure you return constantly to examples of the actual language used, and apply a linguistic analysis to it.

Some practical suggestions follow.

❏ As a means of achieving a focus in analysis, restrict your data to one story on one day across a selection of newspapers, or one story over two weeks, or just the front pages of a day's newspapers. Ask yourself questions such as: how are different groups represented in language? Are different grammatical constructions used consistently for different groups of people? Are words from certain semantic fields used consistently for particular groups? Which groups tend to appear as the subjects of sentences and which as the objects? What evaluative adjectives and adverbs are used? Is there a semantic pattern in the verb choices associated with particular groups?

❏ Most news reports concern people (such as politicians, judges, representatives and commentators) saying things, making speeches, issuing statements, and then debating the utterances made by others. How is all this speech reported? When is speech quoted directly, when is it paraphrased, and when is it summarised? How does the ideological stance of the reporter, newspaper or TV programme have an effect on the choice of representation?

❏ Take Fairclough's notions of metaphorical and congruent configurations of discourse and track their use and sources in other news stories. If metaphorical configurations are discovered, identify the source domains of the metaphors and consider, like Fairclough, how these choices affect the ideology of the text.

❏ What metaphorical configurations are used to represent America and Europe, or your own government and politicians, or countries in the developing world, or democracy, or even sports reports or natural or human disasters? Do the media represent particular relationships in consistent ways?

LANGUAGE CONTACT AND CODE-SWITCHING

D4

In the reading which follows, John Edwards draws the connections between borrowing (or 'copying') and how this contact between languages often results in interference patterns in the target language. Code-switching is often the specific mechanism through which the borrowing of words and constructions happens.

The terms used here were introduced in A4, B4 and C4. The influence of the processes discussed, especially on newer forms of English, was also mentioned in A9, B9 and C9.

D4.1

**John
Edwards**

Borrowing, interference and code-switching

John Edwards (reprinted from *Multilingualism*, Harmondsworth: Routledge, 1995: 72–8)

Outright language choice is obviously available to bilingual individuals, and an illustrative example is found in Paraguay. Here, more than 90 per cent are bilingual in Guaraní and Spanish. Language choice is non-random, and heavily influenced by external constraints, as figure D4.1 shows.

It is also common to find linguistic alteration occurring within one unit of speech directed to one listener. In his classic volume on the subject, Weinreich (1966) stated that all such 'deviation from the norms of either language' may be referred to as *interference*. It seems evident, however, that not every switch from one language to another results from the unwelcome intrusion which the term *interference* suggests; speakers may often switch for emphasis, because they feel that the *mot juste* is found more readily in one of their languages than in another, or because of their perceptions of the speech situation, changes in content, the linguistic skills of their interlocutors, degrees of intimacy and so on. Some writers have thus opted for the more neutral term *transference* which implies, among other things, a greater element of volition. There is certainly a wide range of possibilities, as the following examples suggest:

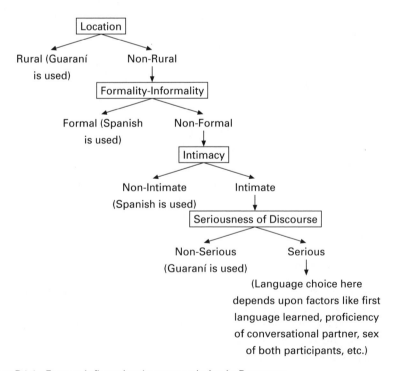

Figure D4.1 Factors influencing language choice in Paraguay
Source: after Rubin, 1968

John Edwards

(1) The proceedings went smoothly, ba? (Tagalog)

(2) This morning I hanter my baby tu dekat babysitter tu lah ('This morning I took my baby to the babysitter'). (Malay–English)

(3) De pompier militaire van de staat . . . loop partout me ne vitesse zoo rapide as de chemin de fer ('The state military fireman . . . runs everywhere with the speed of a railway'). (French–Dutch)

(4) Sano että tulla tänna että I'm very sick ('Tell them to come here that I'm very sick'). (Finnish–English)

(5) Sometimes I'll start a sentence in English y terminó en español ('Sometimes I'll start a sentence in English and end it in Spanish').

These examples of code-switching (some refer to it as code-*mixing*; these and other terms have yet to reach agreed-upon definition) illustrate changes of various types. Example (1) shows 'tag-switching', where a stock element in one language (often interrogatory or exclamatory) is joined to an utterance in another. A common related event is when speakers of German French, for whom the tags *nicht wahr* and *n'est-ce pas* are all-purpose say, in English, something like *She's a nice person, isn't it?* This is plainly a matter of interference. Examples (2) and (3) show *intrasentential* mixing; indeed, (3) is particularly interesting. Is this mainly lexical interference, since the basic structure is Dutch, or is it better seen as repeated switching? Finally, examples (4) and (5) show *intersentential* mixing/switching, where the change occurs at a clause or sentence boundary.

A considerable amount of research has been devoted to the understanding of the linguistic factors which may account for various types of code changing, the constraints which make one form more likely or common than another, and so on. Obviously this has a great deal to do with the grammar and syntax of each of the languages involved.

Different *types* of language transfer can be easily understood. For example, if a Brussels French speaker uses the Dutch *vogelpik* for a game of darts, rather than the standard French *fléchettes*, this is an example of *lexical* transfer. Further, *vogelpik* in this context constitutes a *loanword* since it is an 'intrusion' regularly used in unchanged form. It may, however, be given a French pronunciation, which indicates another type of 'change', an attempt to bring the foreign element into the maternal fold (another familiar example is the French adoption of the English *pullover*, pronounced 'poolovaire').

Sometimes loanwords become very widely used and, if we go far enough, we reach the level of permanent interlanguage borrowing. Here are some 'English' words showing eastern influence:

ALCOHOL (Arabic *al-koh'l*): powdered antimony, then any quintessence (e.g., 'alcohol of wine' via distillation), then just the intoxicating ingredient.

ALGEBRA (Arabic *al-jebr*): the reuniting of broken parts, first used in English to refer to the setting of bones.

ASSASSIN (*hash-shashin*): hashish-eaters, a sect who killed under the influence of cannabis.

BUCKRAM: first meant a high-quality fabric from Bokhara then, later, coarse cloth.

Eunuch (Greek *eunoukhos*): 'bed-guard'.

Gazette (Italian *gazeta* or *gazzetta*): name of a small Venetian copper coin.

Onyx (Greek *onux*): 'claw, fingernail' (pink, with white streaks).

Punch (Hindi *panch*, Sanskrit *panchan*): 'five' (i.e., the five basic ingredients: wine/spirit, water/milk, sugar, lemon and spice).

Tabby: from *Al-'at-tabiya*, a suburb of Baghdad named for Prince Attab where a cloth was made known as *attabi*; this was usually striped. Later applied to cats.

A modern example of words beginning to enter a foreign vocabulary is found in the English of Quebec, where a speaker might now say something like:

> I took the autoroute to the dépanneur [convenience store], stopped at the caisse populaire [credit union] . . . crossed [met] the representative of my syndicate [union], who has been seized with [informed of] my dossier.

It is interesting to note, though, that not all languages can incorporate borrowed elements equally easily. The grammatical constraints may be such – say, between two languages widely removed from one another typologically – that borrowing may be less frequent than it is between closely-related languages. More simply, borrowings from language A may not fit as easily into B as into C. This may have important consequences for B and C if A, for example, is the variety of a 'developed' society and they are not.

Another variety of lexical transfer occurs when loan *translation* occurs: for example, the adoption of the English *skyscraper* into Dutch (as *wolkenkrabber*), German (*wolkenkratzer*), French (*gratte-ciel*) and Spanish (*rascacielos*). Such words are called *calques* (literally, 'copies'). *Morphological* transfers occur when a word in language A is more fully embraced by language B: the Dutch *kluts* (dollop) becomes, in Brussels French, *une clouche*, and *heilbot* (halibut) becomes *un elbot*. *Syntactic* transfer occurs in such examples as *Tu prends ton plus haut chiffre* ('You take your highest figure') – said by a native Dutch speaker, who makes his adjectives precede the noun, as they would in Dutch (*Je neemt je hoogste cijfer*) but not as they would in French. *Phonological* transfer is very common, of course, and is a most difficult area in which to avoid interference (consider fluent adult speakers with 'horrible' accents). Equally, *prosodic* transfer – subtle differences in stress and intonation between languages, such that one's dominant variety influences the other – is also difficult to avoid. In Standard French the appropriate emphasis would be *il faut **pas** dire ça!* ('You mustn't say that!') but in Brussels French the emphasized word is *dire*, on the model of the Dutch *Ge moogt dat niet **zeggen***.

This brief discussion of interference and code-switching only scratches the surface, but it does reveal something of the variety of transference and, more importantly, the variability in terms of conscious intent. That is, bilingual speakers may *choose* to use *vogelpik*, and their choice may be determined by non-linguistic, social factors; syntactic and phonological interference, on the other hand, is presumably less subject to such factors or, more accurately perhaps, is less easily or directly

John
Edwards

influenced by them, necessitating more effort to remove it. In general one might roughly view interference phenomena as those determined by internal factors, and code-switching as more influenced by extralinguistic constraints; however this is only general, as even the few examples given here suggest.

However we divide the subject up, and whatever labels we apply – interference, code-switching, mixing, transference, etc. – it is clear that in all cases something is 'borrowed' from another language. Further, the degree to which the borrowed element is integrated (or can be integrated) into the other code may be of considerable interest for studies of group contact, of relative linguistic prestige, of the perceived or actual ease with which different languages deal with given topics, and so on. Borrowings may be on a 'nonce' basis or may represent more established practice, but the latter grows from the former and presumably reflects stronger and more widespread need. However, a further subdivision has been suggested for these established borrowings; some are indeed necessary – words filling lexical gaps in the other language, for example – but some are 'gratuitous' – there already exists the equivalent item. Why, then, the borrowing? The motivation here is most often perceived status and prestige. Common examples include the use of foreign words or phrases. To say that something is a *sine qua non* or, *mutatis mutandis*, might become *la crème de la crème* (*sensu bono*, of course) in terms of representing the *Zeitgeist*, is perhaps to reach the *Ultima Thule*, *poco a poco*, of prestige – but it can be overdone, *non è vero?* Four hundred years ago, du Bellay also had reservations:

> Among other things, let our poet take care not to use the Latin and Greek proper names, a thing as absurd really as if thou shouldst apply a piece of green velvet to a dress of red velvet. But would it not be an absurd thing to use in a Latin work the proper name of a man or other thing in French, as *Jan currit*, *Loyre fruit*, and other like words? Suit, then, such proper names, of whatever language they be, to the use of thy vulgar tongue . . . say in French *Hercule*, *Thésée*, *Achille*, *Ulysse*, *Virgile*, *Ciceron*, *Horace*. Thou shouldst, however, in this use judgment and discretion, for there are many such names which cannot be appropriated into French: . . . I refer you to the judgment of your ear. As for the rest, use words purely French, not, however, too common, nor yet too rarely used.

At another level, one can observe the trendy status of English which seems to be growing around the world, even among those ignorant of it. It has been reported, for example, that shops in the re-emerging eastern European countries often find it easier to sell their products (when they have any) if they are labelled in English. No English competence is implied or required in either seller or buyer; simple recognition and cachet apparently do the trick. English is the international language, too, of pop music and culture (the coca-colonialism factor). As Michael Luszynski, a Polish singer, wryly noted recently, a phrase like *Słysze warkot pociągu nadjedzie na torze* does not have the same oomph as 'I hear the train a-coming, it's rolling down the line' – even to Polish speakers with no English. In Germany,

John
Edwards

teenagers wear *die Jeans*, in Moscow you can attend a *dzhazz-saission*, you can say *baj-baj* in many countries, and even the French grudgingly acknowledge the appeal of *le drugstore* and *le weekend*. In Japan, English has a social clout which, again, is underpinned by neither knowledge nor grammaticality. Tomato juice may be sold as 'red mix for city actives', a coffee-shop motto is 'world smell in cup, full', a soft drink is called 'Pocari sweat' and one can get advice on 'how to sex'. This omits the use of English words more fully integrated into Japanese, often in abbreviated form (e.g., *hamu tosuto* for a 'toasted ham sandwich', *apaato* for 'apartment' and many others in regular use).

Under the heading 'Pretentious diction', Orwell excoriated the use of many foreign words and expressions – *Weltanschauung*, *status quo*, *ancien régime* and all the rest – which he said are used to 'give an air of culture and elegance'. Some abbreviations – *e.g. i.e.*, and *etc.* – are useful, and Orwell thought that a few other terms might be necessary. He noted, though, that 'if we really need the word *café* . . . it should either be spelled "caffay" or pronounced "cayfe"'. He went on to say that 'bad writers, and especially scientific, political and sociological writers, are nearly always haunted by the notion that Latin or Greek words are grander than Saxon ones'; thus he also saw as unnecessary such terms as *ameliorate*, *deracinated* and *clandestine*. The avoidance of perfectly good English words, he felt, led to 'slovenliness and vagueness'. Finally, Orwell criticized phrases like *a not unjust final assumption* – which he thought should be laughed out of existence: 'One can cure oneself of the *not un-* formation by memorizing this sentence: *A not unblack dog was chasing a not unsmall rabbit across a not ungreen field.*' Well, there is a lot to all of this but, as elsewhere, Orwell's passion and generalization obliterate some useful elements along with many bad ones. I would not like to lose *clandestine*, for example, and phrases like *ancien régime* have resonances which one may quite appropriately wish to summon, and are not easily replaceable with concision.

In still other cases, borrowing may occur for what Weinreich 1996 lightly termed 'cacophemistic purposes'. Citing a study done in the 1930s, he observed that:

> the patois of French Switzerland have no morally favorable terms of German origin, but they swarm with German words for disreputable or badly dressed women, rudeness, coarseness, indolence, sloth [and] avarice, corresponding to the stereotyped ridicule with which the French Swiss regards the German Swiss, his culture, and above all his language, of whose inferiority the former is deeply convinced.

This sort of borrowing is often, too, allied to the desire to produce a comic effect and both this and its unilingual counterpart – alteration of accents, say, within a joke – are well-understood and frequently used devices available to virtually all speakers.

It is interesting, in all of this, to recognize that attitudes towards code-switching are often negative, particularly on the part of monolinguals who are sometimes inclined to dismiss it as gibberish. Terms like *Tex-Mex*, *Franglais*, *Japlish* (and many others) are often used, and often meant pejoratively. Bilinguals, too, are wont to see their behaviour here as 'embarrassing', 'impure', 'lazy', even 'dangerous', but the reasons they give for the practice – fitting the word to the topic, finding a word with a nuance unavailable in the other variety, helping out a listener, strengthening intimacy, and so on – make a great deal of sense. If you have two languages to draw upon, why not maximize this happy circumstance as appropriate? The chimeras of impurity and laziness are exposed when we realize that, very often, switching involves the *repetition* – for emphasis, for intimacy – of the same idea in both languages. We see, then, speakers whose twin bowstrings allow them not only the style-shifting available to monolinguals but also full language-shifting. It is hard to imagine that this is anything but a valuable addition.

Issues to consider

Exploring language interference patterns and code-switching is, of course, much easier if you are bilingual yourself. However, it is also possible to investigate code-switching when the codes concerned are at the level of accent or dialect. Many people switch their accent when on the telephone or when telling a joke or when reporting what someone else said. Most people are multi-dialectal, unless they have the misfortune to have the national standard language as their vernacular dialect. All of these can be investigated and the social motivations for switching points can be suggested.

Some practical project ideas follow.

- ❏ If you are planning a holiday in a different language area soon, collect newspapers, magazines, flyers and posters (especially ones that are local or not very professionally produced) and search them for examples of linguistic code-switching. Alternatively, let the data come to you by sitting at a computer and downloading e-mail discussion groups and chatrooms used by young people in, say, Hong Kong, Singapore, Moscow, Tel-Aviv, Berlin or Amsterdam.
- ❏ Take a passage from any text you can find and use an etymological dictionary to track the historical source of every borrowed word. More complexly, take a passage from several different genres (e.g. a piece of academic writing, a recipe, a child's poem, or a selection of different literary genres) and apply the same etymological analysis to see whether there are generic differences in word choice.
- ❏ Many euphemisms for embarrassing, socially awkward, obscene or taboo notions use foreign language borrowing as a politeness disguise. For example, take as many words as you can think of to refer to a 'toilet' and track the source languages and literal meanings of each. Does a pattern emerge? Try the same analysis for other taboo concepts.
- ❏ Investigate the linguistic principles, borrowing and blending behind hybrid forms of language such as Franglais, Japlish, Tex-Mex, Wenglish, Thaiglish and others.

THE SOCIOLINGUIST'S RESPONSIBILITY

More perhaps than in any other field of linguistics, sociolinguists have long been sensitive to the ethical dimensions of conducting research investigations into the language of ordinary people. Many scholars in the field also take the view that their expertise

Deborah
Cameron

in sociolinguistics should be used in a way that is socially and politically engaged in society, rather than pursuing research in an ivory tower. Sociolinguists, in short, have a responsibility not only for scientific accuracy and thoroughness, but also towards the community and society of which they are a part.

The following article was written by Deborah Cameron in the late 1980s and was circulated amongst colleagues but never published. Many of the criticisms and dangers she identifies have since been addressed by many sociolinguists, largely in response to discussions like this one, and sociolinguistic fieldwork practice has moved on in a positive direction. However, the article is reproduced here in order to represent an important debate within the field and as a reminder to those new to the discipline of their ethical responsibilities.

The methods introduced and discussed throughout this book should be seen in the light of arguments like this (and especially the material treated in A5, B5 and C5).

| D5.1 | **'Respect, please!' Subjects and objects in sociolinguistics** |

Deborah Cameron (previously unpublished)

In the early part of 1985 I got a call from a youth worker at Charterhouse in Southwark. I knew her as a friend of a friend, and she knew I was a sociolinguist who enjoyed talking about my subject. She wondered if I could describe my work to a discussion group that met at Charterhouse.

The group consisted of about eight young people, mainly young women, between the ages of 18 and 22. It was not a closed group, but it so happened that all the core members at the time were Afro-Caribbean (Southwark is a run-down inner city area with a large ethnic minority population). There was a white full-time worker – my contact – and a Black part timer. Because of the circumstances, and although I am no expert (by sociolinguists' standards) on Black English, I decided to focus on topics of special interest to Afro-Caribbeans, i.e. racism in language and creole languages. I wanted to present my work to the group in a way they would see as relevant, and I also hoped to learn something useful from them about their experiences/attitudes.

As it turned out, this decision was a good one, in the sense that the topic generated so much enthusiasm, the group decided to go on exploring it. One evening with me turned into six weeks, and eventually we made a video about language and racism. The title for this video, chosen by the group, was significant: they called it *Respect, Please!* They tried to design it to be shown to both Black and white audiences: for white viewers it depicts the everyday experience of racism, and demands that white people respect their Black compatriots, while for Black viewers it shows how the linguistic heritage of patois (creole) can be seen as a source of Black *self*-respect.

I want to explore the theme of respect, for it is closely bound up with my own feelings about the Southwark project, and my own work in general. What *Respect Please!* represents for me as a linguist is the possibility of doing democratic and accountable research which does not make its *subjects* – nonstandard speakers – into *objects*. This project to some extent enhanced the self-knowledge and under-

Deborah
Cameron

standing of those who participated, raising our consciousness in many different ways. It was politically as well as linguistically valuable, as I hope I can show later on in this report. [. . .]

Towards democratic research methods

Most fundamentally, it seems to me, linguists must bear in mind a principle like the following:

KNOWLEDGE IS NOT THE RESEARCHER'S PROPERTY. IT SHOULD SERVE THE NEEDS OF BOTH RESEARCHER AND RESEARCHED.

To observe this principle, I suggest we would need to conduct research in accordance with four maxims.

MAXIM ONE: *RELEVANCE*. WHEN YOU ARE RESEARCHING IN A PARTICULAR COMMUNITY, MAKE SURE YOU ASK QUESTIONS IN WHICH ITS MEMBERS ARE INTERESTED.

When a researcher goes into a community, clearly s/he has certain preconceptions and areas of interest. Often these are dictated by the state of the literature. Thus, I decided I wanted to make a video about patois. It soon became obvious however that this would not fully reflect the group's concerns. Unlike me, they did not distinguish between the question of patois and that of racism in language; both were instances of lack of respect. Attitudes to patois undervalue the language, and racist language undervalues those who speak it. For the group it was important to address both issues, and I revised my plans accordingly.

Another point which became important through the group's insistence was the differences between different islands in the West Indies. All books on British Black English stress its bias towards Jamaican even when spoken, say, by Bajans, and some suggest this reflects a general 'Black British' as opposed to 'specific island' identity among young people (especially those born in Britain). For this group any such suggestion is inaccurate, though: their roots in St Lucia or Dominica or Barbados are very important and we had interesting discussions of lexical and accent differences (and of the gulf between French and English creole speakers). If I had gone by my own inclinations, conditioned by reading standard texts, this question of inter-island variation would never have arisen.

MAXIM TWO: *ACCOUNTABILITY*. INVOLVE THE INFORMANTS IN THE PROCESS OF RESEARCH: DO NOT LIE TO THEM OR OTHERWISE VIOLATE THEIR TRUST. DISCUSS AND NEGOTIATE THE STEPS OF YOUR RESEARCH.

An atmosphere of trust was particularly important in a project where a white researcher worked with Black informants. I never recorded without permission, left the room when the group performed in patois for the video and did not try to elicit patois on other occasions (it is not the variety used in the youth club and certainly not where white members/workers are present). Another important part of my accountability was to acknowledge the racism of white people which was under discussion, including my own. I was not defensive where white people were criticised and did not attempt to dissociate myself, though this was often painful.

When I took part in a role-play, acting the part of a racist interviewer, I accepted their direction (telling me to be more racist) and was thus faithful to their experience rather than my own. The group dictated the style of the video as well as its content and from the beginning we negotiated what it was to be for, which meant me explaining the context of my work (teaching) in detail to them.

MAXIM THREE: RESPECT FOR INFORMANTS' VIEWS. DO NOT ASSUME THESE CAN BE IGNORED OR SET ASIDE AS 'IGNORANT' AND 'NON-EXPERT'. SHOW RESPECT FOR INTERPRETATIONS AT ODDS WITH YOUR OWN.
One area where this was relevant was in discussing the attitudes of the group's parents to patois (usually pretty negative). I tried to present my own view as an alternative conditioned by my social position (I can afford to believe patois is a triumph of the human spirit under conditions of slavery, because I don't have to put up with the stigma of speaking it, which their parents did) and not as 'God's truth'. We considered why people (including their parents, linguists etc.) believe what they do without ascribing particular authority to certain beliefs a priori.

MAXIM FOUR: ACCESSIBILITY. DO NOT WRITE UP RESEARCH JUST FOR LINGUISTS, IN A WAY THAT ENSURES YOUR INFORMANTS CAN NEVER READ IT. IF POSSIBLE, PRODUCE RESULTS IN A FORM THEY CAN MAKE USE OF, AND THROUGH A MEDIUM WITH WHICH THEY FEEL COMFORTABLE.
One of the most dispiriting experiences I had in Southwark was trying to find things on creoles that the group could read. This opened my eyes to the complexity of sociolinguistic writing even on the most entertaining subjects (e.g. Labov's paper on ritual insults which would have interested my informants could they have deciphered it) and to how little of a truly popular nature is written on the subject of language at all.

For younger people like the Southwark group, I feel that writing is not in any case the optimum means of communication. They do not have the habit of non-fiction reading or writing – it could be acquired, but they would not easily come to regard it as 'theirs' in the way TV and radio are. This is why we decided to make a video, though on the face of it language is a very unvisual topic. Video also has the advantage of requiring a highly collaborative effort with people using different skills. It allows a variety of approaches to a subject: role-play, discussion, information given straight to camera. It would not be ideal for every group (and given the scarcity of good equipment, the results are apt to be technically disappointing, as they were in this case) but for young people it is worth considering. The video we eventually produced is useful to me in teaching and to the group who plan to use it in a number of ways: to demonstrate points about racism and Black identity to club trustees with no direct experience, for instance, and to stimulate discussion of language among Black peers.

D

To sum up, democratic research in sociolinguistics requires at least four things:

Deborah
Cameron

1. The research should be perceived as relevant by informants
2. The process of research should be accountable to them
3. The researcher should not present her/himself as an expert in all things whose views are unchallengeable
4. The end-product should be accessible and useful to all who took part.

There is one further point. In democratic research, the *process* should be considered as important as the *product*. I often wonder what happened to the Jets, the Thunderbirds and the Cobras after Labov and his workers left: were they the same, or were they changed? The Southwark group were changed, in their case consciously and with political goals in view. The knowledge they acquired and the questions they asked will last longer and be more valuable than the grainy and inexpert 20-minute tape we collectively produced, however useful it may be. Since sociolinguistic subjects are not rocks or molecules, to be measured objectively and then just walked away from, this is as it should be. We are dealing with people whose consciousness can be altered by what they experience in a research project; and furthermore, we are people ourselves, who have a lot more to learn from our informants than the height of their vowels.

Issues to consider

D5.2

★ Activity

The issues raised by Cameron should be considered throughout your work in sociolinguistics. Responsible data collection is not always an easy matter, however. For example, it can be difficult to collect naturalistic, unselfconscious examples of language use without violating the maxim of 'accountability'. The observer's paradox shows that informants who are aware their language is being recorded often alter their language as a result. Similarly, it can be a challenge to explain what you are interested in to a non-expert group, and also difficult to express your findings in ways which are scholarly and disciplined but also accessible and transparent. All of these considerations require greater imagination in method design and a more careful and considered style of investigation and writing.

Some specific issues for discussion follow.

❑ Can you apply Cameron's maxims to the readings and studies outlined in this book, in order to discover how many of them represent 'data-raids' on communities of people? Specifically, can you do an 'ethical audit' on each of the students' studies reported in Section B? If you find faults, how would you have redesigned the methodologies along more positive ethical principles?

❑ How would you design a fieldwork study in the following areas, while trying to follow ethical principles in your research?

   ❑ an investigation of the transactional language of violent crack cocaine dealers and their clients;

   ❑ an account of the politeness strategies used by people passing through the connections desk of an airport or railway station;

- ❑ a study of the accent patterns or dialectal choices of children in a school playground;
- ❑ an outline of the natural casual conversational strategies of a group of professional sociolinguists.
❑ Do you agree with Cameron's maxims for ethical fieldwork research? Would you add any other considerations, or would you modify any of them? Can you imagine any circumstances in which you would have to choose between one maxim or another? Can you imagine any circumstances in which it would be legitimate to break the maxims?

D6   THE PROCESS OF STANDARDISATION

You will have realised through your reading of this book that sociolinguistics and the study of language change are very closely related. In many ways, sociolinguistics is the modern successor to the foundations of linguistic study in etymology and philology, which were mainly concerned in the nineteenth century with the historical development and influence of languages. In the following article, James Milroy re-evaluates the continuing legacy of earlier attitudes to language change in the light of sociolinguistic insights.

This article has been included here in order to give you a taste of complex sociolinguistic theoretical argument. It uses many of the concepts and terms that you will have encountered in the course of this book, especially in the area of prestige and standardisation (A6, B6, C6 and also B11 and C11). I have found it one of those pieces that takes time to read carefully, but the effort is rewarded with an understanding of an elegant and precise logical discussion.

D6.1   Some new perspectives on sound change: sociolinguistics and the Neogrammarians

James Milroy (reprinted from *Newcastle and Durham Working Papers in Linguistics* 1: 181–205 (1993))

1 Introduction: sociolinguistics and Neogrammarian theory

This paper is about a very traditional topic – the theory of sound change – and its purpose is to work towards an account of sound change that is more explicitly *sociolinguistic* than those that have been used to date. We have elsewhere been concerned chiefly with the social side of this enterprise discussing *speaker variables* such as social class and network (J. Milroy, 1992a: 164–222; Milroy and Milroy, 1992); in this paper, my main focus is on patterns of language, rather than society. I begin with some general comments.

Sound change is probably the most mysterious aspect of change in language, as it appears to have no obvious function or rational motivation. In a change from [e:] to [i:], for example (as in such items as *meet*, *need*, *keen* in the history of English), it is impossible to see any progress or benefit to the language or its speakers – the use of one vowel-sound rather than another is purely arbitrary: there is apparently no profit and no loss. Of all the theoretical questions about language varia-

James
Milroy

tion that we might wish to address, the question of sound change seems to me the weightiest, and the greatest challenge to our powers of explanation.

The traditional apparatus for dealing with sound change is largely derived from, or related to, the late nineteenth-century Neogrammarian movement. Their basic axiom is that sound change is 'regular': sound 'laws' have no exceptions. Thus, when a sound is observed to have 'changed' in a particular lexical item, the regularity principle predicts that it should also have changed in the same way in all other relevant items: for example, items like (general) English *fat*, *cab*, *have* are believed to undergo same particular vowel-change (e.g., front-raising, as in New York City: Labov, 1966) all at the same time. If there is an apparent exception, this will be accounted for by another regular change.

[. . .]

The Neogrammarians were also interested in how 'sound change', in the narrower sense outlined above (i.e., excluding analogy and borrowing), is implemented. One important Neogrammarian claim is that regular sound change is phonetically gradual but lexically abrupt. According to Bloomfield (1933), it proceeds by 'imperceptible degrees'. Thus, the change from Middle English /e:/ to later English /i:/ (in words of the type *meet*, *need*, *keen*) is assumed not to have been sudden: according to this view, speakers pronouncing these words did not make a sudden leap across phonetic space from [e:] to [i:], the change was so slow and so slight at any given time that it was not noticed by speakers. It is also assumed to have affected all relevant items in the same way at the same time: they all start off from [e:] and, after a slow progress, all reach [i:] at the same time. It will be clear in the remainder of this paper that I do not think that this is a plausible scenario for sound change. However, we must first notice that aside from their prominence in recent sociolinguistic discussion (with which I am mainly concerned here) the Neogrammarian axioms are still very much to the fore in several other branches of linguistic inquiry.

[. . .]

Phonetic gradualness appeared to be a feasible proposition to nineteenth-century scholars because of their tendency to separate languages from their speakers and to focus on language as an object – often likening it to a living thing (for a discussion see J Milroy, 1992a: 22–3). When speakers are excluded in this way, it becomes easy to believe that linguistic change is language-internal, independent of speakers and imperceptible. For the Neogrammarians it proceeds 'with blind necessity' (*mit blinder Notwendigkeit*). It is obvious that sociolinguistic approaches, which necessarily deal with speakers, are not very likely to give support to the idea of 'blind necessity', and we shall return to this point in Section 5, below. First we consider the main general characteristics of the Neogrammarian axioms.

The Neogrammarian axioms have at least three characteristics that are worth noticing here:

1. They tend to be dichotomous;
2. They are non-social in character;
3. Although the Neogrammarians recognized the importance of listening to present-day dialects their main sources are written.

D

**James
Milroy**

At various points I shall mention dichotomies relevant to sound change. It is the third characteristic, above, that I should like to consider first.

The Neogrammarians and nineteenth- to early twentieth-century scholars generally depended on documentary records of (often ancient) languages and could not adequately observe language in the community as we do today. Thus, patterns of linguistic change that they identified (by using the comparative method for the most part) consisted of completed or nearly completed changes in languages that were usually definable as discrete entities (Sanskrit, Gothic, Old Church Slavonic and so on): they could not identify change in progress at early stages and in localized varieties (such as New York City or Belfast). Thus, they did not actually *know* whether sound change was implemented in a phonetically gradual manner: phonetic gradualness was a hypothesis. For similar reasons, social explanations could not be used except in the most generalized ways, and as late as the mid-twentieth century, American structuralists were still assuming that social explanations were not usually feasible. Indeed, quite recently, Lass (1987: 34–5) has dismissed 'external' (i.e., socially or politically-based) explanations as inherently unsatisfactory. Thus, the orthodox non-social view of language change is still very much alive.

Present-day sociolinguistic research differs from the Neogrammarian position in a number of fundamental respects. These involve the data-base available for study and the methods used to study the data-base. For example, scholars now have access to bilingual and multilingual speech communities, in which cross-language patterns of variation can be studied. These approaches strongly question the principle that linguistic change is best studied by reference to monolingual states, as the Neogrammarians and others[1] have assumed. Most relevant here, however, is research on social dialectology following the pattern set by Labov (1966) in New York City. Studies of this kind do not focus on whole languages, but on localized varieties in regional speech communities. It is in the localized variety, rather than in the 'language' (English, French, Spanish etc) that they identify changes in progress. The contrast with orthodox historical methodology is quite evident here. In my own work, I have additionally tried to combine this type of research with a theory of language standardization (following Haugen, 1966 and others), to which I return in Section 5, below. Amongst other things I would like to know how changes originating in localized varieties of the kind studied in the 1960s and 1970s by Labov, Trudgill (1974) and others, succeed (or do not succeed) in entering supralocal or standard varieties of the kind studied by the Neogrammarians. In speech community researches, of course, we are not dealing with well-defined linguistic entities that can be regarded as uniform, but with highly variable states that do not have clearly defined boundaries. Much of our effort has been directed towards developing methods of analysing and describing these highly variable states. Thus, there are clearly great differences in data-base and method between Neogrammarian and sociolinguistic studies of sound change.

[. . .]

For these reasons it is quite illuminating to consider what we might have thought about sound change if recent studies of change in progress had been the first studies of sound change ever undertaken. Suppose that the Neogrammarians had never

James
Milroy

existed and their axioms about sound change had never been proposed, and suppose also that our knowledge of language change was based entirely on recent
sociolinguistic studies of change in regional non-standard speech communities –
would we then consider the Neogrammarian axioms to be fundamental in our enterprise? If we had never heard of them, would we ever think of them as primary
principles – and would we follow out our argumentation in the Neogrammarian
framework? I shall suggest that the answer to this is no – and, further, that the
orthodox framework of argumentation is not capable of dealing adequately with
the phenomena that we actually do observe.

Sociolinguistic findings have in effect laid the groundwork of a new kind of
discourse about language change, in which some of the old axioms are no longer
axiomatic and in which the questions that we ask about sound change are a new
set of questions, overlapping with the old ones but in a different distribution. In
this new perspective the question whether sound change is phonetically gradual or
sudden is no longer fundamental. What *is* fundamental in sociolinguistic inquiries
is how we define sound change itself and, further, how we locate a sound change
when it is in progress.

[. . .]

2 Towards a sociolinguistic modelling of language change

My account here is based on a sociolinguistic approach to the study of language
change that I have been developing over the years in collaboration with Lesley
Milroy (J and L Milroy, 1985b; J Milroy, 1992a, 1993; L and J Milroy, 1992),
and which was partly motivated in the first place by my own dissatisfaction with
well-known binary distinctions of types of language change ('blind' sound change
v borrowing, conditioned *v* unconditional change, etc). This model is differentiated from other sociolinguistic models by its insistence on the methodological pri-
ority of the study of language *maintenance* over the study of language change[2]. It
is assumed that a linguistic change is embedded in a context of language (or dialect)
maintenance. The degree to which change is admitted will depend on the degree
of internal cohesion of the community (the extent to which it is bound by 'strong
ties', which resist change), and change from outside will be admitted to the extent
that there are large numbers of *weak ties* with outsiders. It also follows that if a
change persists in the system, it has again to be *maintained* by social acceptance
and social pressure; thus, we need to explain, not only how communities resist
change, but also how a change is maintained in the system after it has been accepted.

[. . .]

2.1 Linguistic change as change in community norms

A second issue, which constitutes a sub-theme in this paper, is the place of *sound*
change within more general patterns of language shift and language change. What we
have traditionally called sound changes have usually been represented as taking
place at the level of the classical phonemic segment – for example, the change from
[e:] to [i:] in English cited above. In the words of Bloomfield (1933): 'phonemes

James
Milroy

change'. But we must consider the possibility that sound change is not actually triggered at this level: a sound change perceived by observers at the segmental level may be a secondary, and not a primary, phenomenon: although we can observe it at the micro-level (e.g., as a change from [e:] to [i:]), it may be one of a number of a low-level manifestations of a change, or a shift, that originates at a more general level of language use. I have approached this point elsewhere by proposing that linguistic change in general is a result of changes in speaker-agreement on the *norms* of usage in speech communities (J Milroy, 1992a: 91), and there is plenty of anecdotal evidence that a whole 'dialect' can die out as another 'dialect' replaces it, leaving only a few traces behind (see below for some examples). It is fairly clear that the much greater access to spoken language that we now have gives us the opportunity to follow up such questions much more thoroughly than was possible for earlier scholars, and there is much scope for future research on this issue, using *inter alia* instrumental techniques and benefiting from advances in phonological theory.

3 Sound change in historical linguistics

In dealing with sound change of the traditional type, the first substantive point that we need to notice is that there is, in reality, no such thing. Speech 'sounds' do not physically change: what happens is that in the course of time one sound is substituted for another; speakers of a given dialect gradually and variably begin to use sound X in environments where speakers formerly used sound Y. Historical linguistic scholars then observe the result of this essentially social process and apply the term *sound change* to the phenomenon. As Andersen (1989) points out, what historical linguists actually observe in data from the past is not a sound change, but a 'diachronic correspondence' between language states at two or more points in time (formally this is precisely the same thing as a *synchronic* correspondence between two or more states of language at the same time). In effect, they use a system-based term (sound change) for a speaker-based event in time.

   [. . .]

4 Social aspects of sound change

We now turn to questions which seem to be more fundamental than the question whether the implementation of sound change is phonetically gradual or not. Among these questions the meaning of the term 'sound change' is crucial. We have argued elsewhere that it is not explainable as a wholly linguistic phenomenon: it is also inherently and necessarily a *social* phenomenon in that it comes about because speakers in conversation bring it about, speakers often have very strong feelings about it, and it is manifested in speaker-usage. It isn't languages that change – it is speakers who change languages. Such a view is obviously a very long distance away from the Neogrammarian notion that sound change is 'blind'. It does not make sense, from this perspective, to say that sound-change is phonetically gradual either. But it is definitely socially gradual: it passes from speaker to speaker and from group to group, and it is this *social* gradualness that sociolinguists attempt to trace by their quantitative methods.

**James
Milroy**

It seems that scholars in the past may sometimes have equated phonetic gradualness with social gradualness; that is, when they have said that a change is phonetically gradual, they have 'really meant' that it spreads gradually in the social dimension – from speaker to speaker. On the other hand, as Ohala (1993: 266) points out, many have certainly believed in the imperceptibility of change – the idea that sound change takes place in phonetic steps that are too small for the ear to detect. It is surely clear now that this is a mystical view of change, more appropriate to a belief-system than to a science, for, as Ohala also points out, we must surely accept that sound change by definition is implemented in phonetic steps that are large enough to be detected. If this were not so, we could not detect it in progress, as Labov claims we can, nor could speakers imitate it. And if it is not detectable why should we call it a sound change anyway?

The principle of social gradualness supersedes the binary division between 'regular' sound change and lexical diffusion that Labov (1992) discusses. Both processes are socially gradual, both are abrupt replacement patterns, and both can be shown to be regular in some sense. The difference between them in terms of phonetic change now becomes one of greater or lesser phonetic distance between State A (before the change) and State B (after the change). What we have traditionally called gradual phonetic change differs from lexical diffusion (following Labov's account above) in that the new form differs only slightly from the older one, whereas in lexical diffusion (as studied so far) it differs markedly. Thus, from this perspective, the two kinds of sound change are not two *opposing* types, as Labov claims. In phonetic terms, they are two ends of a continuum, with slight phonetic difference at one end and gross phonetic difference at the other.

The axiomatic distinction between regular sound change and lexical diffusion is further undermined by the fact that, as my own work and that of other sociolinguists has amply demonstrated, there is no evidence to support the Neogrammarian assumption that in regular sound change all items in the affected set change at the same time. On the contrary, sound changes have normally been observed to spread gradually through the lexicon. If we had never heard of the Neogrammarians, it seems very unlikely that we would now propose these two categories as axiomatic opposites. As sociolinguists we may now be inclined to propose some sub-divisions of types of sound change – some new taxonomies – but they will presumably be socially-based and thus quite different from the traditional taxonomies. But we must be careful not to propose premature classifications, and I am therefore quite cautious here.

4.1 Varying patterns of change

I shall return below to social processes, but first I would like to observe that sound-change is not necessarily a unilinear process either, and this becomes especially clear if we take a socially- or speaker-oriented point of view. It isn't just a matter of A becoming B in a unidirectional way in the course of time. What Le Page and Tabouret-Keller (1985) have called focusing and diffusion and what I have sometimes called convergence and divergence, are also patterns of change.

James
Milroy

There are other patterns also: at a sub-phonemic level, sound-change can be manifested by reduction in the number of allophonic variants (as in outer-city v inner-city Belfast: J Milroy, 1982) – a trend towards simplification. At much more general levels there are patterns of dialect displacement – displacement of one dialect by another which is, for some reason, socially dominant at some particular time. For example, there is evidence from recordings of persons born around 1860 which can be interpreted as indicating that much New Zealand English in the nineteenth century was southern British in type (favoured by males), and that it was displaced by an Australasian type (favoured by females) with some effects of mixing and residue. The gradual displacement of heavily inflected West Midand dialects of Middle English by weakly inflected East Midland dialects is another example (J Milroy, 1992b) – one which led to morphological simplification of the grammar of English more generally. Changes from more heterogeneous to more homogeneous states (including the process of standardization) are also patterns of linguistic change – even though they are seldom recognized as such in orthodox historical linguistics.

4.2 Changing norms of language

According to our social view, language is a normative phenomenon. The norms of language are maintained and enforced by social pressures. It is customary to think of these norms as standardizing norms – norms that are codified and legislated for, and enforced in an impersonal way by the institutions of society. But the fact that we can recognize different dialects of a language demonstrates that other norms exist apart from the standard ones, and that these norms are observed by speakers and maintained by communities often in opposition to standardizing norms. It is convenient to call these *community norms* or *vernacular norms*. I have tried to show (J Milroy, 1992a: 81–4) that these norms manifest themselves at different levels of generality. Some of them, for example, characterize the dialect as a whole and are recognized by outsiders as markers of that dialect. Others, however, are hardly accessible except by quantitative methods and may function within the community as markers of internal social differences, for example, gender-difference. We have elsewhere demonstrated stable markers of gender-difference in the community (L Milroy, 1982; J Milroy, 1981, 1992a), in which the pattern is maintained over both the generations studied. It follows from this that the stable speech community is not one in which everyone speaks the same way, but one in which there is consensus on a pattern of stable variation. Another way of putting it is to say that community norms can be variable norms – in contrast to standard norms, which are invariant.

All these observations suggest certain important modifications to orthodox views of the nature of linguistic change, and these ultimately have to do with the definition of what actually constitutes a sound change, as distinct from synchronic variation. Just as language stability depends on speaker-agreement on the (variable) norms of language, so linguistic change is brought about by changes in agreement on norms. In the solidary group, which agrees on a stable variation pattern, a linguistic change in progress will show up as a disturbance of this consensus pattern. Sometimes (when the direction of change has not yet been determined) this pattern may seem to be rather inconsistent and unpredictable: in Belfast we found in the outer city a number of patterns which did not seem to have much consistency to them. We interpret this kind of pattern as indicating the break-up of consensus norms of the kind we found in the inner city (see further J Milroy, 1992a: 105–109). At other times – presumably when the direction of change has been more clearly set – there will be a regular social pattern in terms of age, sex, social class and other social variables, and it is through this that we will recognize linguistic change in progress. It should also be noted that the starting point and the end-point of change are not necessarily uniform states. As I tried to show in a paper on /h/-dropping (J Milroy, 1983), a change can persist as a variable state for seven or eight centuries without ever going to 'completion' in the traditional sense.

[. . .]

4.3 Speaker-innovation and linguistic change

The distinction between innovation and change leads, as we have seen, to an associated distinction – the distinction between speaker innovation, on the one hand, and linguistic change, on the other. We have suggested (Milroy and Milroy, 1985b) that the terms *innovation* and *change* should reflect a conceptual distinction: an innovation is an act of the speaker, whereas a change is manifested within the language system. It is speakers and not languages, that innovate. It should also be noted that an innovation, when it occurs, must be unstructured and 'irregular' and not describable by quantitative or statistical methods. It may be observable, but when observed, it is not known that it will lead to a change and is probably thought to be an error or defective usage of some kind (Trudgill, 1986b, discusses such a case in Norwich – labio-dental /r/). It is also quite clear that this distinction between innovation and change has not been sufficiently carefully or consistently observed in historical linguistics, and that many discussions about linguistic change have been in reality about linguistic innovation. Indeed, partly as a result of this conceptual confusion, questions about how linguistic change is implemented have often appealed to phenomena that have to do with synchronic variability rather than change itself. The appearance of phonetic gradualness in the data (as discussed above) is a case in point.

From a speaker-based perspective, we can think of sound-change as moving gradually through a population of speakers, assuming a regular sociolinguistic pattern, rather than postulating gradual movement within the language system (e.g., phonetic gradualness). Quantitative statements do not show how innovations occur; however, they can be interpreted as manifesting the *socially* gradual diffusion of changes. Bloomfield's account of how change may come about through gradual favouring of new variants at the expense of older ones is consistent with this position: 'Historically, we picture phonetic change as a gradual favoring of some non-distinctive features and a disfavoring of others (1933: 365)'. Although he was defending the Neogrammarians, Bloomfield's position is in certain respects also consistent

James
Milroy

with that of lexical diffusionists, as it can be disputed whether the variants involved must always be 'non-distinctive'. Bloomfield's position does not require an assumption of phonetic gradualness: it can apply equally well regardless of whether the two phonetic variants involved are closely similar or grossly different from one another, i.e., whether they are represented as resulting from gradual phonetic movement or from abrupt replacement – it is still a gradual favouring of new variants. But this gradual favouring is a speaker-based social process, rather than an intralinguistic one. It must be speakers rather than languages who 'favour' the new variants. I shall return to this point.

It should also be noted that, although we sometimes say that sound-change can now be 'observed' in progress by sociolinguistic methods, this is a loose formulation which is not strictly accurate. Locating change in progress depends on extensive (normally quantitative) analysis of data that has been collected from a speech community, and the direction and patterning of a change in a monolingual community cannot usually be reliably determined until much careful analysis has been carried out. So we don't just 'observe' it in the community. However, as I have pointed out above and elsewhere (Milroy and Milroy, 1985b), we cannot *successfully* observe innovations either. To put it more precisely, although we can in principle observe linguistic innovations, we do not know when we observe them whether they are innovations that will lead to changes. It must be assumed that the vast majority of innovations are ephemeral and lead nowhere.

It is, however, clear that for a speaker-innovation to become a change, it must be adopted by some community. It must pass from one speaker to others. Thus, the adoption of a linguistic change depends at the speaker-level on a process of *borrowing*. It is appropriate therefore to consider more closely here the effect of our social approach on another Neo-grammarian dichotomy – the distinction between sound change and borrowing.

4.4 Innovation, change and 'borrowing'

The sound change/borrowing distinction is sometimes formulated as a distinction between 'internally' and 'externally' motivated change. This dichotomy has certainly been prominent in the work of many scholars, and although it is a well motivated distinction in certain respects (in vocabulary replacement, for example), it can be problematic at the level of phonological/ morphological structure (for an especially clear discussion of important difficulties see Dorian, 1993). In sociolinguistic investigations, what we call 'sound changes' in progress are often traceable to borrowings from neighbouring dialects. Bloomfield himself, in his defence of the Neogrammarians, cites an example that happens to show very clearly the difficulty of drawing the distinction between sound change and borrowing as it relates to gradual and abrupt change.

> In various parts of Europe, for instance, the old tongue-tip trill [r] has been replaced . . . by a uvular trill. . . . Aside from its spread by borrowing, the new habit . . . could have originated only as a sudden replacement of one trill by another. A replacement of this sort is surely different from the gradual and imperceptible alterations of phonetic change (1933: 390).

D

James Milroy

From a sociolinguistic perspective, the difficulties with Bloomfield's assumptions here are very striking. First, the 'origin' of this abrupt change is equated with the change itself; that is, what Bloomfield calls a change is what I have called a speaker-innovation, and what has to be explained (in Bloomfield's account) is the phonetic event of abrupt replacement, not the adoption of this replacement by a community. Second, it is assumed that the spread of the change is by 'borrowing' and implied that the spread therefore *does not involve* sudden replacement – this is said to be 'aside from its spread by borrowing'. But in fact, whether we are dealing with some original event or with a concatenation of 'borrowings', each single event is equally abrupt – 'a sudden replacement of one trill by another'. In other words, it is possible to argue that each single event of 'borrowing' into a new speech community is just as much an innovation as the presumed original event in the 'original' speech community (and even that some of these events are independent innovations). Furthermore, if we accept the Bloomfieldian distinction, we may be inclined to believe that we can locate the 'original' innovation in some specific community (perhaps Parisian French), when there can be no guarantee at all that this is the original 'sound change' – the *Urquelle* of all the 'borrowings'; we cannot be certain that it had not previously been imported from somewhere else where it was 'more original' – and so backwards ad infinitum with the origin continuously receding and eluding our grasp. In other words, the distinction on which Bloomfield depends here (true sound change *v* phonological borrowing) is poorly motivated.

It is also possible that abrupt events of the kind envisaged by Bloomfield can occur without ever having a long-term effect on the speech community. Thus, a speaker-innovation of uvular [ʁ] may happen again and again without resulting in a linguistic change in the speech community concerned. An innovation is not in itself a change, and it is linguistic *change*, not innovation, that we are trying to explain.

As I have noted above, many consonant alternations that have been studied are manifestly of this sudden replacement type: for example, alternation of alveolar with dental stops and alternation of dental fricatives with zero in inner-city Belfast (J Milroy, 1981, etc). In the work of Trudgill (1974), Mees (1990), Kingsmore (forthcoming) and others, alternation of [t] with the glottal stop (intervocalically and word-finally) is a particularly clear example of sudden replacement and a very common one in British English. In recent years it has been noticed that this 'glottalling' (Wells, 1982: 261) is spreading rapidly in British English, and we hope to investigate this further. The work that has so far been carried out, however, raises a number of issues about the origin, spread and social correlates of glottalling that are relevant to the question of speaker-innovation and linguistic change. Here I can only summarize the main points briefly.

According to Andresen (1968, cited in Kingsmore, forthcoming), the earliest references to the glottal stop are from central Scotland in the 1860s, where it was noticed by Alexander Graham Bell. Subsequently there are references to it in various parts of England, including the London area in the early 1900s. Therefore, it is suggested that from an origin in Central Scotland it spread rapidly to locations in England. This raises some obvious sociolinguistic questions, such as the following: Why should Central Scotland have the kind of 'prestige' required for

D

**James
Milroy**

this rapid spread to England? How could the glottal stop have become so stereo-typical of London and East Anglian English in such a short time? Additionally, from the perspective of this paper, there are other questions to be asked. These are: 1) does the evidence show that the 'original' innovation was in Central Scotland? 2) does the evidence show that the glottal stop diffused by borrowing from Central Scotland to several other places in the period 1860–1900?

The answer to both of these questions must be no. There is no evidence to support a positive answer to either. When the phenomenon was noticed in Central Scotland, it was already a well-established variant that was socially salient. If it had been at a very early stage of development with no social salience, it would not have been noticed – not even by such an excellent observer as Bell. Therefore, the origin of the glottal stop is earlier than 1860. The fact that it is well established in the Ulster Scots of County Antrim suggests (but does not prove) that it may even pre-date the Plantation of Ulster in the seventeenth century. Taking all these matters into account, it seems most unlikely that it spread to other dialects (including London English) from Central Scots. There may be an ultimate common origin for the glottal stop in some variety of early Modern English, or there may be multiple origins. The point of primary innovation and the speaker-innovator are irrecoverable. However, as I have tried to show here, drawing a careful distinction between innovation and change makes a great difference to how we interpret these phenomena.

In many of the cases discussed (including some aspects of the spread of glottalling in modern English), the most immediate explanation for the changes observed is dialect contact – externally motivated change. For Bloomfield and the Neogrammarians, this is not sound-change proper: as we have seen they tended to equate sound-change with innovation internal to the 'dialect' concerned. If Bloomfield's view is accepted, it follows that much of our sociolinguistic research has not been about sound-change at all, but about the diffusion of changes through 'borrowing'. But as I have already pointed out, the logically prior distinction between speaker-innovation and linguistic change greatly alters our understanding of this Neogrammarian distinction.

The main implication of the innovation/change distinction here is that when an innovation is taken up by a speech community, the process involved is funda-mentally a borrowing process, i.e. the implementation of a sound change depends on the 'borrowing' of an innovation: all sound change is implemented by being passed from speaker to speaker, and it is not a linguistic change until it has been adopted by more than one speaker. Indeed, perhaps we need a stronger require-ment: a change is not a change until it has assumed a social pattern of some kind in a speech community. To put it in another way – all sound-change must be socially conditioned, simply because those so-called changes that arise spontaneously are not actually changes: they are *innovations*, and they do not become changes until they have assumed a social pattern in the community. If, as often happens, these innovations are not adopted by some community, then they do not become changes at all. It is obviously important to try to explain how spontaneous innovations arise (and much of our intralinguistic research has been in reality about innovations), but this is not the central question that we seek to answer, which is: how do we specify the conditions under which some of these innovations, and not others, are

James Milroy

admitted into linguistic systems as linguistic changes? From this perspective, a linguistic change is by definition a sociolinguistic phenomenon (it has both linguistic and social aspects): it comes about for reasons of marking social identity, stylistic difference and so on. If it does not carry these social meanings, then it is not a linguistic change. Similarly, if we think in traditional terms about 'sound change' and 'borrowing', we must accept that all sound change depends on a process of borrowing. Change is negotiated between speakers, who 'borrow' new forms from one another.

I have discussed the innovation/change distinction more fully elsewhere (J Milroy, 1992a, b). Here, we need to recall that we have to determine whether and in what manner the innovation (say, a uvular [ʁ]) will feed into the system as a patterned change. As long as it occurs as a variant, it is possible for it to feed into the system in this way, but although there are billions of occasions on which this is possible, it may not happen at all – even when favourable structural conditions exist in the language. For the change to take place it is necessary for the social conditions to be favourable. Thus, if we explain the phonetic and other intra-linguistic conditions that lead to this possible change, we have not thereby explained why this particular change took place, and not some other change: what we have explained are the linguistic circumstances that made possible a speaker-innovation. We have not explained why it entered the linguistic system at some particular time and place and in particular social circumstances. This, of course, is the actuation problem itself (why did it happen at this particular time and place, and not at some other time and place?). This is a problem that is not ever likely to be completely solved, but our empirical studies of language in speech communities have certainly enabled us to get considerably closer to it than was previously possible. From all this, we can reasonably conclude that, in micro-level studies of sound change, the traditional distinction between 'regular sound change' and 'borrowing' is otiose, and to apply it at this level simply leads to confusion.

We have also tried to specify elsewhere (Milroy and Milroy, 1985b) what the social conditions for linguistic change are likely to be, arguing that as close social ties tend to maintain stability, a large number of weak ties must be present for linguistic changes to be communicated between people. I believe that the 'weak-tie' model of change can lead us to more satisfactory accounts of change in many traditional areas of interest than have been offered to date, for example in the history of English and in some aspects of Indo-European studies (and I had these things in mind when I embarked on empirical sociolinguistic research in the first place). Here my main point is that a linguistic change is a change in linguistic structure which necessarily has a social distribution. If it does not manifest such a distribution, it should not be counted as a linguistic change.

5 Some broader perspectives

[. . .]

It has become very clear that the historical linguistic tradition has itself been greatly influenced by the consequences of living in a standard language culture, and this has affected judgements on the implementation and diffusion of sound change. The main influence is what I have elsewhere called *the ideology of the standard language* (Milroy and Milroy 1985a). The principles of historical linguistics have been largely based on the study of uniform states and standard or near-standard languages. Therefore, changes have frequently been envisaged as originating in 'languages' (well-defined entities such as English and French) or in fairly widely spoken 'dialects' (i.e., in linguistic abstractions), rather than in speech communities.

[. . .]

From a sociolinguistic perspective, standard languages are not 'normal' languages. They are created by the imposition of political and military power; hence the sound-patterns in them and the changes that come about in these sound patterns do *not* come about *through blind necessity*, as the Neogrammarians argued, and they are not wholly explainable by reference to phenomena internal to the *structure* of language. These language states are planned by human beings and maintained through prescription (Milroy and Milroy 1985a). The idea that there are discrete languages that can be treated as if they were physical entities is in itself a consequence of standardization and literacy – discreteness of languages is not inherent in the nature of 'language' as a phenomenon. Standard languages are carefully constructed in order to appear as if they are discrete linguistic entities – and the ideology of standardization causes people to believe that they are indeed discrete physical entities – whereas dialects and languages that have not been standardized have fuzzy boundaries and are indeterminate. The idea that the sound changes differentiating these well-defined socially-constructed entities must always come about *blindly* and independently of socially-based human intervention is, on the face of it, absurd: it is another consequence of believing in the ideology of standardization. Standard languages are not merely the structural entities that linguists have believed them to be: they are also socio-political entities dependent on powerful ideologies which promote 'correctness' and uniformity of usage (it is likely that they are in some senses more regular than non-standard forms, but further empirical research is needed into this). Thus, although regularity of the Neogrammarian kind remains as part of the general picture, it can no longer provide an adequate backdrop for the study of the origins of sound changes in the variable language states that are found in real speech communities.

Another reason for this inadequacy is that whereas standard languages (being idealizations) provide the investigator with relatively 'clean' data which have already been largely normalized, the vernaculars that we actually encounter in the speech community are relatively intractable: the data we encounter is to a greater extent 'dirty' data. To the extent that the data-base of sociolinguistic investigations presents itself as irregular and chaotic, progress in understanding linguistic change will largely depend on our ability to cope with these 'dirty' data and expose the systematicity behind them. To the extent that traditional thinking has been affected by the 'standard ideology', it has supported the emphasis on the uniform, unilinear and normalized language histories which have dominated the tradition. Now we may be better able to understand these histories for what they actually are.

Issues to consider

D6.2

★ Activity

James
Milroy

In general, standardisation and the ideology of standardisation are fascinating areas to investigate. Some standardisation is a result of official and quite explicit language planning by governments or other authorities. Certain dialects or individual features are adopted, codified and promoted, and others are proscribed as 'errors'. The consequences of such language planning are especially noticeable and important when it is applied oppressively by autocratic regimes and is resisted by local speech communities. In areas where language or dialect is especially regarded as a marker of ethnic identity, there will be interesting conflicts to be explored. Attempts in history to eradicate 'Scotticisms' in English writing, or the language of the Basques by Franco's fascist regime in Spain, or the promotion of modern Hebrew in Israel, or the non-recognition of African-American English as a grammatical code are all situations that would reward reading and research.

Some practical suggestions for exploration follow.

❏ Concrete evidence for historical language change is available even in the absence of a time machine as a sociolinguistic tool. For example, documents from the past, whether literary, legal, ecclesiastical or practical, can make very useful comparisons with the equivalent modern texts. The modern English spelling system largely represents a medieval system of pronunciation. You could list as many words as you can think of which are no longer pronounced 'as seen', and use your reading to discover when their pronunciations changed.

❏ Milroy emphasises the innovations of speakers and communities of speakers as a major factor in linguistic change. The rate of influence and change depends on the degree of creativity of the individual and their range of social connections. Do you know someone who is linguistically creative or adept at telling jokes or stories or imitating voices, for example? Are their innovations likely to be taken up by others? You could also investigate the enormous amount of creative uses of language in everyday conversation, where puns, rhyme, impromptu jokes, poetic metaphor and other witticisms occur constantly. Alternatively, you could list the buzzwords that people have adopted this year in your area or community and trace where they come from.

❏ It is possible to investigate apparent change in time by comparing the language of old and young people from the same community. Select a particular dimension of language (an accent variation, the use of particular words or constructions, prevalence of certain idioms or proverbs, and so on) and devise a means of comparing a set of grandparents and their grandchildren.

MEN'S AND WOMEN'S NARRATIVES

D7

Many recent studies of genderlects and gendered practices in language use have moved away from looking at differences in word choice and are instead exploring the different discursive strategies used by men and women. In this article, for example, Janet Holmes uses some real examples of story-telling to draw out patterns of narrative organisation.

Issues in language and gender which you studied in A7, B7 and C7 are developed here. You could also compare the data presented in B10, and B13 and C13.

Story-telling in New Zealand women's and men's talk

Janet Holmes (reprinted from Ruth Wodak (ed.) *Gender and Discourse*, London: Sage, 1997: 263–93)

[. . .]

It has been suggested that New Zealand is a particularly gendered culture, 'a culture in which the structures of masculinity and femininity are central to the formation of society as a whole' (James and Saville-Smith, 1989: 6). Gender has been identified by feminist sociologists as the major preoccupation of New Zealand culture. Because of the pervasive influence of symbols of the pioneer origins of New Zealand Pakeha society such as 'man alone' and 'dependent women', it is suggested that women and men are more effectively trapped in gender roles still in New Zealand than in European societies such as Britain.

[. . .]

Stories provide one way in which women and men construct their gender identity. Within a social constructionist framework, language is viewed as 'a set of strategies for negotiating the social landscape' (Crawford, 1995: 17). Language is the site of the cultural production of gender identity: subjectivity is discursively constituted (see also Weedon, 1987; Butler, 1990). In other words, each person's subjectivity is constructed and gendered within the social, economic and political discourse to which they are exposed (Weedon, 1987: 21). Using this approach people operate within subject positions, positions created and sustained by the use of language (Fairclough, 1989; 1995a); speakers are regarded as constantly 'doing gender', and the different ways in which women and men behave are accounted for by the gendered social contexts in which they operate.

[. . .]

In the stories analysed in this chapter, I will show that New Zealand women and men tend to construct relatively conservative gender identities for themselves within the social contexts they select for their narrative settings, though there are also indications that feminist ideology has had some influence on women's perceptions of appropriate gender identities.

[. . .]

Through their choice of story topics, as well as their different treatment of these topics, New Zealand women and men construct themselves as differently gendered.

Female identity

Coates (1996) points to the importance of narrative in women's lives as a way of keeping in touch with friends. For women, updating friends on the ongoing story of one's life is an important component in 'doing friendship'. The narratives in the New Zealand corpus illustrate this very well. Without exception, at least one, and typically most, of the women's stories in each of the recorded conversations functioned to update the other person on recent events in the narrator's life (cf.

Janet
Holmes

Linde, 1993). But, of course, when we update someone on our life story we are inevitably selective. We can choose to focus on successes and events that have gone smoothly, for example, or we can focus on disasters and worries. Similarly, we can present ourselves as 'in charge', controlling events, or as the hapless victim of circumstances or luck. The aspect of this selection process that I want to highlight in this section is the ways in which women and men use stories to 'do gender'. In a variety of ways, the stories told by the New Zealand women functioned to construct or reinforce a particular kind of gendered identity for the narrator. This identity was typically a rather conservative one, even when the protagonist was a professional woman working full-time.

[. . .]

'We tried to go to the pool today'

This narrative occurs in a conversation between two close friends, Helen and Joan, both middle-aged Pakeha women pursuing professional careers. The first part of the conversation consists of Joan describing her newly established cottage garden. She then asks, 'but tell me about Jason I was thinking about him as I came up.' Jason is Helen's father who has been very ill. The story 'We tried to go to the pool today' is embedded within a long discussion of Jason's state of health, including a description of ways in which Helen is looking after him (with visits and meals), what his doctors have recommended, and so on. The conversation develops into a general discussion of the way doctors treat old people, and then moves to a discussion of Helen's mother's final illness. It provides an excellent example of the way women's conversations often move easily back and forward between descriptions of specific experiences and discussion of more general issues, and particularly of the way a specific story can lead into a more abstract discussion, as described by Coates (1996).

The story which is the focus of discussion is an account of Helen's attempt to take herself and her children to the swimming pool (see Appendix 2). The pool story is a classic narrative, recapitulating past experience using a sequence of temporally ordered clauses to do so (Labov, 1972a: 359–60). Its structure is in some respects reminiscent of that of many fairy stories: the protagonist makes three attempts to achieve her goal and succeeds only on the third attempt. It can be summarized as follows:

1 I wanted to go to aqua-fitness at the Kilbirnie Pool – but didn't succeed.
2 I tried the Freyburg pool – but that wasn't satisfactory.
3 I decided to go to the Karori pool:
    (a) on the way we stopped in and saw Jason;
    (b) Andrea did seven lengths of the pool.
4 Resolution: it all ended up fine.
5 Coda: Jason's state of health.

The resolution completes both subsection 3 and subsection 3(a), each of which could be regarded as mini-stories, as well as rounding off the whole story. The coda relates the story back to the larger response to Joan's initial inquiry about Jason's health.

A superficial look at this story might leave one wondering what was its point. The most important 'point' is far from explicit: the evaluative component is deeply embedded in the context within which the story is told. At one level, its point is simply to bring Joan up to date on what Helen has been doing: it is a story about a visit to the swimming pool. At another level it is one component in a complex answer to Joan's inquiry about Jason's health. At yet another level (the level on which I am focusing), the story constructs Helen's identity as a 'good' daughter and a 'good' mother. Both these identities are very important to her. Of three daughters, she is the only one who lives near her father; and she is a solo parent. Though in many respects her life does not conform to the norms of conservative New Zealand society, in these two areas she clearly strives to so conform. She takes her roles as 'daughter' and 'mother' very seriously, and likes others to recognize and appreciate the extent to which she meets society's prescriptions in these areas. This message is conveyed in the story 'We tried to go to the pool today', but it is not always conveyed explicitly. It is also worth noting that Joan is a much more conservative woman than Helen in a number of respects, and it is probably not accidental that she is the audience for this particular story. (As Linde, 1993: 72, points out, participants must agree on the evaluative component of a narrative.)

Helen first presents herself as a good mother, concerned for her children's comfort and well-being. This is most obvious in the following three utterances:

so we gathered up Susie and everybody and their togs . . .
it's lane swimming only which is no good for the little kids . . .
and actually it was rather sort of muggy and hot to be driving round Wellington with a
    car full of children . . .

While the message is easily inferred from the latter two utterances, it is not quite so clear from the first. In fact, this utterance indicates Helen's willingness to take an extra child Susie on this outing, thus providing a playmate for her youngest child, Andrea, another indication of her thoughtful mothering.

Helen also constructs her identity as a good daughter. Here the most obviously relevant sections of the story are:

so on the way to the Karori pool we stopped in and saw Jason . . .
and I said why don't you stay with Jason and make him some lunch
so we went in and visited him
and I said Annie'll stay with you and make you some lunch
and she gets on quite- and she chats away with Jason . . .
so she stayed with him for an hour . . .
so Annie stayed there and made Jason some lunch
and then we went back afterwards . . .

These utterances represent Helen as looking after her father's needs: he is provided with the companionship of his granddaughter, with whom we are told he gets on well, and also with his lunch.

More subtly, Helen constructs her identity as good mother and daughter in the account she provides of the way she 'manages' Annie, and in the analysis she presents of Annie's relationship with Jason. Annie is a somewhat difficult teenager, as Joan knows, and as indicated earlier in this story by her reluctance to cooperate with Helen's attempts to rescue their outing:

so then we get I don't want to go to – Annie didn't want to go to Freyburg . . .
and Annie was saying I don't want to go in will you drop me home

Helen presents herself skilfully persuading her daughter to look after her grandfather's needs, and, at the same time, she constructs a much more positive identity both for her difficult daughter and for her rather grouchy father:

and she gets on quite- and she chats away with Jason
and they have quite a nice . . .
well she's good with him too
I don't know they sort of get along nicely
and um better than the other two do really you know
she sort of somehow gets it right with him
and he seems to make an effort too

Similarly, the picture Helen presents of her youngest daughter is extremely positive:

Andrea did SEVEN lengths
with a little breaks in between
but she's never swum a length of that pool before
and she just suddenly discovered she could swim a length [laughs]
and got so keen she didn't want to stop
she said I'll just do another one and then I'll do another one
so that was quite sweet she looked like a [laughs]
s- Liz was there with her friend John
and he said she looked like a goldfish you [laughs] know
s- (there's) a little head (rolling) in the water
[laughs] and legs sort of sagging in the water o-
and breaststroking away you know
but she was obviously really sort of getting a kick out of the achievement

There is firstly an explicitly admiring account of Andrea's achievement, but, in addition, this section of the story achieves its effect through the use of diminutives and attenuators which construct Andrea's identity as a small, sweet, endearing little girl. The positive effect of the explicit phrase *quite sweet* is further supported and developed by attenuating words such as *just* and *little*, the pragmatic particles *sort of* and *you know*, the adverb particle *away* in the phrase *breaststroking away* and the repetition of phrases and syntactic patterns (*I'll just do another one and then I'll do another one*). These components all contribute to Helen's affectionate picture of her little girl swimming gamely away, as does the paralinguistic laughter, and the attribution to an observer of a comment (*there's a little head*) that emphasizes how sweet and amusing Andrea's behaviour is.

In this story, we see some of the ways in which Helen presents herself to her friend in her role as a loving mother and daughter. But, there are hints of another discourse here, too. As David Lee points out:

> Texts are typically the site of contestation between conflicting perspectives, and linguistic processes constitute the mechanism for the resolution of these conflicts.
>
> (1992: 136)

The conflicting discourse is kept relatively suppressed, but it surfaces at various points. It is a discourse which on other occasions Helen may choose to voice more extensively and explicitly – the expression of Annie's lack of cooperation, the glancing reference to the fact that her other two children do not get on so well with Jason, the presentation of herself as authoritative and decisive, brooking no argument (*so I said 'we're going to Freyburg we've got this far'*), and the implied criticism of her father, the hint that he is not always cooperative (*he seems to make an effort too*). From a poststructuralist perspective, there is some evidence here of the relative nature of the individual's identity, of reflexivity and slippage (Weedon, 1987: 106). Ultimately, however, this particular narrative resolves into Helen's construction of herself as a normatively good mother and daughter, and in addition, she constructs conservatively gendered identities for her two daughters.

Many of the New Zealand women's stories in the sample can be similarly interpreted as underlining and emphasizing the women's roles as 'good' mothers, daughters, wives and friends.

[. . .]

Male identity
The men too used stories to construct a gendered identity for themselves and others. But they tended to do so in rather different ways than the women, and in a different overall context. Men's stories were generally not ways of bringing their addressees up to date on the story of their lives as the women's usually were. There were certainly stories which recounted recent events in the men's lives, but these were decidedly a minority. Often the men would use stories to illustrate more general points, or as ancillary devices in the discussion of an issue such as 'urban transport' or 'homosexuality', or a particular topic such as 'painting the house' or 'developing a good football team'.

On the other hand, like the women's stories, the men's stories constructed a clearly gendered identity for those featuring in their stories.

[. . .]

The stories often reflect a concern with status, and with giving an impression of worldly wisdom. In men's stories, 'doing gender' involves presenting themselves as in control, knowledgeable, competent or, if things go wrong, as self-aware, sophisticated, and reflective.

'I drove our video last night'
These points are illustrated in a male narrative from a conversation between two friends and colleagues, Tom and Gary, both middle-aged Pakeha men who work

Janet
Holmes

in salaried professional jobs. This is one of the relatively few male conversations which focus on recent activities. In the first part of the conversation they talk about what they have been doing earlier in the day. It is probably not irrelevant that this conversation takes place over a coffee at work, rather than in one of their homes. The identities constructed in the stories told in this conversation are no doubt influenced by the social context. Tom introduces the first topic by volunteering to explain 'Why I haven't been in my office all day'. He then gives an account of meeting a visitor at the airport, chairing a meeting, and solving problems for clients. By contrast Gary frames his day as 'much more prosaic', but goes on to provide a similarly detailed account of his activities. The story 'I drove our video last night' follows a discussion of the tape recorder and similar technical apparatus. Tom tells how he eventually overcame the problem of getting his video machine to record a film, and his story is followed by a discussion of the inadequacies of the television company in providing accurate programme information to viewers.

In this video story, Tom constructs himself as competent and intelligent by describing in detail his achievement in mastering the programming of the video (see Appendix 3). He describes each step in the process, giving the impression of an orderly, methodical approach to the challenge he faced.

I looked at- looked up where the programme was on in the pap- you know in the paper
I picked up the video thingy you know the the remote one . . .
I pushed the appropriate buttons
and it ALL worked

The use of the same syntactic pattern through several constructions reinforces Tom's presentation of his behaviour as orderly and systematic. Utterances like

I had to set the time and the date from scratch . . .
I set it up and it recorded at exactly the right time . . .
everything was perfect . . .

underline the complexity of the task and the level of his achievement. As he presents it:

th- the whole point about this is
I solved the technology problem
I had programmed the video

Tom is constructing his identity as a competent manager of technology. He also indicates, however, that external forces undermined his best efforts.

and do you know what went wrong . . .
the p- programme schedule was completely screwed up . . .

The interfering factors are constructed as beyond his control and the word *silly* recurs repeatedly in his account (*it was silly, the silly (remote), the silly rugby sevens*), expressing his attitude to the subverting factors.

**Janet
Holmes**

One of the most interesting aspects of this story is the fact that, having clearly framed it as a triumph of his skill over modern technology, Tom then admits in the course of the account that things were not quite as much under his control as he had suggested – nor as he had intended to convey when he began the story. This subsequent undermining of the identity he has constructed is presented in a rather wry and somewhat self-conscious manner, and, interestingly, this too is not atypical of the men's stories. There was often an ironic comment or an indication that the constructed identity of an effective or powerful person, totally in control of events, did not represent the whole picture. The mocking attitude to their younger selves apparent in Example 2 is somewhat similar, though the narrators maintain distance by telling a story about an earlier time. In a number of cases, as in Tom's narrative, the story peters out towards the end with qualifications and caveats, as the narrator permits reality, or some degree of reflexivity, to intervene and prevent the story reaching a heroic climax.

no that's right I couldn't undo the programming
'cause having programmed the damn thing
having got all that set up I couldn't then undo the programming
I couldn't figure out how to do it
I tried that I tried I I I
in the end I decided I have to undo the whole lot start again
but I couldn't change anything . . .
no I solved part of the of 'cause I couldn't figure out to turn it off
I couldn't undo the programming once it had started once it started . . .
I thought it was just me
maybe maybe it's the way the Japanese make videos

So, in the men's narratives too there is often an alternative discourse competing with the explicit message – a slightly ironic, self-mocking discourse. In Tom's story it is hinted at in the comic framing of his story with the introductory utterance (*I drove our video last night*), but it gradually becomes more evident and almost takes over at the end of the story, suggesting Tom is aware of an alternative view of his behaviour. It is further indicated by words such as *thingy* to refer to the digital scanner, as well as by the somewhat wry tone with which some utterances are imbued. Another male conversationalist, Ken, tells a story about recording a radio programme without a script. Ken's story appears to be making the point that because he was an experienced broadcaster he managed to achieve this goal, thus proving undeserved the scepticism expressed by the producer. But in fact, as the story progresses, Ken admits that things did not go as smoothly as he had intended, and some patching up of his presentation was necessary. Nevertheless, at the most obvious level, Tom's story is intended to demonstrate his competence, just as Ken's ends with a statement emphasizing that the results of the recording session were fine. Tom presents himself as an able person who has successfully mastered the workings of a complex piece of machinery. The reason all does not go well is due to forces beyond his control. This is as much a gendered identity as that reflected in Helen's story which presents her as a paradigmatically dutiful

Janet
Holmes

mother and daughter. Tom's story emphasizes a typical normative masculine identity in New Zealand culture – someone who can control modern technology.

It is possible, though not common, to find stories in which men present themselves in ways more usually framed as 'feminine'. One man recounts a story about
the rejection of his work by an expert, clearly seeking his friend's sympathy; another's story describes a problem at work. But such stories are exceptional. It seems
likely that stories constructing alternative, less stereotypically masculine identities
occur in more intimate contexts. This is an obvious area for further research.

One final feature worth comment which is illustrated by these stories is the
extent to which the evaluative component of the women's stories was more likely
to be relatively implicit or embedded in the story structure, while the men were
more likely to make the 'point' of the story explicit. Labov suggests that explicit
or 'external evaluation' is a common trait of middle-class narrative (1972b: 372).
Middle-class narrators, he claims, frequently interrupt their narratives to underline the point of the story, ensuring that their audience is not missing it. By contrast,
he illustrates how the young working-class black men he recorded tend to embed
their evaluations within the narrative: they may quote themselves responding at
the time to the events described, or, more subtly, they may attribute the evaluative component to a co-participant in the events. This kind of embedded evaluative component was common in the New Zealand women's stories: another participant
is often quoted expressing astonishment at what the narrator has experienced, or
admiration for what the narrator has achieved. In the pool story, this process is
taken one step further. At one level, the pool narrative, like the video narrative,
is a success story – Helen finally managed to get to the pool. But I have suggested that its main function is to construct Helen's identity as 'a good mother'
and 'a good daughter'. In the pool story Helen constructs these identities without drawing explicit attention to the process, either through her own commentary or through the words of another. The point is conveyed very indirectly.

Tom, by contrast, makes the point of his story quite explicit. Despite all the
odds, and the interference of external forces beyond his control, he succeeded
in 'driving' his video machine. He draws explicit attention to this point at two
different stages in his account. The first is when the interfering forces are
introduced:

and do you know what went wrong
'cause it you know that something went wrong
otherwise I wouldn't be telling you this story
(quite-) quite pointless if nothing

And the second is at the end of the story when he again underlines his point quite
explicitly:

but BUT th- the whole point about this is
I solved the technology problem
I had programmed the video

D

Janet Holmes

While there is clearly an element of subjectivity in identifying the main point of a story, especially when it is not made explicit, there is nonetheless evidence in the sample that men were generally more likely than women to assert the point of their stories explicitly. In a number of ways, then, these two stories serve to illustrate gender-differentiated patterns which are typical of a number of stories in the sample.

CONCLUSION

[. . .]

The analysis has demonstrated how stories may serve to construct and rein-force the dominant societal ideology concerning gender roles, reaffirming conser-vative normative social and cultural values. As Coates says:

> through our story-telling we create and re-create our identities and experi-ment with possible selves, in a context of mutuality and trust. Conversational narrative is our chief means of constructing the fictions that are our lives and of getting others to collude in them. (1996: 115)

The topics of women's and men's narratives assert the fundamental importance of everyday experience and activities. But they also reflect the different preoccupa-tions of the daily lives of women and men. The women focus on relationships and people, affirm the importance of their family roles, family connections and friendships. The men focus on work and sport, events, activities and things, and affirm the importance of being in control, even when they don't achieve it. These different preoccupations contribute to and reinforce the gender identities women and men construct through their talk.

[. . .]

APPENDIX 1: TRANSCRIPTION CONVENTIONS

All names are pseudonyms.

YES	capitals indicate emphatic stress
[laughs]	paralinguistic features in square brackets
+	pause of up to one second
.../.....\...	simultaneous speech
.../.....\...	
(hello)	transcriber's best guess at an unclear utterance
?	rising or question intonation
–	incomplete or cut-off utterance

APPENDIX 2: THE POOL STORY

H: and so today we wen- we tried to go to the pool today I tri- I wanted to go to aqua fitness at eleven

J: oh good on you

H: well I wanted to go to aqua fitness at eleven so we gathered up Susie and everybody and their togs and we tear over there just- get there about three minutes before the class is supposed to start and the pool is all closed for some other spe- you know they're not /no\

J: /oh a\

H: aqua- aqua fitness is cancelled some

J: /sport thing\

H: /sporting thing\

J: oh

H: and I th- so I thought oh god I thought you know after we'd s- go- spent half an hour getting there so then I said let's go to Freyburg so then we get I don't want to go to- Annie didn't want to go to Freyburg and the other two DID and you know w- so I said we're going to Freyburg we've got this far /so we\ get round to Freyburg it's lane

J: /right\

H: swimming only which is no good for the little kids [tut] so I thought + oh god this really isn't working out at all and actually it was rather sort of /muggy an hot to be driving round Wellington with a car full of children\

J: /[laughs] I mean (only car) I know\

H: so then /I said oh well\ we'll go and we'll

J: /you've got to (deal)\

H: go to um the Karori pool what the hell\ we'll go to the Karori pool

J: mm mm

H: and we'll just swim there wh- well we could have done that in the first place except that I couldn't have done my class and /the\ w- and it's

J: /no\

H: not quite as w- good as those bigger pools so on the way to the Karori pool we stopped in and saw Jason and i- and Annie was saying I don't want to go in will you drop me home and I said why don't you stay with Jason /and\ make

J: /mm\

H: him some lunch

J: mm

H: so we went in and visited him and I said Annie'll stay with you and make you some lunch and she gets on quite- and she chats away with Jason and they have quite a nice-

J: /she's very good with\ adults isn't she

H: /yes she is\ she's- well she's good with him too I don't know they sort of get along /nicely\ and um better

J: /mm\

H: than the other two do really /you know\

J: /mm\

H: She sort of somehow gets it right with him and he seems to make an effort too so she stayed with him for an hour we went- the other two and I went and swam at the pool Andrea did SEVEN lengths

J: goodness me

H: with a little breaks in between but she's never swum a length of that pool before /and she just suddenly discovered\

J: /(that's so good)\

H: she could swim a length [laughs] and got so keen she didn't want to stop she
        said I'll just do another one and then /I'll do another one so

J: /that's terrific\

H: that\was quite sweet she looked quite sweet like a [laughs] s- Liz was there with
        her friend John and he said /she\ looked like a goldfish you [laughs]

J: /mm\

H: /know s- (there's) a little head ( )\

J: /[laughs]\ (he'd find out when we-) yeah

H: a- a (rolling) in the water

J: /[laughs] oh\

H: [laughs] and legs sort of sagging in the water o- and breaststroking away

J: /good on her\

H: /you know\ but she obviously really sort of getting a kick out of the achievements

J: /that's so good\

H: so Annie stayed there and made Jason some lunch and then we went back
        afterwards so I mean he's sort of all right he's pottering around but he's- he's
        walking with a stick

APPENDIX 3: THE VIDEO STORY

T: I I drove our video last night

G: [laughs]

T: I did I I looked at- looked up where the programme was on in the pap- you know
        in the paper

G: mm

T: [drawls] and I picked up the video thingy you know the

G: is this the g code?

T: /the remote one no no\

G: /no\

T: no no no just [drawls] the just an ordinary remote and I pushed the appropriate
        buttons and it ALL worked and I had to set the time and the date from scratch
        and I set it up and it recorded at exactly the right time and do you know what
        went wrong 'cause it you know that something went wrong /otherwise\ I
        wouldn't

G: /( ) [laughs]\

T: be telling you this story/ (quite-)\

G: /you got\ the wrong channel

T: quite pointless if nothing no no no everything was perfect

G: oh

T: no it was silly um the silly (remote) er

G: the programme schedule was /( )\

T: /yeah the p- programme schedule\ was completely screwed up /the\ the um it
        was it was Channel Two and I

G: /yeah\

T: was suppose
a Ken Russell

G: oh

T: Ken Russell horror stor
instead the silly rugby sev

G: mm

T: went on until twelve thirty so I'd
wouldn't have mattered too much ca
but I /didn't\ know when they finished

G: /mm\ yeah

T: and it was a three hour tape and I didn't know
White Worm went on for /because Ken\ Russell c

G: /[laughs]\

T: make some pretty long movies

G: /[laughs]\ yes [laughs]

T: and so [drawls] um I had to take (undo- it) no that's right I coul
programming 'cause having programmed the damn thing having g
I couldn't then undo /the\ programming

G: /yeah\ that's right you've got to unless you just undo the whole lot and s

T: I couldn't figure out how to do it I tried that I tried I I I in the end I decided
to undo the whole lot start again but I couldn't change anything so as far as I
know having set it up it still turned itself off at two o'clock and there's probably
another half an hour of [film title] The Lair of the White Worm

G: /(yeah)\

T: /unrecorded\

G: a- and and the thrilling climax

T: yes

G: (oh)

T: but BUT th- the whole point about this is I solved the technology problem I had
programmed the video no I solved part of the of 'cause I couldn't figure out to
turn it off I couldn't undo the programming once it had started /once it\ started

G: /yeah\ no I've had that problem with our o- o- original simple one

T: I thought it was just me maybe /maybe\ it's

G: /yeah\

T: the way the Japanese make videos

Issues to consider

The inter-relationship of gender and power as social variables complicates all investigations into this area. In many societies across the world, feminism and economic
changes in wealth and the workplace have either changed the social position of
women and men or have at least made the issue one that is foregrounded and
discussed. Ascribing a variation in the use of a linguistic feature to gender rather than
power relations, or even distinguishing between the two, is not straightforward. All

d to be recording [film title] The Lair of the White Worm [laughs] it's

y and it was supposed to start at five to twelve ++ and

ns went on you know the rugby league sevens

carefully set this thing up now if I'd left it it

tching half an hour of the silly rugby sevens

how long [film title] The Lair of the

an

dn't undo the

t all that set up

tart again

have

Janet
Holmes

D

you an insight into their attitudes to genderlects. You can then use this to make notes on a discussion between the groups.

❏ You could try to replicate Holmes' study of narrative organisation to see if similar patterns hold for your own community.

D8

THE ORIGINS OF PIDGINS AND CREOLES

Since the birth and early development of new languages can be observed at first hand in pidgins and creoles, their study has become very important in sociolinguistics. In particular, theories of the origins of widely-used creoles have enormous consequences for different theories of language development. In this extract, Ronald Wardhaugh neatly surveys the main competing theories in the area.

The passage builds on your study from A8, B8 and C8, and is also a development of material in A9, B9 and C9.

Theories of origin

Ronald Wardhaugh (reprinted from *Introduction to Sociolinguistics* (1998, third edition), Oxford: Blackwell, pp. 70–5)

Linguists who have studied pidgins and creoles have long been intrigued by the similarities they have found among them. Pidgins from very different parts of the world exhibit remarkable similarities in structure even when the standard languages with which they are associated are quite different. Furthermore, pidgins and creoles based on the same standard language but found in places far distant from one another may have a high degree of mutual intelligibility, e.g., the various pidginized and creolized varieties of French found geographically as far apart as the Caribbean, the Indian Ocean, and the South Pacific. How can we account for these similarities?

One theory about the origins of pidgins is easily dismissed. This is the idea that pidgins arise because the people among whom they are found lack the ability to learn the standard languages with which the pidgins are associated. Such a view may sometimes be associated with another one, that European languages are somehow 'better' than others and that many people speak 'primitive' languages, i.e., languages that are 'deficient' in certain respects. Such deficiencies may then be cited as evidence that the people themselves are inferior. We must note that linguists have been unable to locate a single such 'primitive language', that claims about associated intellectual deficiencies are largely 'racist', and that this theory about the origins of pidgins ignores many important facts.

There is no evidence either for any *'foreigner-talk'* or *'baby-talk'* theory (see Bloomfield 1933: 472–3) for the origin of pidgins and creoles, i.e., that they result from Europeans deliberately simplifying their languages in order to communicate with others. According to this theory, these simplified forms then serve to provide pidgins with their basic structures and vocabularies. There are too many structural similarities among pidgins and creoles associated with very different European languages to make such a theory of origin plausible, e.g., between the English-based creole of Jamaica and the French-based one of Haiti. If there is evidence of simplification, it is evidence of some very different process at work than any kind of 'talking down', 'baby-talk', or 'mimicry' can explain. Moreover, pidgins are far less frequently used between Europeans and non-Europeans than among non-Europeans. In fact, many Europeans who must deal regularly with pidginized varieties of their languages speak them very badly indeed, failing to understand some of the basic structural characteristics of the pidgins. Finally, there is plenty of evidence that it is Europeans who learn the pidgins from non-Europeans rather than the opposite, although the use of so much European vocabulary may tend to conceal that fact.

Pidgins are not imperfectly learned standard languages, the imperfections in learning arising from lack of either the ability or the opportunity to learn the standard varieties thoroughly; nor are they the consequence of very simple processes of simplification. What is more, all pidgins apparently share some of the same features, no matter which languages they are based on. The 'foreigner-talk' or 'baby-talk' theory fails to offer an adequate account of these similarities.

Ronald
Wardhaugh

One theory, the theory of *polygenesis*, is that pidgins and creoles have a variety of origins; any similarities among them arise from the shared circumstances of their origins. For example, speakers of English have had to make themselves understood for the purposes of trade and those trading with them have had to be understood. Consequently, certain simplified forms of English have developed independently in a number of places, giving rise to varieties of pidgin English. Because in every case the target language is English, these local varieties will have certain similarities. In this view a 'pidgin X' or 'creolized Y' is a variety of X or Y, much as Cockney English is a variety of English. Then, more generally, since English, French, Spanish and Portuguese are really not so different – they are all Indo-European languages – we might expect similarities. We can go even further to claim that a 'simplification' process for any language would produce much the same results everywhere: a simpler set of sounds, no inflections, basic word order patterns, short uncomplicated utterances, and so on. Various other explanations have been offered for the resulting similarities including the similar social contexts of their origin, the similar communicative needs of those who use them, and most plausible of all a shared *substratum*.

This last idea seems particularly appropriate to explain many similarities among the Atlantic Ocean and possibly certain Indian Ocean pidgins and creoles on the one hand and Pacific Ocean pidgins and creoles on the other. The former are said to have an African substrate and the latter an Oceanic one, i.e., each contains certain language characteristics of the native ancestral languages of their speakers. In this view Atlantic pidgins and creoles retain certain characteristics of ancestral African languages. African slaves were often multilingual, spoke languages of similar structure but different vocabulary, and tended to treat English and French, and to a lesser extent Portuguese, in the same way. Therefore, the pidgins and creoles are European-language-based and were freshly created in different places. What similarities they have they owe to this fusion of European and African components (see Holm 1988: Chapters 3–50).

We can contrast such *polygenetic* views with *monogenetic* ones. One such view of the similarities among Atlantic pidgins and creoles requires us to examine the very beginnings of the pidginization process. For example, according to McWhorter (1995), their similarities can be accounted for if we look back to the beginnings of the slave trade and the existence of English and French slave forts on the West African coast. In these forts contact languages developed. These contact languages provided the bases for most of the pidgins and creoles that later developed across the Atlantic. McWhorter points to the relative paucity of Spanish-based creoles in the New World as evidence which supports this claim as well as to the fact that such creoles are also missing from places we might expect to find them, e.g., Puerto Rico and Cuba. (The Spanish creoles that do exist, e.g., Papiamentu, are relexified (see following pages) Portuguese ones.) McWhorter points out that Spain came late to the sugar industry, did not use labor-intensive cultivation systems, sometimes took areas from Portugal, and did not have large slave forts and settlements in Africa. This view of the development of pidgins and creoles is a monogenetic view, claiming as it does that a single source accounts for the perceived similarities among the varieties we find.

Ronald
Wardhaugh

Another variant of such a monogenetic theory is that the similarities among pidgins and creoles might be attributable to a common origin in the language of sailors in some kind of nautical jargon. It is a well-known fact that the crews of ships were – and sometimes still are – often drawn from a variety of sources. For example, Nelson's flagship *Victory* is said to have been crewed by sailors of fourteen different nationalities. A common shipboard lingua franca, of nautical jargon, developed among the members of the sailing community. In this view, it was that lingua franca, rather than a pidginized variety of a standard language, that was carried along the shipping routes. However, the evidence for this theory is weak, consisting of a few sea-based terms in different pidgins. Moreover, it almost completely ignores the more serious structural similarities among existing pidgins and creoles, similarities that seem to require a more profound explanation.

The theory of *relexification* is an attempt to offer such an explanation. According to this theory, all the present European-language-based pidgins and creoles derive from a single source, a lingua franca called Sabir used in the Mediterranean in the Middle Ages. In the fifteenth and sixteenth centuries the Portuguese *relexified* this language; that is, they introduced their own vocabulary into its grammatical structure, so that a Portuguese-based pidgin came into widespread use as a trade language. Later, this pidgin was in turn relexified into pidginized French, English, and Spanish. In each case the underlying grammatical structure remained largely unaffected, but a massive shift occurred in vocabulary. It is also argued that Portuguese relics still remain after relexification, e.g., *savvy* and *piccaninny* (from Portuguese *saber,* 'know,' and *pequeno,* 'little'), in English-based creoles.

Such a theory attempts to provide a serious explanation for the fact that pidgins and creoles associated with different standard languages have certain common structural features but quite different vocabularies. In this view a pidgin English is therefore an Anglicized version of the original pidgin and a pidgin French is a Gallicized version. The theory leads creolists such as Todd (1974) to go so far as to use a version of the classical comparative method of reconstruction in an attempt to show how various pidgins and creoles have descended from a Portuguese-based ancestor. Todd provides a family-tree type model for pidgins and creoles, which shows them originating in Sabir. Sabir then becomes Proto-Portuguese Pidgin, which in turn splits into two distinct branches, Atlantic Portuguese Pidgin and Indo-Pacific Portuguese Pidgin. The former has sub-branches with Portuguese varieties (e.g., Guiné Crioule), Hispanic varieties (e.g., Papiamentu), Anglicized varieties (e.g., Jamaican), and Gallicized ones (e.g., Louisiana, Haitian); the latter has its sub-branches too – Gallicized ones (e.g., Seychelles), Nederlandized ones (e.g. Afrikaans), and Anglicized ones (e.g., Tok Pisin).

The theory of relexification is not without its problems. One is that pidgins are so stripped down that they lack most of the features that linguists usually rely on to relate one language to another. The similarities among them are very general, and it is quite possible that some alternative theory may better explain them, e.g., the general principles of language acquisition. Relexification also asks us to believe that, in learning a language, people somehow can learn the grammar quite independently of the vocabulary and that they do indeed learn the first but com-

D

pletely replace the second during the process of learning. We might also expect more Portuguese to have survived.

There is actually some good evidence that relexification has occurred. If we look at Saramaccan, it seems to be a pidgin in the process of relexification from Portuguese to English (hence the disagreement I noted earlier about its classification). It was 'frozen' in this intermediate, transitional stage when its speakers were cut off from England in 1667 when the colony became a Dutch possession. There is also some evidence that in parts of West Africa such kinds of replacement do occur, that people know the vocabularies of different languages but use a kind of common grammar in speaking them so that when they come across a new language they employ the 'new' vocabulary in the 'old' grammatical framework and manage to make themselves understood (Todd 1974: 38). We could argue, however, that all we have in this case is a reintroduction of the substratum theory in a new and subtle form; in any case, such a theory seems inadequate on other grounds. There is also no apparent relexification possible for varieties such as Pitcairnese (spoken by descendants of the *Bounty* mutiny of 1790), Sango, and Chinook jargon. At least some pidgins and creoles cannot owe their origin to this process.

One of the severest condemnations of relexification comes from Bickerton (1977: 66–83), who argues that: 'We are asked to believe that an original contact language could be disseminated round the entire tropical zone, to peoples of widely differing language background, and still preserve a virtually complete identity in its grammatical structure wherever it took root, despite considerable changes in its phonology and virtually complete changes in its lexicon.' Bickerton considers that relexification asks us to accept too many improbabilities. Instead, he offers (1981) an alternative theory to account for the similarities we find: his *bioprogram* hypothesis or the theory of *universal language learning*.

Bickerton (1983) claims that only one hypothesis adequately explains the similarities among creoles and that is that universal principles of first language acquisition are involved. Jespersen (1922: 234) had previously pointed out certain similarities between pidgins and creoles and children's language. Bickerton argues that it is better to focus on what pidgins and creoles *have* and *do* than on what they *lack*. Typically, creoles are developed by children who find themselves born into a multilingual environment in which the most important language for peer contact is a pidgin. Children are compelled to develop that language because each child has a *bioprogram* to develop a full language. Children use this bioprogram in the same way wherever they happen to be and the consequence is that 'the grammatical structures of creoles are more similar to one another than they are to the structures of any other language' (p. 121). Bickerton further develops this thesis, claiming that children have certain innate language abilities that they are actually forced to suppress as they learn languages like English and French. 'It [is] only in pidgin-speaking communities, where there [is] no grammatical model that could compete with the child's innate grammar, that the innate grammatical model [is] not eventually suppressed' (p. 121). It is in just these circumstances that creoles arise. Bickerton says that the essential difference between pidginization and creolization is that pidginization is second-language learning with restricted input and creolization is first-language learning, also with restricted input. There has been considerable discussion of Bickerton's ideas but they have found only lukewarm support; they give too much weight to the role of children in the development of creoles and too little to the role of expanded pidgins, the diversity found in creoles, and the amount of time the creolization process takes place.

Ronald Wardhaugh

Issues to consider

D8.2

✪ Activity

You should consider your own response to the various theories of creolisation. Examine the logic of each of the approaches, and find examples of published studies that represent each one. You can then decide where you consider the weight of evidence to be. You should also consider the social consequences of 'buying into' any one of these theories. There are ideological and political implications, implications for our approach to language and linguistics, as well as consequences for educational policy that follow from the adoption of every one of these theories. You should consider what these are.

The issues of prestige and stigmatisation are also important in relation to pidgin and creole users. There are various means of exploring the relative prestige values attached to different varieties, depending on the range of factors introduced in A6.

Some practical suggestions follow.

❑ You can test the perceived prestige value of a particular pidgin or creole using Bell's criteria (A6). Before making any decisions on these dimensions, you will have to decide which variety of the creole you are focusing on, and you must also consider the context and environment of its usage: the prestige of a creole alters radically when considered in its original, native context as compared with the variety spoken by people who have emigrated to another country and live amongst a different speech community.

❑ You should look around your own region to see if any creole languages are spoken by communities that are accessible to you. Do they have a written form or are they taught locally either formally or informally? Is the creole recognised in your local school system?

❑ If you do not have the fortune to be planning a trip to the Caribbean, West Africa, Pacific Islands or Papua New Guinea in the near future, you can still explore a lot of creole data using the internet. University linguistics departments in these locations are especially good sources of interesting material, often with commentary included.

❑ Consider the use made of pidgins and creoles, and the representation of their speakers, in literature and film. You could compare the representation with what you can discover about the reality of the situation.

WORLD ENGLISHES AND CONTACT LITERATURE

D9

Many teachers of English as a second or foreign language use creative writing or the reading of literary texts as a teaching tool. In the article that follows, Braj Kachru demonstrates the creativity involved in the practice of bilingualism, and argues for an awareness of the processes involved in creating and reading 'contact literatures'. Sometimes literature is not seen as authentic sociolinguistic data, since it is in a sense 'artificial' rather than 'real'. However, I would argue that literature is a language event like any other and so is amenable to a sociolinguistic analysis.

The article develops concepts that were discussed in A9, B9 and C9, but it also touches upon issues of ethnicity and multilingualism (from A4 and C4).

The bilingual's creativity: discoursal and stylistic strategies in contact literatures

Braj Kachru (reprinted from Larry Smith (ed.) *Discourse Across Cultures: Strategies in World Englishes*, New York: University of Illinois Press, 1987: 125–40)

The bilingual's creativity in English on a global scale, and the issues concerning nativization of discourse patterns, discourse strategies and speech acts, are a natural consequence of the unprecedented world-wide uses of English, mainly since the early 1920s. The phenomenon of a language with fast-increasing diaspora varieties – and significantly more non-native users than native speakers – has naturally resulted in the pluricentricity of English. The sociolinguistic import of this pluricentricity is that the non-native users of English can choose to acquire a variety of English which may be distinct from the native varieties. As a result, two types of model of English have developed: native and institutionalized non-native (see Kachru, 1982c). It is with reference to these models that the innovations, creativity and emerging literary traditions in English must be seen. Each model has its own linguistic and literary norms – or a tendency to develop such norms. This is the linguistic reality of English in its world context. Attitudinally, however, the way people react to this situation opens up an entirely different can of worms, not directly related to the discussion in this chapter.

The concept 'pluricentricity' of English is a useful beginning point for this chapter. I will address certain issues which, it seems to me, are related to both Western and non-Western pluricentricity of the English language. I will first raise a theoretical question concerning linguists' common perception of a speech community, particularly their understanding of the linguistic behaviour of the members of a speech community which alternately uses two, three or more languages depending on the situation and function. One might ask: How valid is a theory of grammar which treats monolingualism as the norm for description and analysis of the linguistic interaction of traditional multilingual societies? Yet in linguistic description – save a few exceptions – the dominant paradigms have considered monolingualism as the norm (i.e. judgements based on the ideal speaker–hearer). My second concern – not unrelated to the first point – is with description and methodology: Are the models proposed for discourse and text-analysis of monolinguals' linguistic interaction observationally, descriptively, and explanatorily adequate for the analysis of bilinguals' language use? My third aim is to discuss some underlying processes of nativization and innovations which characterize *literariness* (both formal and contextual) of selected texts manifesting the bilingual's creativity. The examples have been taken primarily from what has earlier been termed 'contact literature'. Finally, I shall refer to the issue of relationship between this creativity and underlying thought patterns of bilinguals.

I believe that the theoretical and methodological tracks followed to date in the study of contact literatures in English fail on several counts. The foremost limitation one detects in a majority of studies is that of using almost identical approaches for the description of the bilingual's and monolingual's creativity. Literary creativity in English has until now been studied within the Western Judeo-Christian heritage and its implications for understanding English literature. True, the English language shows typical characteristics of a 'mixed' language development in its layer after layer of borrowings, adaptations, and various levels of language contact. But even there, the earlier main intrusion has been essentially European and more or less consistent with the Hellenistic and Roman traditions.

However, the prolonged colonial period substantially changed that situation in the linguistic fabric of the English language, and extended its use as a medium for ethnic and regional literatures in the non-Western world (e.g. Indian English, West African English; see Kachru, 1980). The extreme results of this extension can be observed in the 'Sanskritization' and 'Kannadaization' of Raja Rao's English, and in the 'Yorubaization' and 'Igboization' of Amos Tutuola and Chinua Achebe. The labels indicate that these authors have exploited two or more linguistic – and cultural – resources which do not fit into the paradigms of what Kaplan (1966) terms 'the Platonic-Aristotelian sequence' and the dominant Anglo-Saxon thought patterns of the native speakers of English. Recognition of this mixing of Western and non-Western resources has implications for our use of terms such as *cohesion* or *coherence*, and even *communicative competence*. We should also be cautious in suggesting typologies of culture-specific speech acts in various varieties of English (see Chishimba, 1983 and Magura, 1984).

In contact literature the bilingual's creativity introduces a nativized thought process (e.g. Sanskritic, Yoruba, Malaysian) which does not conform to the recognized canons of discourse types, text design, stylistic conventions, and traditional thematic range of the English language, as viewed from the major Judeo-Christian traditions of literary and linguistic creativity.

The linguistic realization of the underlying traditions and thought processes for a bilingual may then entail a *transfer* of discoursal patterns from one's other (perhaps more dominant) linguistic code(s) and cultural and literary traditions. That such organization of discourse strategies – conscious or unconscious – arises in different ways in different cultures has been shown in several studies on non-Western languages.

'CONTACT' IN CONTACT LITERATURES

What does the term 'contact literatures' imply? The term refers to the literatures in English written by the users of English as a second language to delineate contexts which generally do not form part of what may be labelled the traditions of English literature (African, Malaysian, Indian and so on). Such literatures, as I have stated elsewhere, are 'a product of multicultural and multilingual speech communities' (Kachru, 1982b: 330). Furthermore:

Braj Kachru

The concept of 'contact literature' is an extension of 'contact language'. A language in contact is two-faced; it has its own face, and the face it acquires from the language with which it has contact. The degree of contact varies from lexical borrowing to intensive mixing of units. Contact literatures (for example, non-native English literatures of India, Nigeria or Ghana; the Francophone literatures; or the Indian-Persian literature) have certain formal and thematic characteristics which make the use of the term 'contact' appropriate (Kachru, 1982b: 341).

It has already been shown that contact literatures have both a national identity and a linguistic distinctiveness (e.g., *Indianness, Africanness*). The 'linguistic realization' of such identities is achieved in several ways: the text may have both a surface and an underlying identity with the native varieties of English; it may show only partial identity with the native norms; or it may entail a culture-specific (e.g. African, Asian) identity both at the surface and the underlying levels and share nothing with the native variety. Thus contact literatures have several linguistic and cultural faces: they reveal a blend of two or more linguistic textures and literary traditions, and they provide the English language with extended contexts of situation within which such literatures may be interpreted and understood. In such literatures there is a range of discourse devices and cultural assumptions distinct from the ones associated with the native varieties of English. One must extend the scope of the historical dimension and cultural traditions from that of Judeo-Christian traditions to the different heritages of Africa and Asia. This kind of historical and cultural expansion results in a special type of linguistic and literary phenomenon: such texts demand a new literary sensibility and extended cultural awareness from a reader who is outside of the speech fellowship which identifies with the variety.

It is in this sense that English writing has become, to give an example, 'our national literature', and English 'our national language' in Nigeria as claimed by Nnamdi Azikiwe, the first President of Nigeria (quoted in Thumboo, 1976: vii). The same is, of course, true of most of the former British and American colonies or areas of influence, such as India, Singapore, and the Philippines.

Thumboo (1976: ix) is making the same point in connection with Commonwealth writers in English when he says that

> language must serve, not overwhelm, if the Commonwealth writer is to succeed. Mastering it involves holding down and breaching a body of habitual English associations to secure that condition of verbal freedom cardinal to energetic, resourceful writing. In a sense the language is remade, where necessary, by adjusting the interior landscape of words in order to explore and mediate the permutations of another culture and environment.

And discussing the problems of such writers, Thumboo adds (xxxiv):

> The experience of peoples crossing over into a second language is not new, though the formalization of the move acts as a powerful rider. What amounts to the re-location of a sensibility nurtured by, and instructed in one culture, within another significantly different culture, is complicated in the outcome.

DISCOURSAL THOUGHT PATTERN AND LANGUAGE DESIGN

The relationship between underlying thought patterns and language designs has been well illustrated by Achebe in a very convincing way. In his *Arrow of God*, Achebe (1969) provides two short texts as an illustration – one nativized (Africanized) and the other Englishized – and then gives reasons for choosing to use the former. In explaining his choice he says that it will '. . . give some idea of how I approach the use of English'. In the passage, the Chief Priest is telling one of his sons why it is necessary to send him to church. Achebe first gives the Africanized version:

> I want one of my sons to join these people and be my eyes there. If there is nothing in it you will come back. But if there is something then you will bring back my share. The world is like a mask, dancing. If you want to see it well, you do not stand in one place. My spirit tells me that those who do not befriend the white man today will be saying, 'had we known', tomorrow.

Achebe then asks, 'supposing I had put it another way. Like this for instance:

> I am sending you as my representative among those people – just to be on the safe side in case the new religion develops. One has to move with the times or else one is left behind. I have a hunch that those who fail to come to terms with the white man may well regret their lack of foresight.

And he rightly concludes: 'The material is the same. But the form of the one is in character and the other is not. It is largely a matter of instinct but judgement comes into it too.'

It is thus a combination of creative *instinct* and formal *judgement* which makes a text language- or culture-specific within a context of situation (e.g. Yoruba speech, Chicano English, Kannada influence, Punjabi English).

Furthermore, if we accept Kaplan's claim that the preferred dominant 'thought patterns' of English are essentially out of 'the Anglo-European cultural patterns' based on 'a Platonic-Aristotelian sequence', the logical next step is to recognize that in the case of, for example, Raja Rao or Mulk Raj Anand, the underlying thought patterns reflect the traditions of Sanskrit and the regional or national oral lore. And in the case of Amos Tutuola and Chinua Achebe they stem from Yoruba and Igbo traditions, respectively.

Raja Rao makes it clear that such transfer of tradition is part of his creativity.

> There is no village in India, however mean, that has not a rich *sthala-purana* or legendary history, of its own. . . . The *Puranas* are endless and innumerable. We have neither punctuation nor the treacherous 'ats' and 'ons' to bother us – we tell one interminable tale. Episode follows episode, and when our thoughts stop our breath stops, and we move on to another thought. This was and still is the ordinary style of our story telling. I have tried to follow it myself in this story [*Kanthapura*] (Rao, 1963: vii–viii).

Raja Rao's narration of an 'interminable tale' results in breaking the Western norms of punctuation and prose rhythm, and he shares it, for example, with the writers on another continent, West Africa. Tutuola has a 'peculiar use of punctuation, resulting in an unending combination of sentences', which he 'owes to his Yoruba speech' (Taiwo, 1976: 76).

> When he tried all his power for several times and failed and again at that moment the smell of the gun-powder of the enemies' guns which were shooting repeatedly was rushing to our noses by the breeze and this made us fear more, so my brother lifted me again a very short distance, but when I saw that he was falling several times, then I told him to leave me on the road and run away for his life perhaps he might be safe so that he would be taking care of our mother as she had no other sons more than both of us and I told him that if God saves my life too then we should meet again, but if God does not save my life we should meet in Heaven (*Bush of Ghosts*, p. 20; quoted in Taiwo, 1976: 76).

In addition to this characteristic, Taiwo (1976: 111) argues that Tutuola and his compatriot Achebe 'exhibit in their writings features which may be described as uniquely Nigerian'. Taiwo further explains (1976: 75) that Tutuola 'has carried Yoruba speech habits into English and writes in English as he would speak in Yoruba. . . . He is basically speaking Yoruba but using English words.' And 'the peculiar rhythms of his English are the rhythms of Yoruba speech' (1976: 85). With regard to Achebe, Taiwo (1976: 116–117) observes that in the following scene which he quotes from *Things Fall Apart*, Achebe 'has had to rely heavily on the resources of Igbo language and culture to dramatise the interrelation between environment and character:'

> 'Umuofia kwenu!' shouted the leading *egwugwu*, pushing the air with his raffia arms. The elders of the clan replied. 'Yaa!'
> 'Umuofia kwenu!'
> 'Yaa!'
> 'Umuofia kwenu!'
> 'Yaa!'
> Evil Forest then thrust the pointed end of his rattling staff into the earth. And it began to shake and rattle, like something agitating with a metallic life. He took the first of the empty stools and the eight other *egwugwu* began to sit in order of seniority after him.

THE BILINGUAL'S GRAMMAR: SOME HYPOTHESES

It seems to me that for understanding the bilingual's creativity one must begin with a distinct set of hypotheses for what has been termed 'the bilingual's grammar' (or multilingual's grammar). I am, of course, not using the term 'grammar' in a restricted sense: it refers to the productive linguistic processes at different linguistic levels (including discourse and style) which a bilingual uses for various linguistic functions.

The bilingual's grammar has to be captured in terms of what sociolinguists term 'verbal repertoire' or 'code repertoire', with specific reference to a speech community (or a speech fellowship). Such speech communities have a formally and functionally determined range of languages and/or dialects as part of their competence for linguistic interaction.

A characteristic of such competence is the faculty and ease of mixing and switching, and the adoption of stylistic and discoursal strategies from the total verbal repertoire available to a bilingual. One has to consider not only the blend of the formal features, but also the assumptions derived from various cultural norms, and the blending of these norms into a new linguistic configuration with a culture-specific meaning system. There are several salient characteristics of the creativity of such a person. I shall discuss some of these below.

First, the processes used in such creativity are based on multinorms of styles and strategies. We cannot judge such devices on the basis of one norm derived from one literary or cultural tradition (see Parthasarathy, 1983).

Second, nativization and acculturation of text presupposes an altered context of situation for the language. Traditionally accepted literary norms with reference to a particular code (say, Hindi or English) seem to fail here. A description based on an approach which emphasizes the monolingual 'speaker-hearer' is naturally weak in terms of its descriptive and explanatory power.

Third, the bilingual's creativity results in the configuration of two or more codes. The resultant code, therefore, has to be contextualized in terms of the new uses of language.

Finally, such creativity is not to be seen merely as a formal combination of two or more underlying language designs, but also as a creation of cultural, aesthetic, societal and literary norms. In fact, such creativity has a distinct context of situation.

It is this distinctive characteristic which one might say on the one hand formally *limits* the text and on the other hand *extends* it, depending on how one looks at linguistic innovations. The creative processes used in such texts have a *limiting* effect because the conventional 'meaning system' of the code under use is altered, lexically, grammatically, or in terms of cohesion (see Y. Kachru, 1983a, b). A reader-hearer 'outside' the shared or re-created meaning system has to familiarize himself or herself with the processes of the design and formal reorganization, the motivation for innovations, and the formal and contextual implications of such language use. In other words, to borrow Hallidayan terms (1973: 43) one has to see what a multilingual 'can say' and 'can mean'. The *range in saying* and the *levels of meaning* are distinct, and one has to establish 'renewal of connection' with the context of situation.

What is, then, inhibiting (limiting or unintelligible) in one sense may also be interpreted as an extension of the codes in terms of the new linguistic innovations, formal experimentation, cultural nuances, and addition of a new cultural perspective to the language. If the linguistic and cultural 'extension' of the code is missed, one also misses the interpretation at the linguistic, literary, socio-linguistic and cultural levels. One misses the relationship between *saying* and *meaning*, the core of literary creativity.

What does it take from a reader to interpret such creativity? It demands a lot: it almost demands an identification with the literary sensibility of the bilingual in tune with the ways of *saying* and the levels of new *meaning*.

D

LINGUISTIC REALIZATION OF DISTINCTIVENESS

This altered 'meaning system' of such English texts is the result of various linguistic processes, including nativization of context, of cohesion and cohesiveness, and of rhetorical strategies.

Nativization of context

One first thinks of the most obvious and most elusive process which might be called *contextual* nativization of texts, in which cultural presuppositions overload a text and demand a serious cultural interpretation. In Raja Rao's *Kanthapura*, to take a not-so-extreme example, such contextualization of the following exemplary passage involves several levels.

> 'Today,' he says, 'it will be the story of Siva and Parvati.' And Parvati in penance becomes the country and Siva becomes heaven knows what! 'Siva is the three-eyed,' he says, 'and Swaraj too is three-eyed: Self-purification, Hindu-Moslem unity, Khaddar.' And then he talks of Damayanthi and Sakunthala and Yasodha and everywhere there is something about our country and something about Swaraj. Never had we heard *Harikathas* like this. And he can sing too, can Jayaramachar. He can keep us in tears for hours together. But the *Harikatha* he did, which I can never forget in this life and in all lives to come, is about the birth of Gandhiji. 'What a title for a *Harikatha*!' cried out old Venkatalakshamma, the mother of the Postmaster.
>
> 'It is neither about Rama nor Krishna.' – 'But,' said her son, who too has been to the city, 'but, Mother, the Mahatma is a saint, a holy man.' – 'Holy man or lover of a widow, what does it matter to me? When I go to the temple I want to hear about Rama and Krishna and Mahadeva and not all this city nonsense,' said she. And being an obedient son, he was silent. But the old woman came along that evening. She could never stay away from a *Harikatha*. And sitting beside us, how she wept! . . . (Rao, 1963: 10).

In this passage it is not so much that the underlying narrative technique is different or collocational relationships are different, but the 'historical' and 'cultural' presuppositions are different from what has been traditionally the 'expected' historical and cultural milieu for English literature. One has to explain Siva and Parvati with reference to the multitude of the pantheon of Hindu gods, and in that context then *three-eyed* (Sanskrit *trinetra*) makes sense: it refers to Lord Siva's particular manifestation when he opens his 'third eye', located on his forehead, spitting fire and destroying the creation. Damayanthi [Damayantī], Sakunthala [Sakuntalā], and Yasodha [Yasodā] bring forth the epic tradition of Indian classics: Damayanthi, the wife of Nala; Sakunthala, who was later immortalized in Kalidasa's [Kālidāsa: 5th century AD?] play of the same name; and Yasodha, the mother of Krishna, the major character of the epic *Mahābhārata*. The contemporariness of the passage is in reference to Gandhi (1869–1948), and the political implications of Hindu-Muslim unity and *khaddar* (handspun cloth). The *Harikatha* man is the traditional religious storyteller who has woven all this in a fabric of story.

Now, this is not unique: this is in fact characteristic of context-specific texts in general. But that argument does not lessen the *interpretive* difficulties of such texts. Here the presupposition of discourse interpretation is at a level which is not grammatical. It is of a special lexical and contextual nature. It extends the cultural load of English lexis from conventional Greek and Roman allusions to Asian and African myths, folklore, and traditions. It universalizes English, and one might say 'de-Englishizes' it in terms of the accepted literary and cultural norms of the language.

Nativization of cohesion and cohesiveness

The second process involves the alteration of the native users' concept of *cohesion* and *cohesiveness*: these concepts are to be redefined in each institutionalized variety within the appropriate universe of discourse (see Y. Kachru, 1983a, b). This is particularly true of types of lexicalization, collocational extension and the use or frequency of grammatical forms. A number of such examples are given in my earlier studies.

The lexical *shift*, if I might use that term, is used for various stylistic and attitudinal reasons. The lexicalization involves not only direct lexical transfer but also entails other devices, too, such as hybridization and loan translation. Such English lexical items have more than one interpretive context: they have a surface 'meaning' of the second language (English) and an underlying 'meaning' of the first (or dominant) language. The discoursal interpretation of such lexicalization depends on the meaning of the underlying language – say Yoruba, Kannada, Punjabi, Malay, etc.

Nativization of rhetorical strategies

The third process is the nativization of rhetorical strategies in close approximation to the devices a bilingual uses in his or her other code(s). These include consciously or unconsciously devised strategies according to the patterns of interaction in the native culture, which are transferred to English.

A number of such strategies are enumerated below. First, one has to choose a style with reference to the stylistic norms appropriate to the concepts of 'high culture' and 'popular culture'. In India, traditionally, high culture entails Sanskritization, and in certain contexts in the north, Persianization. We see such transfer in the much-discussed and controversial work of Raja Rao, *The serpent and the rope*. On the other hand, in *Kanthapura*, Rao uses what may be called a 'vernacular style' of English. His other work, *The cat and Shakespeare*, introduces an entirely new style. In devising these three styles for Indian English, Rao has certainly demonstrated a delicate sense for appropriate style, but such experimentation has its limitations, too. These innovations make his style linguistically 'deviant' from a native speaker's perspective, and culturally it introduces into English a dimension alien to the canons of English literature.

In the expansion of the style range, the African situation is not different from the South Asian. In Achebe we find that 'he has developed not one prose style but several, and in each novel he is careful to select the style or styles that will best suit his subject' (Lindfors, 1973: 74). It is for this reason that, as Lindfors says, 'Achebe has devised an African vernacular style' (74).

Once the choice of the style is made, the next step is to provide authenticity (e.g. *Africanness, Indianness*) to the speech acts, or to the discourse types. How is this accomplished? It is achieved by 'linguistic realization' of the following types:

(1) the use of native similes and metaphors (e.g. Yoruba, Kannada, Malay) which linguistically result in collocational deviation;
(2) the transfer of rhetorical devices for 'personalizing' speech interaction;
(3) the translation ('transcreation') of proverbs, idioms, etc.;
(4) the use of culturally dependent speech styles; and
(5) the use of syntactic devices.

Let me now illustrate these five points one by one. First the use of native similes and metaphors. It is through such similes that Achebe, for example, is able to evoke the cultural milieu in which the action takes place (Lindfors, 1973: 75). Examples of such similes are: *like a bush-fire in the harmattan, like a yam tendril in the rainy season, like a lizard fallen from an iroko tree, like pouring grains of corn into a bag full of holes* (also see B. Kachru, 1965 [1983: 131 ff]).

Second, the transfer of rhetorical devices for contextualizing and authenticating speech interaction. Such devices provide, as it were, the 'ancestral sanction' to the interaction, a very important strategy in some African and Asian societies. It is one way of giving 'cultural roots' to English in African and Asian contexts, particularly to its 'vernacular style'. One might say it is a device to link the past with the present. Onuora Nzekwu (*Wand of noble wood*) accomplishes this by the use of what may be called 'speech initiators' which appear 'empty' to one who does not share the cultural and linguistic presuppositions. But for contextualizing the text, these are essential. Consider among others the following: *our people have a saying; as our people say; it was our fathers who said; the elders have said.* Stylistically this also preserves the 'orality' of the discourse.

A third strategy is that of 'transcreating' proverbs and idioms from an African or Asian language into English. The culture-embeddedness of such linguistic items is well recognized and, as Achebe says, they are 'the palm-oil with which words are eaten' (1964: viii). The function of such expression is to universalize a specific incident and to reduce the harshness of an utterance. Achebe's use of proverbs, in Lindfors' view (1973: 77), sharpens characterization, clarifies conflict, and focuses on the values of the society. In other words, to use Herskovits' term (1958), the use of such a device provides a 'grammar of values'. Consider, for example, the use of the following proverbs by Achebe: *I cannot live on the bank of the river and wash my hand with the spittle; if a child washed his hands he could eat with kings*, and *a person who chased two rats at a time would lose one.* It is through the proverbs and word play that the wit and wisdom of the ancestors is passed on to new generations. I have shown earlier (B. Kachru, 1965, 1966) how this device is used to nativize speech functions such as abuses, curses, blessings, and flattery.

A fourth characteristic is to give the narrative and the discourse a 'naive tall-tale style' typical of the earthy folk style (Lindfors, 1973: 57). This is typical of

Tutuola, or of Raja Rao's *Kanthapura*. This, as Jolaoso observes (quoted by Lindfors, 1973: 57), 'reminds one very forcibly of the rambling old grandmother telling her tale of spirits in the ghostly light of the moon' (see also Afolayan, 1971 and Abrahams, 1983: 21–39).

The fifth strategy is the use of particular syntactic devices. An example is the enhancement of the above folk style by using the device of a traditional native village storyteller and occasionally putting questions to the audience for participation. This assures a reader's involvement. Tutuola makes frequent use of asking direct questions, or asking rhetorical questions in the narration. In Raja Rao's case the Harikathaman or the grandmother uses the same devices, very effective indeed for passing on the cultural tradition to new generations and for entertaining other age groups.

One might ask here: Is there evidence that the discourse of Indians reflects features which according to Lannoy represent a 'culture of sound'? (1971: 275) Would one agree with him that one consequence of belonging to such a culture is 'the widespread tendency of Indians to use language as a form of incantation and exuberant rhetorical flourish on public occasions. Orators rend the air with verbose declamations more for the pleasure of the sound than for the ideas and facts they may more vaguely desire to express'? (176). One wonders, is Babu English (see Widdowson, 1979: 202–211) a manifestation of such 'culture of sound' in the written mode?

[. . .]

CONCLUSION

The study of the bilingual's creativity has serious implications for linguistic theory, and for our understanding of culture-specific communicative competence. It is of special interest for the study and analysis of the expanding body of the non-native literatures in English and of the uses of English in different cultures.

The universalization of English may be a blessing in that it provides a tool for crosscultural communication. But it is a double-edged tool and makes several types of demands: a new theoretical perspective is essential for describing the functions of English across cultures. In other words, the use of English is to be seen as an integral part of the socio-cultural reality of those societies which have begun using it during the colonial period and, more important, have retained it and increased its use in various functions in the post-colonial era.

In recent years many such proposals for a theoretical reorientation have been made, not necessarily with reference to international uses of English, by Gumperz (1964), Halliday (1973), Hymes (1967) and Labov (1972b), among others. And in 1956, when Firth suggested (in Palmer, 1968: 96–97) that 'in view of the almost universal use of English, an Englishman must de-Anglicize himself', he was, of course, referring to the implications of such universalization of the language. In his view, this de-Anglicization was much more than a matter of the readjustment of linguistic attitudes by the Englishmen; it entailed linguistic pragmatism in the use of English across cultures.

The diaspora varieties of English are initiating various types of changes in the English language. More important is the decanonization of the traditionally recognized literary conventions and genres of English. This change further extends to the introduction of new Asian and African cultural dimensions to the underlying cultural assumptions traditionally associated with the social, cultural, and literary history of English. The shared conventions and literary milieu between the creator of the text and the reader of English can no more be taken for granted. A text thus has a unique context. English is unique in another sense too: it has developed both national English literatures, which are specific and *context-bound*, and certain types of *context-free* international varieties. The national varieties show more localized organizational schemes in their texture, which may be 'alien' for those who do not share the canons of literary creativity and the traditions of underlying culture which are manifest in such varieties.

The national English literatures are excellent resources for culture learning through literature, a topic which has attracted considerable attention in recent years. However, for such use of these texts one has to acquire the appropriate interpretive methodology and framework for identifying and contextualizing the literary creativity in English, especially that of its non-native bilingual users. It is only by incorporating such pragmatic contexts, as has been recently shown, for example in Chishimba (1983), that the functional meaning and communicative appropriateness of the new discourse strategies and discourse patterns will be understood and appreciated.

Issues to consider

Kachru raises large issues that are at the heart of linguistics. Do you agree that there is a link between stylistic expression and particular cultural views or thoughts? This would mean that – as several of his quoted sources imply – certain world views could only be expressed in the appropriate language. What do you think of this link between language and thought?

You might also consider the place of literature in this area of bilingual linguistics. Is there a trade off between the authenticity of the language and the accessibility of the text to a wider audience? Universality is often suggested as a feature of literature, but the specific nature of 'contact literature' might not share this feature. You could also consider which cultural knowledge is assumed by a specific text, and which pieces of knowledge are provided by the text for readers who do not have access to the source culture. Obviously, the main way into this area is to read some 'contact literature' and investigate its sociolinguistic aspects.

Some suggestions follow.

❑ If you examine a literary text which arises out of a language-contact situation, can you discern a stylistic distinctiveness that indicates its origins? Is this distinctiveness at the level of word choice, metaphor construction, syntax, or other interference patterns at the level of discourse organisation? Essentially you will be investigating the stylistic representation of characterisation, whether it is through the speech and thought of actual characters in the novel or through the 'voice' of the narrator. You might evaluate how successful the text is as a piece of literature.

❏ Using a descriptive linguistic account of the source language, you could evaluate the degree of 'authenticity' in Kachru's terms. It is likely in a literary text that the author has selected certain features of the source language and culture rather than trying to represent its detail exactly. What can you surmise from the selection process and what image does it give you of the stereotypes involved?

❏ You could try to copy the creative process yourself. If you have a competence in another language, you might try to write a brief narrative which represents your own native culture in that language. You could also try to do this using another dialect of your own language to represent your own local culture. This is actually quite difficult, and so you should also consider why it is not easy.

Emanuel Schegloff and Harvey Sacks

CLOSING TURNS

D10

Emanuel Schegloff and Harvey Sacks produced one of the most influential frameworks for the analysis of conversational structure in terms of 'turn-taking'. In the reading that concludes this book, their article on conversational closure develops their framework in a systematic way.

The passage builds on concepts introduced in A10, B10 and C10, and also B13. It can usefully be explored in relation to the extracts given in B7 and B8.

Opening up closings

D10.1

Emanuel A. Schegloff and Harvey Sacks (reprinted from *Semiotica* 7: 289–327).

OUR AIM IN THIS PAPER is to report in a preliminary fashion on analyses we have been developing of closings of conversation. Although it may be apparent to intuition that the unit 'a single conversation' does not simply end, but is brought to a close, our initial task is to develop a technical basis for a closing problem. This we try to derive from a consideration of some features of the most basic sequential organization of conversation we know of – the organization of speaker turns. [. . .]

This project is part of a program of work undertaken several years ago [this paper was first delivered to the American Sociological Association in 1969] to explore the possibility of achieving a naturalistic observational discipline that could deal with the details of social action(s) rigorously, empirically, and formally. For a variety of reasons that need not be spelled out here, our attention has focused on conversational materials; suffice it to say that this is not because of a special interest in language, or any theoretical primacy we accord conversation. Nonetheless, the character of our materials as conversational has attracted our attention to the study of conversation as an activity in its own right, and thereby to the ways in which any actions accomplished in conversation require reference to the properties and organization of conversation for their understanding and analysis, both by participants and by professional investigators. This last phrase requires emphasis and explication.

D

**Emanuel
Schegloff
and Harvey
Sacks**

We have proceeded under the assumption (an assumption borne out by our research) that insofar as the materials we worked with exhibited orderliness, they did so not only for us, indeed not in the first place for us, but for the coparticipants who had produced them. If the materials (records of natural conversations) were orderly, they were so because they had been methodically produced by members of the society for one another, and it was a feature of the conversations that we treated as data that they were produced so as to allow the display by the coparticipants to each other of their orderliness, and to allow the participants to display to each other their analysis, appreciation, and use of that orderliness. Accordingly, our analysis has sought to explicate the ways in which the materials are produced by members in orderly ways that exhibit their orderliness, have their orderliness appreciated and used, and have that appreciation displayed and treated as the basis for subsequent action.

In the ensuing discussion, therefore, it should be clearly understood that the 'closing problem' we are discussing is proposed as a problem for conversationalists; we are not interested in it as a problem for analysts except insofar as, and in the ways, it is a problem for participants. (By 'problem' we do not intend puzzle, in the sense that participants need to ponder the matter of how to close a conversation. We mean that closings are to be seen as achievements, as solutions to certain problems of conversational organization.) [. . .]

The materials with which we have worked are audiotapes and transcripts of naturally occurring interactions (i.e., ones not produced by research intervention such as experiment or interview) with differing numbers of participants and different combinations of participant attributes. There is a danger attending this way of characterizing our materials, namely, that we be heard as proposing the assured relevance of numbers, attributes of participants, etc., to the way the data are produced, interpreted, or analyzed by investigators or by the participants themselves. Such a view carries considerable plausibility, but for precisely that reason it should be treated with extreme caution, and be introduced only where warrant can be offered for the relevance of such characterizations of the data from the data themselves.

[. . .]

It seems useful to begin by formulating the problem of closing technically in terms of the more fundamental order of organization, that of turns. Two basic features of conversation are proposed to be: (1) at least, and no more than, one party speaks at a time in a single conversation; and (2) speaker change recurs. The achievement of these features singly, and especially the achievement of their co-occurrence, is accomplished by co-conversationalists through the use of a 'machinery' for ordering speaker turns sequentially in conversation. The turn-taking machinery includes as one component a set of procedures for organizing the selection of 'next speakers', and, as another, a set of procedures for locating the occasions on which transition to a next speaker may or should occur. The turn-taking machinery operates utterance by utterance. That is to say [. . .] it is within any current utterance that possible next speaker selection is accomplished, and upon possible completion of any current utterance that such selection takes effect and transition to a next speaker becomes relevant. We shall speak of this as the 'transition relevance' of

Emanuel Schegloff and Harvey Sacks

possible utterance completion. [. . .] Whereas these basic features [. . .] deal with a conversation's ongoing orderliness, they make no provision for the closing of conversation. A machinery that includes the transition relevance of possible utterance completion recurrently for any utterance in the conversation generates an indefinitely extendable string of turns to talk. Then, an initial problem concerning closings may be formulated: HOW TO ORGANIZE THE SIMULTANEOUS ARRIVAL OF THE CO-CONVERSATIONALISTS AT A POINT WHERE ONE SPEAKER'S COMPLETION WILL NOT OCCASION ANOTHER SPEAKER'S TALK, AND THAT WILL NOT BE HEARD AS SOME SPEAKER'S SILENCE. The last qualification is necessary to differentiate closings from other places in conversation where one speaker's completion is not followed by a possible next speaker's talk, but where, given the continuing relevance of the basic features and the turn-taking machinery, what is heard is not termination but attributable silence, a pause in the last speaker's utterance, etc. It should suggest why simply to stop talking is not a solution to the closing problem: any first prospective speaker to do so would be hearable as 'being silent' in terms of the turn-taking machinery, rather than as having suspended its relevance. [. . .]

How is the transition relevance of possible utterance completion lifted? A proximate solution involves the use of a 'terminal exchange' composed of conventional parts, e.g., an exchange of 'good-byes'. [. . .] We note first that the terminal exchange is a case of a class of utterance sequences which we have been studying for some years, namely, the utterance pair, or, as we shall refer to it, the adjacency pair. [. . .] Briefly, adjacency pairs consist of sequences which properly have the following features: (1) two utterance length, (2) adjacent positioning of component utterances, (3) different speakers producing each utterance. The component utterances of such sequences have an achieved relatedness beyond that which may otherwise obtain between adjacent utterances. That relatedness is partially the product of the operation of a typology in the speakers' production of the sequences. The typology operates in two ways: it partitions utterance types into 'first pair parts' (i.e., first parts of pairs) and second pair parts; and it affiliates a first pair part and a second pair part to form a 'pair type'. 'Question-answer', 'greeting-greeting', 'offer-acceptance/refusal' are instances of pair types. [. . .] Adjacency pair sequences, then, exhibit the further features (4) relative ordering of parts (i.e. first pair parts precede second pair parts) and (5) discriminative relations (i.e., the pair type of which a first pair part is a member is relevant to the selection among second pair parts). [. . .]

In the case of that type of organization which we are calling 'overall structural organization', it may be noted that at least initial sequences (e.g., greeting exchanges), and ending sequences (i.e., terminal exchanges) employ adjacency pair formats. It is the recurrent, institutionalized use of adjacency pairs for such types of organization problems that suggests that these problems have, in part, a common character, and that adjacency pair organization [. . .] is specially fitted to the solution of problems of that character. [. . .]

But it may be wondered, why are two utterances required for either opening or closing? [. . .] What two utterances produced by different speakers can do that one utterance cannot do it: by an adjacently positioned second, a speaker can show that he understood what a prior aimed at, and that he is willing to go along with that. Also, by virtue of the occurrence of an adjacently produced second, the doer of a first can see that what he intended was indeed understood, and that it was or was not accepted. [. . .]

We are then proposing: If WHERE transition relevance is to be lifted is a systematic problem, an adjacency pair solution can work because: by providing that transition relevance is to be lifted after the second pair part's occurrence, the occurrence of the second pair part can then reveal an appreciation of, and agreement to, the intention of closing NOW which a first part of a terminal exchange reveals its speaker to propose. Given the institutionalization of that solution, a range of ways of assuring that it be employed have been developed, which make drastic difference between one party saying 'good-bye' and not leaving a slot for the other to reply, and one party saying 'good-bye' and leaving a slot for the other to reply. The former becomes a distinct sort of activity, expressing anger, brusqueness, and the like, and available to such a use by contrast with the latter, it is this consequentiality of alternatives that is the hallmark of an institutionalized solution. [. . .]

In referring to the components of terminal exchanges, we have so far employed 'good-bye' as an exclusive instance. But, it plainly is not exclusively used. Such other components as 'ok', 'see you', 'thank you', 'you're welcome', and the like are also used. Since the latter items are used in other ways as well, the mere fact of their use does not mark them as unequivocal parts of terminal exchanges. [. . .]

The adjacency pair is one kind of 'local', i.e., utterance, organization. It does NOT appear that FIRST parts of terminal exchanges are placed by reference to that order of organization. While they, of course, occur after some utterance, they are not placed by reference to a location that might be formulated as 'next' after some 'last' utterance or class of utterances. Rather, their placement seems to be organized by reference to a properly initiated closing SECTION.

The [relevant] aspect of overall conversational organization concerns the organization of topic talk. [. . .] If we may refer to what gets talked about in a conversation as 'mentionables', then we can note that there are considerations relevant for conversationalists in ordering and distributing their talk about mentionables in a single conversation. There is, for example, a position in a single conversation for 'first topic'. We intend to mark by this term not the simple serial fact that some topic gets talked about temporally prior to others, for some temporally prior topics such as, for example, ones prefaced by 'First, I just want to say . . .', or topics that are minor developments by the receiver of the conversational opening of 'how are you' inquiries, are not heard or treated as 'first topic' is to accord it to a certain special status in the conversation. Thus, for example, to make a topic 'first topic' may provide for its analyzability (by coparticipants) as 'the reason for' the conversation, that being, furthermore, a preservable and reportable feature of the conversation. In addition, making a topic 'first topic' may accord it a special importance on the part of its initiator [. . .].

These features of 'first topics' may pose a problem for conversationalists who may not wish to have special importance accorded some 'mentionable', and who

Emanuel
Scheqloff
and Harvey
Sacks

may not want it preserved as 'the reason for the conversation'. It is by reference to such problems affiliated with the use of first topic position that we may appreciate such exchanges at the beginnings of conversations in which news IS later reported, as:

A: What's up.
B: Not much. What's up with you?
A: Nothing.

Conversationalists, then, can have mentionables they do not want to put in first topic position, and there are ways of talking past first topic position without putting them in.

A further feature of the organization of topic talk seems to involve 'fitting' as a preferred procedure. That is, it appears that a preferred way of getting mentionables mentioned is to employ the resources of the local organization of utterances in the course of the conversation. That involves holding off the mention of a mentionable until it can 'occur naturally', that is, until it can be fitted to another conversationalist's prior utterance [. . .]

There is, however, no guarantee that the course of the conversation will provide the occasion for any particular mentionable to 'come up naturally'.

This being the case, it would appear that an important virtue for a closing structure designed for this kind of topical structure would involve the provision for placement of hitherto unmentioned mentionables. The terminal exchange by itself makes no such provision. By exploiting the close organization resource of adjacency pairs, it provides for an immediate (i.e., next turn) closing of the conversation. That this close-ordering technique for terminating not exclude the possibility of inserting unmentioned mentionables can be achieved by placement restrictions on the first part of terminal exchanges, for example, by requiring 'advance note' or some form of foreshadowing.

[. . .]

The first proper way of initiating a closing section that we will discuss is one kind of (what we will call) 'pre-closing'. The kind of pre-closing we have in mind takes one of the following forms, 'We-ell . . .', 'O.K . . .', 'So-oo', etc. (with downward intonation contours), these forms constituting the entire utterance. These pre-closings should properly be called 'POSSIBLE pre-closing', because providing the relevance of the initiation of a closing section is only one of the uses they have. One feature of their operation is that they occupy the floor for a speaker's turn without using it to produce either a topically coherent utterance or the initiation of a new topic. With them a speaker takes a turn whose business seems to be to 'pass', i.e., to indicate that he has not now anything more or new to say, and also to give a 'free' turn to the next, who, because such an utterance can be treated as having broken with any prior topic, can without violating topical coherence take the occasion to introduce a new topic [. . .] When this opportunity is exploited [. . .] then the local organization otherwise operative in conversation, including the fitting of topical talk, allows the same possibilities which obtain in any topical talk. The opening [. . .] may thus result in much more ensuing talk

Emanuel
Schegloff
and Harvey
Sacks

than the initial mentionable that is inserted [. . .] The extendability of conversation to great lengths past a possible pre-closing is not a sign of the latter's defects
with respect to initiating closings, but of its virtues in providing opportunities for
further topic talk that is fitted to the topical structure of conversation.

[. . .] The other possibility is that co-conversationalists decline an opportunity to insert unmentioned mentionables. In that circumstance, the pre-closing may
be answered with an acknowledgement, a return 'pass' yielding a sequence such as:

A: O.K.
B: O.K.

thereby setting up the relevance of further collaborating on a closing section. When
the possible pre-closing is responded to in this manner, it may constitute the first
part of the closing section.

[. . .]

Clearly, utterances such as 'O.K.', 'We-ell', etc. (where those forms are the
whole of the utterance), occur in conversation in capacities other than that of
'pre-closing'. It is only on some occasions of use that these utterances are treated
as pre-closings. [. . .]

[They] operate as possible pre-closings when placed at the analyzable (once
again, TO PARTICIPANTS) end of a topic.

[. . .] Not all topics have an analyzable end. One procedure whereby talk moves
off a topic might be called 'topic shading', in that it involves no specific attention to ending a topic at all, but rather the fitting of differently focused but related
talk to some last utterance in a topic's development. But co-conversationalists may
specifically attend to accomplishing a topic boundary, and there are various mechanisms for doing so; these may yield 'analyzable ends', their analyzability to participants being displayed in the effective collaboration required to achieve them.

For example, there is a technique for 'closing down a topic' that seems to be
a formal technique for a class of topic types, in the sense that for topics that are
of the types that are members of the class, the technique operates without regard
to what the particular topic is. [. . .] We have in mind such exchanges as:

A: Okay?
B: Alright

Such an exchange can serve, if completed, to accomplish a collaboration on the
shutting down of a topic, and may thus mark the next slot in the conversational
sequence as one in which, if an utterance of the form 'We-ell', 'O.K.', etc. should
occur, it may be heard as a possible pre-closing.

Another 'topic-bounding' technique involves one party's offering of a proverbial or aphoristic formulation of conventional wisdom which can be heard as the
'moral' or 'lesson' of the topic being thereby possibly closed. Such formulations
are 'agreeable with'. When such a formulation is offered by one party and agreed
to by another, a topic may be seen (by them) to have been brought to a close.
Again, an immediately following 'We-ell' or 'O.K.' may be analyzed by its placement as doing the alternative tasks a possible pre-closing can do.

Emanuel Schegloff and Harvey Sacks

Dorrinne: Uh-you know, it's just like bringin the – blood up.
Theresa: Yeah well, THINGS UH ALWAYS WORK OUT FOR THE / / BEST
Dorrinne: Oh certainly. Alright / / Tess.

(1)   **Theresa:**   Oh huh,
      Theresa: Okay,
      Dorrinne: G'bye.
      Theresa: Goodnight,

(2)   **Johnson:**   . . . and uh, uh we're gonna see if we can't uh tie in our plans a little better.
      Baldwin: Okay / / fine.
      Johnson: ALRIGHT?
      Baldwin: RIGHT.
      Johnson: Okay boy,
      Baldwin: Okay
      Johnson: Bye / / bye
      Baldwin: G'night

[. . .]

What the preceding discussion suggests is that a closing section is initiated, i.e., turns out to have begun, when none of the parties to a conversation care or choose to continue it. Now that is a WARRANT for closing the conversation, and we may now be in a position to appreciate that the issue of placement, for the initiation of closing sections as for terminal exchanges, is the issue of warranting the placement of such items as will initiate the closing at some 'here and now' in the conversation. The kind of possible pre-closing we have been discussing – 'O.K.', 'We-ell', etc. – is a way of establishing one kind of warrant for undertaking to close a conversation. Its effectiveness can be seen in the feature noted above, that if the floor offering is declined, if the 'O.K.' is answered by another, then together these two utterances can constitute not a possible, but an actual first exchange of the closing section. The pre-closing ceases to be 'pre-' if accepted, for the acceptance establishes the warrant for undertaking a closing of the conversation at some 'here'.

We may now examine other kinds of pre-closings and the kinds of warrants they may invoke for initiating the beginning of a closing section. The floor-offering-exchange device [above] is one that can be initiated by any party to a conversation. In contrast to this, there are some [. . .] devices whose use is restricted to particular parties. We can offer some observations about telephone contacts, where the formulation of the parties can be specified in terms of the specific conversation, i.e., caller – called. What we find is that there are, so to speak, 'caller's techniques' and 'called's techniques' for inviting the initiation of closing sections. [. . .]

One feature that many of them have in common [is] that they employ as their warrant for initiating the closing the interests of the other party. It is in the specification of those interests that the techniques become assigned to one or another party. Thus, the following invitation to a closing is caller-specific and makes reference to the interests of the other.

**Emanuel
Schegloff
and Harvey
Sacks**

A discussion about a possible luncheon has been proceeding:

A: Uhm livers 'n an gizzards 'n stuff like that makes it real yummy. Makes it too rich
for *me* but: makes it yummy.

A: *Well* I'll letchu go. I don't wanna tie up your phone.

And, on the other hand, there are such called-specific techniques, also making reference to the other's interests, as

A: This is costing you a lot of money.

There are, of course, devices usable by either party which do not make reference to the other's interests, most familiarly, 'I gotta go'.

[. . .]

The 'routine' questions employed at the beginnings of conversations, e.g., 'what are you doing?', 'where are you going?', 'how are you feeling?', etc., can elicit those kinds of materials that will have a use at the ending of the conversation in warranting its closing, e.g., 'Well, I'll let you get back to your books', 'why don't you lie down and take a nap?', etc. By contrast with our earlier discussion of such possible pre-closings as 'O.K.' or 'We-ell', which may be said to accomplish or embody a warrant for closing, these may be said to announce it. That they do so may be related to the possible places in which they may be used.

[. . .]

It is the import of some of the preceding discussion that there are slots in conversation 'ripe' for the initiation of closing, such that utterances inserted there may be inspected for their closing relevance. To cite an example, 'why don't you lie down and take a nap' properly placed will be heard as an initiation of a closing section, not as a question to be answered with a 'Because [. . .]' (although, of course, a coparticipant can seek to decline the closing offering by treating it as a question). To cite actual data:

B has called to invite C, but has been told C is going out to dinner:

B: Yeah. Well get on your clothes and get out and collect some of that free food and
we'll make it some other time Judy then.

C: Okay then Jack

B: Bye bye

C: Bye bye

While B's initial utterance in this excerpt might be grammatically characterized as an imperative or a command, and C's 'Okay' as a submission or accession to it, in no sense but a technical syntactic one would those be anything but whimsical characterizations. While B's utterance has certain imperative aspects in its language form, those are not ones that count; his utterance is a closing initiation; and C's utterance agrees not to a command to get dressed (nor would she be inconsistent if she failed to get dressed after the conversation), but to an invitation to close the conversation. The point is that no analysis – grammatical, semantic, pragmatic, etc. – of these utterances taken singly and out of sequence, will yield their import

Emanuel
ScheGloff
and Harvey
Sacks

in use, will show what coparticipants might make of them and do about them. That B's utterance here accomplishes a form of closing initiation, and C's accepts the closing form and not what seems to be proposed in it, turns on the placement of these utterances in the conversation. Investigations which fail to attend to such considerations are bound to be misled. [Schegloff and Sacks go on to discuss 'pre-topic closing offerings', utterances like 'Did I wake you up?', which offer listeners a means of moving into a closing section.]

[. . .]

Once properly initiated, a closing section may contain nothing but a terminal exchange and accomplish a proper closing thereby. Thus, a proper closing can be accomplished by:

A: *O.K.*
B: O.K.
A: Bye Bye
B: Bye

Closing sections may, however, include much more. There is a collection of possible component parts for closing sections which we cannot describe in the space available here. Among others, closings may include 'making arrangements', with varieties such as giving directions, arranging later meetings, invitations, and the like; reinvocation of certain sorts of materials talked of earlier in the conversation, in particular, reinvocations of earlier-made arrangements (e.g., 'See you Wednesday') and reinvocations of the reason for initiating the conversation (e.g., 'Well, I just wanted to find out how Bob was'), not to repeat here the earlier discussion of materials from earlier parts of the conversation to do possible pre-closings; and components that seem to give a 'signature' of sorts to the type of conversation, using the closing section as a place where recognition of the type of conversation can be displayed (e.g., 'Thank you'). Collections of these and other components can be combined to yield extended closing sections, of which the following is but a modest example:

B: Well that's why I *said* 'I'm not gonna say anything, I'm not making *any comments* //
    about anybody'
C: Hmh
C: Ehyeah
B: Yeah
C: Yeah
B: *Al*righty. Well *I'll* give you a call before we decide to come down. O.K.?
C: O.K.
B: *Al*righty
C: O.K.
B: We'll see you then
C: O.K.
B: *Bye* bye
C: Bye

Emanuel
Schegloff
and Harvey
Sacks

However extensive the collection of components that are introduced, the two crucial components (FOR THE ACHIEVEMENT OF PROPER CLOSING; other components may be important for other reasons, but not for closing *per se*) are the terminal exchange which achieves the collaborative termination of the transition rule, and the proper initiation of the closing section which warrants the undertaking of the routine whose termination in the terminal exchange properly closes the conversation.

[. . .]

To capture the phenomenon of closings, one cannot treat it as the natural history of some particular conversation; one cannot treat it as a routine to be run through, inevitable in its course once initiated. Rather, it must be viewed, as much conversation as a whole, as a set of prospective possibilities opening up at various points in the conversation's course; there are possibilities throughout a closing, including the moments after a 'final' good-bye, for reopening the conversation. Getting to a termination, therefore, involves work at various points in the course of the conversation and of the closing section; it requires accomplishing. For the analyst, it requires a description of the prospects and possibilities available at the various points, how they work, what the resources are, etc., from which the participants produce what turns out to be the finally accomplished closing.

[. . .]

Symbols used in transcriptions

/	– indicates upward intonation
//	– indicates point at which following line interrupts
(n.0)	– indicates pause of n.0 seconds
( )	– indicates something said but not transcribable
(word)	– indicates probable, but not certain, transcription
but	– indicates accent
emPLOYee	– indicates heavy accent
DO	– indicates very heavy accent
::::::	– indicates stretching of sound immediately preceding, in proportion to number of colons inserted
becau-	– indicates broken word

D10.2

Activity

Issues to consider

Recent advances in recording technology have enormously improved our ability to investigate conversation, especially in its natural setting rather than in the experimental context of a classroom or interview room. This means you can undertake your own studies with relative ease.

Perhaps the first difference you will notice between many transcriptions of speech and real examples is the number and extent of silences and long pauses in normal conversational exchanges. Since these are obviously a prominent feature of spoken discourse, you might want to think of ways of categorising different types of silence.

A framework for conversational analysis often assumes both an orderliness in the structure and 'recipient design': that is, an assumption that speakers tailor their utterance for optimal communicativeness for the addressee. Schegloff and Sacks make this assumption in their article. However, how would you deal analytically with different situations: when someone is being wilfully obscure; or has a very idiosyncratic style of speech that seems more like a monologue; or is engaged in argument and domination? What about the conversational structure of small children, especially when talking to adults? And how are the patterns of conversational structure exploited in absurdist drama?

Some other suggestions follow.

❑ Many conversations, especially those involving older people, often conclude with the citation of an idiom or proverbial saying. There are two connected hypotheses here: some conversations end with idioms; and the practice is dying out, using the age distinction as an apparent change over time. How would you design a study that would test whether these hypotheses were the case?

❑ In addition to the non-normative situations of dialogue mentioned above, how would you adapt the Schegloff and Sacks framework to analyse conversations in which one person is desperate to leave and the other wants to prolong the conversation?

❑ Though Schegloff and Sacks acknowledge the social context in conversation, theirs is more a pragmatic model than a sociolinguistic one, in the sense that it focuses on intentions and meanings rather than the social factors of the speakers. Consider the effect of the different social variables that might attach to speakers in a conversation, and how this would affect the structure and language choices in the dialogue.

REFERENCES

Abrahams, R.D. (1983) *The Man-of-Words in the West Indies: Performance and the Emergence of Creole Culture*, Baltimore, MD: Johns Hopkins University Press.

Achebe, C. (1964) 'Foreword', in W.H. Whitley (ed.) *A Selection of African Prose*, Oxford: Clarendon Press.

Achebe, C. (1969) *Arrow of God*, New York: Doubleday.

Addington, D.W. (1968) 'The relationship of selected vocal characteristics to personality perception', *Speech Monographs* 25: 492–503.

Adler, M.K. (1978) *Naming and Addressing: A Sociolinguistic Study*, Hamburg: Helmut Buske.

Afolayan, A. (1971) 'Language and sources of Amos Tutuola', in C. Heywood (ed.) *Perspectives on African Literature*, London: Heinemann.

Aitchison, J. (1991) *Language Change: Progress or Decay?* (2nd edition), Cambridge: Cambridge University Press.

American Civil Liberties Union (1996) 'Briefing paper', http://www.aclu.org/library/pbp20.html

Andersen, H. (1989) 'Understanding linguistic innovations', in L. Breivik and E.H. Jahr (eds) *Language Change: Contributions to the Study of its Causes*, Berlin: Mouton de Gruyter, pp. 56–83.

Andersson, L. and Trudgill, P. (1990) *Bad Language*, Oxford: Basil Blackwell.

Ashcroft, B., Griffiths, G. and Tiffin, H. (1989) *The Empire Writes Back: Theory and Practice in Post-Colonial Literatures*, London: Routledge.

Aston, G. and Burnard, L. (1998) *The BNC Handbook: Exploring the British National Corpus with SARA*, Edinburgh: Edinburgh University Press.

Bailey, R.W. and Görlach, M. (eds) (1984) *English as a World Language*, Ann Arbor, MI: University of Michigan Press.

Bain, R., Fitzgerald, B. and Taylor, M. (eds) (1992) *Looking into Language: Classroom Approaches to Knowledge about Language*, London: Hodder & Stoughton.

Barber, C. (1976) *Early Modern English*, Edinburgh: Edinburgh University Press.

Barnbrook, G. (1996) *Language and Computers: A Practical Introduction to the Computer Analysis of Language*, Edinburgh: Edinburgh University Press.

Baugh, A.C. and Cable, T. (1978) *A History of the English Language* (1st edition), London: Routledge & Kegan Paul.

Baugh, A.C. and Cable, T. (1993) *A History of the English Language* (3rd edition), London: Routledge.

Beardsmore, H.B. (1982) *Bilingualism: Basic Principles*, Clevedon: Tieto.

Bell, R.T. (1976) *Sociolinguistics: Goals, Approaches and Problems*, London: Batsford.

Bernstein, B. (1971) *Class, Codes and Control* (3 vols), London: Routledge & Kegan Paul.

Bernstein, B. (1990) *The Structuring of Pedagogic Discourse: Class, Codes and Control Volume 4*, London: Routledge.

Bex, A.R. and Watts, R. (eds) (1999) *Standard English: The Widening Debate*, London: Routledge.

Biber, D., Conrad, S. and Reppen, R. (1998) *Corpus Linguistics: Investigating Language Structure and Use*, Cambridge: Cambridge University Press.

Biber, D. and Finegan, E. (eds) (1994) *Sociolinguistic Perspectives on Register*, Oxford: Oxford University Press.

Biber, D., Johanssen, S., Leech, G., Conrad, S. and Finegan, E. (1999) *The Longman Grammar of Spoken and Written English*, London: Longman.

Bickerton, D. (1977) 'Pidginization and creolization: language acquisition and language universals', in A. Valdman (ed.) *Pidgin and Creole Linguistics*, Bloomington, IN: Indiana University Press, pp. 60–83.

Bickerton, D. (1981) *Roots of Language*, Ann Arbor, MI: Karoma.

Bickerton, D. (1983) 'Creole languages', *Scientific American* 249(1): 116–22.

Bickerton, D. (1990) *Language and Species*, Chicago, IL: University of Chicago Press.

Birch, D. (1989) *Language, Literature and Critical Practice: Ways of Analysing Text*, London: Routledge.

Bloomfield, L. (1933) *Language*, London: Allen and Unwin.

Boden, D. and Zimmerman, D. (eds) (1991) *Talk and Social Structure*, Oxford: Polity Press.

Braun, F. (1988) *Terms of Address*, Berlin: Mouton de Gruyter.

Brown, P. and Levinson, S. (1979) 'Social structure, groups and interaction', in K.R. Scherer and H. Giles (eds) *Social Markers in Speech*, Cambridge: Cambridge University Press, pp. 76–98.

Brown, P. and Levinson, S. (1987) *Politeness: Some Universals of Language Use*, Cambridge: Cambridge University Press.

Brown, R. and Gilman, A. (1960) 'The pronouns of power and solidarity', in T.A. Sebeok (ed.) *Style in Language*, New York: John Wiley, pp. 58–71.

Bruck, P.A. (ed.) (1989) *A Proxy for Knowledge: The News Media as Agents for Arms Control and Verification*, Ottawa: Norman Paterson School of International Affairs.

Burton, D. (1980) *Dialogue and Discourse*, London: Routledge & Kegan Paul.

Butler, J. (1990) *Gender Trouble*, New York: Routledge.

Caldas-Coulthard, C.R. and Coulthard, M. (eds) (1996) *Texts and Practices: Readings in Critical Discourse Analysis*, London: Routledge.

Cameron, D. (ed.) (1990) *The Feminist Critique of Language: A Reader*, London: Routledge.

Cameron, D. (1992) *Feminism and Linguistic Theory* (2nd edition), London: Macmillan.

Cameron, D. (1995) *Verbal Hygiene*, London: Routledge.

Carter, R.A. (ed.) (1990) *Knowledge about Language and the Curriculum*, London: Hodder & Stoughton.

Carter, R.A. (1995) *Keywords in Language and Literacy*, London: Routledge.

Carter, R.A. (1997) *Investigating English Discourse: Language, Literacy, Literature*, London: Routledge.

Carter, R.A. and McRae, J. (eds) (1996) *Language, Literature and the Learner: Creative Classroom Practice*, London: Longman.

Cassidy, F.G. and Le Page, R.B. (eds) (1980) *Dictionary of Jamaican English* (2nd edition), Cambridge: Cambridge University Press.

Chambers, J.K. (1997) *Sociolinguistic Theory: Linguistic Variation and its Social Significance*, Toronto: University of Toronto Press.

Chambers, J.K. and Trudgill, P. (1980) *Dialectology*, Cambridge: Cambridge University Press.

Cheshire, J. (1978) 'Present tense verbs in Reading English', in P. Trudgill (ed.) *Sociolinguistic Patterns in British English*, London: Edward Arnold, pp. 45–55.

Cheshire, J. (ed.) (1991) *English Around the World: Sociolinguistic Perspectives*, Cambridge: Cambridge University Press.

Chilton, P. (ed.) (1985) *Language and the Nuclear Arms Debate*, London: Pinter.

Chilton, P. (1986) 'Metaphor, euphemism, and the militarization of language', paper presented at the Biannual Meeting of the International Peace Research Associa-tion, Sussex.

Chilton, P. (1988) *Orwellian Language and the Media*, London: Pluto Press.

Chilton, P. (1996) *Security Metaphors: Cold War Discourse from Containment to Common House*, New York: Peter Lang.

Chilton, P., Ilyin, M.V. and Mey, J.L. (eds) (1998) *Political Discourse in Transition in Europe, 1989–1991*, Amsterdam: Benjamins.

Chishimba, M. (1983) *African Varieties of English: Text in Context*, unpublished doctoral dissertation, University of Illinois.

Christy, C. (1983) *Uniformitarianism in Linguistics*, Amsterdam: John Benjamins.

Coates, J. (1993) *Women, Men and Language* (2nd edition), London: Longman.

Coates, J. (1996) *Women Talk: Conversation Between Women Friends*, Oxford: Blackwell.

Coates, J. and Cameron, D. (eds) (1986) *Women in Their Speech Communities*, London: Longman.

Coggle, P. (1993) *Do You Speak Estuary?* London: Bloomsbury.

Crawford, J. (ed.) (1992) *Language Loyalties*, Chicago: University of Chicago Press.

Crawford, M. (1995) *Talking Difference: On Gender and Language*, London: Sage.

Crewe, W. (ed.) (1977) *The English Language in Singapore*, Singapore: Eastern Universities Press.

Crowley, T. (1989) *The Politics of Discourse*, London: Macmillan.

Crystal, D. (1995) *The Cambridge Encyclopedia of the English Language*, Cambridge: Cambridge University Press.

Davis, L.M. (1983) *English Dialectology: An Introduction*, Tuscaloosa, AL: University of Alabama Press.

Davis, L.M. (1990) *Statistics in Dialectology*, Tuscaloosa, AL: University of Alabama Press.

Dobson, E.J. (1968) *English Pronunciation 1500–1700* (vol. I, 2nd edition), Oxford: Oxford University Press.

Dorian, N. (1993) 'Internally and externally motivated change in language contact settings: doubts about dichotomy', in C. Jones (ed.) *Historical Linguistics: Problems and Perspectives*, London: Longman, pp. 131–89.

Downes, W. (1984) *Language and Society*, London: Fontana.

Edwards, J. (1989) *Language and Disadvantage* (2nd edition), London: Cole and Whurr.

Edwards, J. (1995) *Multilingualism*, Harmondsworth: Penguin.

Edwards, V. (1986) *Language in a Black Community*, Clevedon: Multilingual Matters.

Eiser, J.R. (ed.) (1984) *Attitudinal Judgement*, New York: Springer-Verlag.

Ellis, D.S. (1967) 'Speech and social status in America', *Social Forces* 45: 431–7.

Fairclough, N. (1989) *Language and Power*, London: Longman.

Fairclough, N. (1991) *Discourse and Social Change*, Cambridge: Polity.

Fairclough, N. (1995a) *Critical Discourse Analysis: The Critical Study of Language*, London: Longman.

Fairclough, N. (1995b) *Media Discourse*, London: Edward Arnold.

Fasold, R. (1990) *The Sociolinguistics of Language*, Oxford: Basil Blackwell.

Ferguson, C.A. (1964) 'Diglossia', in D.H. Hymes (ed.) *Language in Culture and Society: A Reader in Linguistics and Anthropology*, New York: Harper & Row, pp. 423–38.

Ferguson, C.A. and Heath, S.B. (eds) (1981) *Language in the USA*, Cambridge and New York: Cambridge University Press.

Fishman, J. (ed.) (1968) *Readings in the Sociology of Language*, The Hague: Mouton.

Fishman, J. (1972) *The Sociology of Language: An Interdisciplinary Social Science Approach to Language in Society*, Rowley, MA: Newbury House.

Fishman, J. (1974) *Advances in Language Planning*, The Hague: Mouton.

Fishman, J. (ed.) (1978) *Advances in the Study of Societal Multilingualism*, The Hague: Mouton.

Foley, J.A., Kandiah, T., Bao Zhiming, Fraser-Gupta, A., Alsagoff, L., Ho Chee Lick, Wee, L., Talib, I.S. and Bokhorst-Heng, W. (eds) (1998) *English in New Cultural Contexts: Reflections from Singapore*, Singapore: Oxford University Press.

Fowler, R. (1981) *Literature as Social Discourse*, London: Batsford.

Fowler, R. (1986) *Linguistic Criticism*, Oxford: Oxford University Press.

Fowler, R. (1991) *Language in the News: Discourse and Ideology in the Press*, London: Routledge.

Fowler, R., Hodge, R., Kress, G. and Trew, T. (eds) (1979) *Language and Control*, London: Routledge & Kegan Paul.

Francis, W.N. (1983) *Dialectology*, Harlow: Longman.

Fraser-Gupta, A. (1991) 'Acquisition of diglossia in Singapore English', in A. Kwan-Terry (ed.) *Child Language Development in Singapore and Malaysia*, Singapore: Singapore University Press, pp. 119–60.

Fraser-Gupta, A. (1992) 'The pragmatic particles of Singapore colloquial English', *Journal of Pragmatics* 17(3): 39–65.

Garcia, O. and Otheguy, R. (1988) 'The language situation of Puerto Ricans', in S.L. McKay and S-L.C. Wong (eds) *Language Diversity: Problem or Resource?* Boston: Heinle & Heinle, pp. 140–65.

Giglioli, P.P. (ed.) (1972) *Language and Social Context: Selected Readings*, Harmondsworth: Penguin.

Giles, H. (1970) 'Evaluative reactions to accents', *Educational Review* 22: 211–27.

Giles, H. and Powesland, P.F. (1975) *Speech Style and Social Evaluation*, London: Academic Press.

Giles, H. and Coupland, N. (1991) *Language: Contexts and Consequences*, Milton Keynes: Open University Press.

Graddol, D., Leith, D. and Swann, J. (1996) *English: History, Diversity and Change*, Milton Keynes: Open University Press.

Graddol, D. and Swann, J. (1989) *Gender Voices*, Oxford: Blackwell.

Greenbaum, S. (ed.) (1996) *Comparing English World-wide: The International Corpus of English*, Oxford: Oxford University Press.

Grimes, M.F. (ed.) (1992) *Ethnologue: Languages of the World*, http://wwwala.doc.ic.ac.uk/~rap/Ethnologue

Grundy, P. (2000) *Doing Pragmatics* (2nd edition), London: Arnold.

Gumperz, J.J. (1964) 'Linguistic and social interaction in two communities', in J.J. Gumperz and D. Hymes (eds) *The Ethnography of Communication* (special edition) *American Anthropologist* 66(2): 137–53.

Gumperz, J.J. (1982) *Discourse Strategies*, Cambridge: Cambridge University Press.

Gumperz, J.J. and Hymes, D.H. (eds) (1972) *Directions in Sociolinguistics: The Ethnography of Communication*, New York: Holt, Rinehart and Winston.

Halliday, M.A.K. (1973) *Explorations in the Functions of Language*, London: Edward Arnold.

Halliday, M.A.K. (1985) *An Introduction to Functional Grammar*, London: Edward Arnold (2nd edition, 1994).

Haugen, E. (1966) 'Dialect, language, nation', *American Anthropologist* 68: 922–35.

Heller, M. (ed.) (1988) *Codeswitching*, Berlin: Mouton de Gruyter.

Herskovits, M.J. (1958) *Dahomean Narrative*, Evanston, IL: Northwestern University Press.

Hewitt, R. (1986) *White Talk, Black Talk: Interracial Friendship and Communication Amongst Adolescents*, Cambridge: Cambridge University Press.

Hildebrandt, H.W. (1977) *A Treatise of Schemes and Tropes (1550) by Richard Sherry: A Facsimile Reproduction*, New York: Scholars' Facsimiles and Reprints.

Hock, H.H. (1986) *Principles of Historical Linguistics*, Berlin: Mouton de Gruyter.

Hodge, R. and Kress, G. (1988) *Social Semiotics*, Cambridge: Polity Press.

Hoey, M. (1983) *On the Surface of Discourse*, London: Allen & Unwin.

Holm, J. (1988, 1989) *Pidgins and Creoles* (2 vols), Cambridge: Cambridge University Press.

Holmes, J. (1992) *An Introduction to Sociolinguistics*, London: Longman.

Honey, J. (1989) *Does Accent Matter? The Pygmalion Factor*, London: Faber and Faber.

Hopper, R. and Williams, F. (1973) 'Speech characteristics and employability', *Speech Monographs* 46: 296–302.

Hughes, A. and Trudgill, P. (1979) *English Accents and Dialects*, London: Edward Arnold.

Hymes, D. (1967) 'Models of the interaction of language and social setting', *Journals of Social Issues 23*(2): 8–28.'

Hymes, D.H. (1974) *Foundations in Sociolinguistics: An Ethnographic Approach*, Philadelphia, PA: University of Pennsylvania Press.

James, B. and Savile-Smith, K. (1989) *Gender, Culture and Power: Challenging New Zealand's Gendered Culture*, Auckland: Oxford University Press.

Jespersen, O. (1922) *Language: Its Nature, Development and Origin*, New York: W.W. Norton.

Johnson, S. and Meinhof, U.H. (eds) (1997) *Language and Masculinity*, Oxford: Blackwell.

Joseph, J.E. (1987) *Eloquence and Power*, London: Pinter.

Kachru, B.B. (1965) 'The *Indianness* in Indian English', *Word* 21: 391–410.

Kachru, B.B. (1966) 'Indian English: a study in contextualization', in C.E. Bazell (ed.) *In Memory of J.R. Firth*, London: Longman.

Kachru, B.B. (1980) 'The new Englishes and old dictionaries: directions in lexicographical research on non-native varieties of English', in L. Zgusta (ed.) *Theory and Method in Lexicography: A Western and Non-Western Perspective*, London: Hornbeam Press.

Kachru, B.B. (1982a) 'The bilingual's linguistic repertoire', in B. Hardford (ed.) *Issues in International Bilingual Education: The Role of the Vernacular*, New York and London: Plenum Press.

Kachru, B.B. (ed.) (1982b) *The Other Tongue: English Across Cultures* (1st edition), Urbana, IL: University of Illinois Press.

Kachru, B.B. (1982c) 'Models for non-native Englishes', in B.B. Kachru (ed.) *The Other Tongue: English Across Cultures* (1st edition), Urbana, IL: University of Illinois Press.

Kachru, B.B. (1983) *The Indianization of English*, Delhi: Oxford University Press.

Kachru, B.B. (1988) *The Alchemy of English: The Spread, Functions and Models of Non-Native Englishes*, Oxford: Pergamon.

Kachru, B.B. (1992) *The Other Tongue: English Across Cultures* (2nd edition), Chicago, IL: University of Chicago Press.

Kachru, Y. (1983a) 'Cross-cultural texts, discourse strategies and discourse interpretation', paper presented at the Conference on English as an International Language: Discourse Patterns Across Cultures, East-West Center, Honolulu.

Kachru, Y. (1983b) 'Linguistics and written discourse in particular languages: contrastive studies: English and Hindi', in R. Kaplan (ed.) *Annual Review of Applied Linguistics*, Rowley, MA: Newbury House.

Kaplan, R.B. (1966) 'Cultural thought patterns in intercultural education', *Language Learning* 16: 1–20.

Kingsmore, R. (forthcoming) *Variation in an Ulster Scots Dialect: A Sociolinguistic Study*, Birmingham, AL: University of Alabama Press.

Kress, G. and Hodge, R. (1993) *Language as Ideology* (2nd edition), London: Routledge & Kegan Paul.

Labov, W. (1963) 'The social motivation of a sound change', *Word* 19: 273–309 (reprinted in Labov 1972b).

Labov, W. (1966) *The Social Stratification of English in New York City*, Washington, DC: Center for Applied Linguistics.

Labov, W. (1972a) *Language in the Inner City: Studies in the Black English Vernacular*, Philadelphia, PA: University of Pennsylvania Press.

Labov, W. (1972b) *Sociolinguistic Patterns*, Philadelphia, PA: University of Pennsylvania Press.

Labov, W. (1992) 'Evidence for regular sound change in English dialect geography', in M. Rissanen (ed.) *History of Englishes: New Methods and Interpretations in Historical Linguistics*, Berlin: Mouton de Gruyter, pp. 42–71.

Labov, W. (1994) *Principles of Linguistic Change: Internal Factors*, Oxford: Basil Blackwell.

Lakoff, R. (1975) *Language and Woman's Place*, New York: Harper & Row.

Lakoff, R. (1990) *Talking Power*, New York: Basic Books.

Lambert, W.E., Frankel, H. and Tucker, G.R. (1966) 'Judging personality through speech: a French-Canadian example', *Journal of Communication* 16: 305–21.

Lannoy, R. (1971) *The Speaking Tree: A Study of Indian Culture and Society*, New York: Oxford University Press.

Lass, R. (1987) *The Frame of English*, London: Dent.

Laver, J. (1975) 'Communicative functions of phatic communion', in A. Kendon, R.M. Harris and M.R. Key (eds) *Communication in Face to Face Interaction*, Berlin: Mouton, pp. 73–92.

Lawton, D. (1968) *Social Class, Language and Education*, London: Routledge & Kegan Paul.

Lee, C-R. (1995) *Native Speaker*, New York: Riverhead Books.

Lee, D. (1992) *Competing Discourses: Perspective and Ideology in Language*, London: Longman.

Leech, G.N. (1983) *Principles of Pragmatics*, London: Longman.

Leith, D. (1983) *A Social History of English* (1st edition), London: Routledge & Kegan Paul.

Leith, D. (1997) *A Social History of English* (3rd edition), London: Routledge.

Le Page, R. and Tabouret-Keller, A. (1985) *Acts of Identity*, Oxford: Blackwell.

Levinson, S. (1983) *Pragmatics*, Cambridge: Cambridge University Press.

Lindfors, B. (1973) *Folklore in Nigerian Literature*, New York: Africana.

Linde, C. (1993) *Life Stories: The Creation of Coherence*, New York and Oxford: Oxford University Press.

Lippi-Green, R. (1997) *English with an Accent: Language, Ideology and Discrimination in the United States*, London: Routledge.

McArthur, T. (1998) *The English Languages*, Cambridge: Cambridge University Press.

McCarthy, M. (1991) *Discourse Analysis for Language Teachers*, Cambridge: Cambridge University Press.

McCarthy, M. (1998) *Spoken Language and Applied Linguistics*, Cambridge: Cambridge University Press.

McCarthy, M. and Carter, R.A. (1994) *Language as Discourse: Perspectives for Language Teaching*, London: Longman.

McCrum, R., Cran, R. and MacNeil, R. (eds) (1992) *The Story of English* (revised edition), London: Faber and Faber.

McWhorter, J.H. (1995) 'The scarcity of Spanish-based creoles explained', *Language in Society* 24: 213–44.

Magura, B. (1984) *Style and Meaning in African English: A Sociolinguistic Study*, unpublished PhD dissertation, University of Illinois.

Mahony, P. (1985) *Schools for the Boys? Co-education Reassessed*, London: Hutchinson.

Mahony, P. and Jones, C. (eds) (1989) *Learning our Lines: Sexuality and Social Control in Education*, London: Women's Press.

Makkai, A. (1972) *Idiom Structure in English*, The Hague: Mouton.

Mees, I. (1990) 'Patterns of sociophonetic variation in the speech of Cardiff schoolchildren', in N. Coupland (ed.) *English in Wales: Diversity, Conflict and Change*, Avon: Multilingual Matters, pp. 167–94.

Meinhof, U. and Richardson, K. (1994) *Text, Discourse and Context: Representations of Poverty in Britain*, London: Longman.

Mills, S. (1995a) *Feminist Stylistics*, London: Routledge.

Mills, S. (1995b) *Language and Gender*, London: Longman.

Milroy, J. (1981) *Regional Accents of English: Belfast*, Belfast: Blackstaff.

Milroy, J. (1982) 'Probing under the tip of the iceberg: phonological normalisation and the shape of speech communities', in S. Romaine (ed.) *Sociolinguistic Variation in Speech Communities*, London: Edward Arnold, pp. 35–47.

Milroy, J. (1983) 'On the sociolinguistic history of /h/-dropping in English', in M. Davenport, E. Hansen and H.F. Nielsen (eds) *Current Topics in English Historical Linguistics*, Odense: Odense University Press, pp. 37–53.

Milroy, J. (1992a) *Linguistic Variation and Change*, Oxford: Blackwell.

Milroy, J. (1992b) 'Middle English dialectology', in N. Blake (ed.) *The Cambridge History of the English Language* (vol. 2), Cambridge: Cambridge University Press, pp. 156–206.

Milroy, J. (1993) 'On the social origins of language change', in C. Jones (ed.) *Historical Linguistics: Problems and Perspectives*, London: Longman, pp. 215–36.

Milroy, J. and Milroy, L. (1985a) *Authority in Language* (1st edition), London: Routledge.

Milroy, J. and Milroy, L. (1985b) 'Linguistic change, social network and speaker innovation', *Journal of Linguistics* 21: 339–84.

Milroy, J. and Milroy, L. (1992) 'Social network and social class: toward an integrated sociolinguistic model', *Language in Society* 21: 1–26.

Milroy, J. and Milroy, L. (eds) (1993) *Real English: The Grammar of English Dialects in the British Isles*, London: Longman.

Milroy, J. and Milroy, L. (1999) *Authority in Language: Investigating Standard English* (3rd edition), London: Routledge.

Milroy, L. (1978) 'Belfast: change and variation in an urban vernacular', in P. Trudgill (ed.) *Sociolinguistic Patterns in British English*, London: Arnold, pp. 7–34.

Milroy, L. (1982) 'Social network and linguistic focusing', in S. Romaine (ed.) *Sociolinguistic Variation in Speech Communities*, London: Arnold, pp. 141–52.

Milroy, L. (1987a) *Language and Social Networks* (2nd edition), Oxford: Basil Blackwell.

Milroy, L. (1987b) *Observing and Analysing Natural Language*, Oxford: Basil Blackwell.

Milroy, L. and Muysken, P. (eds) (1995) *One Speaker, Two Languages: Cross-Disciplinary Perspectives on Code-Switching*, Cambridge: Cambridge University Press.

Mohanen, K.P. (1992) 'Describing the phonology of non-native varieties of a language', *World Englishes* 2(3): 111–28.

Morgan, M. (ed.) (1994) *Language and the Social Construction of Identity in Creole Situations*, Los Angeles: Center for Afro-American Studies, UCLA.

Mugglestone, L. (1995) *Talking Proper: The Rise of Accent as Social Symbol*, Oxford: Oxford University Press.

Mühlhäusler, P. and Harré, R. (1990) *Pronouns and People*, Oxford: Basil Blackwell.

Myers-Scotton, C. (1993a) *Duelling Languages: Grammatical Structure in Code-Switching*, Oxford: Clarendon Press.

Myers-Scotton, C. (1993b) *Social Motivation for Code-Switching*, Oxford: Clarendon Press.

Ochs, E., Schegloff, E. and Thompson, S. (eds) (1996) *Interaction and Grammar*, Cambridge: Cambridge University Press.

Ohala, J. (1993) 'The phonetics of sound change', in C. Jones (ed.) *Historical Linguistics: Problems and Perspectives*, London: Longman, pp. 237–78.

Ortony, A. (ed.) (1993) *Metaphor and Thought* (2nd edition), Cambridge: Cambridge University Press.

Pakir, A. (1994) 'English in Singapore: the codification of competing norms', in S. Gopinathan, A. Pakir, Ho Wah Kam and S. Vanithamani (eds) *Language and Education in Singapore: Issues and Trends*, Singapore: Times Academic Press, pp. 221–34.

Palmer, F.R. (ed.) (1968) *Selected Papers of J.R. Firth, 1952–59*, Bloomington, IN: Indiana University Press.

Parthasarathy, R. (1983) 'South Asian literature in English: culture and discourse', paper presented at the Conference on English as an International Language: Discourse Patterns Across Cultures, East-West Center, Honolulu.

Pateman, T. (1981) 'Linguistics as a branch of critical theory', *UEA Papers in Linguistics* 14/15: 1–29.

Penfield, J. and Ornstein-Galicia, J.L. (1985) *Chicano English: An Ethnic Contact Dialect*, Amsterdam and Philadelphia: John Benjamins.

Pennycook, A. (1994) *The Cultural Politics of English as an International Language*, London: Longman.

Perera, K. (1984) *Children's Writing and Reading*, Oxford: Blackwell.

Pettit, A. (1980) *Images of the Mexican-American in Fiction and Film*, College Station, TX: Texas A & M University Press.

Petyt, K.M. (1980) *The Study of Dialect: An Introduction to Dialectology*, London: André Deutsch.

Platt, J.T. and Platt, H.K. (1975) *The Social Significance of Speech: An Introduction to and Workbook in Sociolinguistics*, Amsterdam: North-Holland.

Platt, J.T. and Weber, H. (1980) *English in Singapore and Malaysia: Status, Features, Function*, Kuala Lumpur: Oxford University Press.

Platt, J.T., Weber, H. and Ho, M.L. (1984) *The New Englishes*, London: Routledge & Kegan Paul.

Poynton, C. (1985) *Language and Gender: Making the Difference*, New York: Deakin University Press.

Pride, J.B. and Holmes, J. (eds) (1972) *Sociolinguistics: Selected Readings*, Harmondsworth: Penguin.

Pyles, T. and Algeo, J. (1993) *The Origins and Development of the English Language* (4th edition), London: Harcourt Brace Jovanovich.

Quirk, R. and Widdowson, H. (eds) (1985) *English in the World*, Cambridge: Cambridge University Press.

Rao, R. (1963) *Kanthapura*, New York: New Dimensions.

Richardson, K. (1987) 'Critical linguistics and textual diagnosis', *Text* 7(2): 145–63.

Richardson, K. and Meinhof, U. (1999) *Worlds in Common? Television Discourse in a Changing Europe*, London: Routledge.

Romaine, S. (1988) *Pidgin and Creole Languages*, London: Longman.

Romaine, S. (1989) *Bilingualism*, Oxford: Blackwell.

Rosewarne, D. (1994) 'Estuary English – tomorrow's RP?' *English Today* 10(1): 3–8.

Rosewarne, D. (1996) 'Estuary as a world language', *Modern English Teacher* 5: 13–17.

Rubin, J. (1968) *National Bilingualism in Paraguay*, The Hague: Mouton.

Sacks, H. (1992) *Lectures on Conversation*, Oxford: Blackwell.

Sacks, H., Schegloff, E. and Jefferson, G. (1974) 'A simplest systematics for the organization of turn-taking for conversation', *Language* 50: 696–735.

Sajavaara, K., Marsh, D. and Keto, T. (eds) (1991) *Communication and Discourse across Cultures and Languages*, Jyväskyla: University of Jyväskyla Press.

Schiffrin, D. (1987) *Discourse Markers*, Cambridge: Cambridge University Press.

Schiffrin, D. (1994) *Approaches to Discourse*, Oxford: Basil Blackwell.

Sebba, M. (1993) *London Jamaican: A Case Study in Language Contact*, London: Longman.

Sebba, M. (1997) *Contact Languages: Pidgins and Creoles*, London: Macmillan.

Seligman, C.R., Tucker, G.R. and Lambert, W.E. (1972) 'The effects of speech style and other attributes on teachers' attitudes towards pupils', *Language in Society* 1: 131–42.

Simmen, E. (ed.) (1971) *The Chicano: From Caricature to Self-Portrait*, New York: Mentor Books.

Sinclair, J. (ed.) (1992) *Collins COBUILD English Usage*, London and Birmingham: Collins COBUILD and University of Birmingham Press.

Sinclair, J.M. and Coulthard, M. (1975) *Towards an Analysis of Discourse: The English Used by Teachers and Pupils*, Oxford: Oxford University Press.

Sinclair, J.M., Hoey, M. and Fox, G. (eds) (1993) *Techniques of Description: Spoken and Written Discourse*, London: Routledge.

Smith, L.E. (ed.) (1983) *Readings in English as an International Language*, Oxford: Pergamon Press.

Smith, L.E. (ed.) (1987) *Discourse Across Cultures: Strategies in World Englishes*, London: Prentice-Hall.

Spender, D. (1985) *Man Made Language*, London: Routledge & Kegan Paul.

Stenström, A.B. (1994) *An Introduction to Spoken Interaction*, London: Longman.

Strang, B. (1970) *A History of English*, London: Methuen.

Stubbs, M. (1976) *Language, Schools and Classrooms*, London: Methuen.

Stubbs, M. (1980) *Language and Literacy*, London: Routledge & Kegan Paul.

Stubbs, M. (1983) *Discourse Analysis: The Sociolinguistic Analysis of Natural Language*, Oxford: Basil Blackwell.

Stubbs, M. (1986) *Educational Linguistics*, Oxford: Blackwell.

Stubbs, M. (1996) *Text and Corpus Analysis*, Oxford: Blackwell.

Sutcliffe, D. (1982) *British Black English*, Oxford: Blackwell.

Sutcliffe, D. and Figueroa, J. (1992) *System in Black Language*, Clevedon: Multilingual Matters.

Sutcliffe, D. and Wong, A. (1986) *The Language of the Black Experience: Cultural Expression through Word and Sound in the Caribbean and Black Britain*, Oxford: Blackwell.

Swales, J.M. (1990) *Genre Analysis*, Cambridge: Cambridge University Press.

Taiwo, O. (1976) *Culture and the Nigerian Novel*, New York: St Martin's Press.

Tannen, D. (1992) *You Just Don't Understand: Women and Men in Conversation*, London: Virago.

Thorne, B. (1983) *Language, Gender and Society*, London: Newbury House.

Thorne, B. and Henley, N. (eds) (1975) *Language and Sex: Difference and Dominance*, London: Newbury House.

Thumboo, E. (1976) *The Second Tongue: An Anthology of Poetry from Malaysia and Singapore*, Singapore: Heinemann Educational Books.

Todd, L. (1974) *Pidgins and Creoles*, London: Routledge & Kegan Paul.

Trudgill, P. (1972) 'Sex, covert prestige and linguistic change in the urban British English of Norwich', *Language and Society* 1: 179–95.

Trudgill, P. (1974) *The Social Differentiation of English in Norwich*, Cambridge: Cambridge University Press.

Trudgill, P. (1975) *Accent, Dialect and the School*, London: Edward Arnold.

Trudgill, P. (ed.) (1978) *Sociolinguistic Patterns in British English*, London: Edward Arnold.

Trudgill, P. (1983) *On Dialect: Social and Geographical Perspectives*, Oxford: Basil Blackwell.

Trudgill, P. (ed.) (1984) *Language in the British Isles*, Cambridge: Cambridge University Press.

Trudgill, P. (1986a) *Dialects in Contact*, Oxford: Basil Blackwell.

Trudgill, P. (1986b) 'The apparent time paradigm: Norwich revisited', paper presented to the Sociolinguistics Symposium VI, University of Newcastle-upon-Tyne.

Trudgill, P. (1988) 'Norwich revisited: recent linguistic changes in an English urban dialect', *English World-Wide* 9: 33–49.

Trudgill, P. (1990) *The Dialects of England*, Oxford: Basil Blackwell.

Trudgill, P. (1995) *Sociolinguistics: An Introduction to Language and Society* (revised edition), Harmondsworth: Penguin.

Trudgill, P. (1998) 'Standard English: what it isn't', paper presented to Poetics and Linguistics Association Conference, University of Bern.

Trudgill, P. and Hannah, J. (1982) *International English: A Guide to Varieties of Standard English*, London: Edward Arnold.

United States Census Bureau (1990) *Social and Economic Characteristics: Metropolitan Areas*, Washington, DC: USCB.

United States Census Bureau (1994) *1990 Census of Population and Housing* (revised edition), Washington, DC: USCB.

Valdés, G. (1988) 'The language situation of Mexican Americans', in S.L. McKay and S.-L.C. Wong (eds), *Language Diversity: Problem or Resource? A Social and Educational Perspective on Language Minorities in the United States*, Boston, MA: Heinle & Heinle, pp. 111–39.

Veltman, C. (1983) 'Anglicization in the United States: language environment and language practice of American adolescents', *International Journal of the Sociology of Language* 44: 99–114.

Ventola, E. (1987) *The Structure of Social Interaction*, London: Frances Pinter.

Watts, R., Ide, S. and Ehlich, K. (eds) (1999) *Politeness in Language: Studies in its History, Theory and Practice*, Berlin: Mouton de Gruyter.

Weedon, C. (1987) *Feminist Practice and Poststructuralist Theory*, Oxford: Basil Blackwell.

Weinreich, U. (1966) *Languages in Contact*, The Hague: Mouton.

Wells, J.C. (1973) *Jamaican Pronunciation in London*, Oxford: Blackwell.

Wells, J.C. (1982) *Accents of English*, Cambridge: Cambridge University Press.

Wells, J.C. (1994) 'What is Estuary English?' *English Teaching Professional* 3 (April): 46–7.

Wells, J.C. (1997) 'Transcribing Estuary English', *Speech Hearing and Language* 8: 261–7.

Whiteley, W.H. (ed.) (1971) *Language Use and Social Change: Problems of Multilingualism with Special Reference to Eastern Africa*, London: Oxford University Press.

Widdowson, H. (1979) *Pidgin and Babu: Explorations in Applied Linguistics*, London: Oxford University Press.

Wilkinson, A. (1965) 'Spoken English', *Educational Review* 6: 17.

Wilkinson, J. (1995) *Introducing Standard English*, Harmondsworth: Penguin.

Wodak, R. (ed.) (1990) *Language, Power and Ideology: Studies in Political Discourse*, Amsterdam and Philadelphia: John Benjamins.

Wodak, R. (ed.) (1997) *Gender and Discourse*, London: Sage.

Wood, F.T. and Hill, R.J. (1989) *Dictionary of English Colloquial Idioms*, London: Macmillan.

Zentella, A.C. (1988) 'The language situation of Puerto Ricans', in S.L. McKay and S-L.C. Wong (eds) *Language Diversity: Problem or Resource?* Boston: Heinle & Heinle, pp. 140–65.

Zentella, A.C. (1996) 'The "Chiquitafication" of US Latinos and their languages, or why we need an anthropological linguistics', *SALSA III* (Proceedings of the Third Annual Symposium about Language and Society), Austin, TX: University of Texas, pp. 1–18.

GLOSSARIAL INDEX

The first occurrence of a keyword is highlighted in **bold**; this is where a definition is provided or the term is used in a context which makes its meaning clear. Other page references are to places in the book where the term is also used.